D0891998

# The Taste of the Pineapple

## Essays on C.S. Lewis as Reader, Critic, and Imaginative Writer

Edited by Bruce L. Edwards
Preface by Owen Barfield

Bowling Green State University Popular Press
Bowling Green, Ohio

Library of Congress Catalogue Card No.: 87-73554
ISBN: 0-87972-406-4 Paperback
0-87972-407-2 Clothbound

**Cover design by Gary Dumm**

## Dedication

To my children, Matthew, Mary Elizabeth, Justin, and Michael, who have suffered through yet another of daddy's projects. May they learn, with Professor Lewis, that life in this world is but a rehearsal for one "further up and further in."

# Contents

# Acknowledgements

Grateful acknowledgement is paid to Mr. Owen Barfield, longtime friend of C.S. Lewis and literary executor of his estate, for writing the preface to this volume. Mr. Barfield is himself one of the most provocative and insightful—and yet undervalued—language theorists of the twentieth century. His work on metaphor and "speaker's meaning" in particular deserve to be better known and evoked among rhetoricians and linguists than is presently the case. Mr. Barfield has now taught four generations to beware the peril of "chronological snobbery," the historical heresy that declares the new and the recent are, because new and recent, thereby true.

I offer my special thanks to Pat Browne, editor of Popular Press here at Bowling Green State University, for her belief in the value of this anthology for Lewis scholars and her graciousness in overseeing its publication.

I am pleased to acknowledge as well the contribution of my wife Joan to this volume. She retyped a number of the essays included here, assisted me in preparing the index, and generally encouraged me to continue pursuing publication of this work over several years even when its prospects seemed dim.

Finally, I offer my sincere gratitude to the following publishers for permission to reprint these essays and portions of essays from their pages:

Margaret P. Hannay, "Provocative Generalizations: *The Allegory of Love* in Retrospect" and Kath Filmer, "The Polemic Image: Metaphor and Symbol in the Fiction of C. S. Lewis." Reprinted from *Seven: An Anglo-American Literary Review, Volume 7, 1986:* Copyright © 1986 by Bookmakers Guild Inc., Longmont, Colorado. Published by Bookmakers Guild, Inc., in cooperation with The Marion E. Wade Center, Wheaton College, Wheaton, Illinois. Reprinted by permission of Bookmakers Guild, Inc.

Kathryn Lindskoog and Gracia Fay Ellwood, "C.S. Lewis: Natural Law and the Law in Our Hearts." Copyright 1984, Christian Century Foundation. Reprinted by permission from the November 14, 1984 issue of *The Christian Century.*

Portions of my essay, "Rehabilitating Reading: C. S. Lewis and Contemporary Critical Theory," have appeared in various forms in the following publications: *Journal of the Evangelical Theological Society; CSL: The Journal New York C.S. Lewis Society; This World;* and *Literature and Belief.* I am grateful to the editors of these journals for permission to print a fully revised and updated version of these materials in this anthology.

# Preface

**Owen Barfield**

I am finding it very difficult to believe that a quarter of a century has elapsed since the death of C.S. Lewis. But if the subjective difficulty became so great as to require objective evidence for its overcoming, I believe I should find enough of that in the sheer quantity of comment—personal and biographical, literary, theological—that has been published about him during those years. I cannot claim acquaintance with anything like the whole of it, but I have read enough of it to lead me to the following conclusion.

A fairly unsophisticated person who had never had any personal contact with Lewis, but who, omitting the biographical parts, had read the whole or most of what has been written about him, might be pardoned for wondering if it were not one writer, but three with whom he was becoming acquainted; three men who just happened to have the same name and same peculiar vigor of thought and utterance. Such a reader (I will venture to put myself in his shoes) might, to avoid confusion, adopt the nomenclature L1, L2 and L3, L1 being a distinguished and original literary critic, L2 a highly successful author of fiction and L3 the writer and broadcaster of popular Christian apologetics. Having established his scheme, and proceeding to survey it, he would almost certainly notice two things. First that, by and large, competent and admiring readers of L1 have little, if any, interest in L3, and vice versa that readers of both L1 and L3 *are* interested, to some extent in a different way, in L2. The second thing he would notice is that quantitatively at all events, L1 has received up to date very much less attention than the other two. Though he has certainly not been ignored, it would hardly be too much to say that L1 has been "swamped" by L2 and L3. I have always felt this to be a pity and it is for that reason that I especially welcome the appearance of the selection that follows. It should make a much needed contribution to the redressing of a balance.

Apart from the fact that they concentrate especially on Lewis's critical and scholarly writings, many of the essays deal in one way or another—most explicitly in Robert Boenig's "Critical and Fictional Pairing in C.S. Lewis," but elsewhere also—with a theme that has received even less notice than his scholarly work taken as a whole, namely the special relation between L1 and L2. I confess it is something to which I myself had hitherto given no attention.

If it is somewhat artificial, the device of distinguishing numerically between different Lewises is nevertheless tempting. And it occurs to me that it might with equal justification be applied diachronically as well as synchronically. Cutting out the jargon that means that, in his biography too, we can hardly help discerning not three this time, but two different Lewises, the one before and the other after his conversion. That has little to do with the subject matter of the book before us, and I mention it only because it adds to the significance of what I am going on to say.

On the one hand there are these three or, as the case may be, five Lewises. But on the other hand—I am not going to say "paradoxically" or "ironically," because I am tired of seeing these two adverbs recklessly scattered about by journalists and academics alike in places where they add nothing, and I am no fonder of "verbicide" than Lewis himself was—on the other hand the *unity* of all these Lewises is to my feeling as impressive, or even more impressive, than their diversity. Others, of course, have drawn attention to it, but I am not sure that anyone has succeeded in locating it. Some have pointed to his "style," but it goes deeper than that. "Consistency?" Noticeable enough in spite of an occasional inconsistency here or there. His unswerving "sincerity" then? That comes much nearer, but still does not satisfy me. Many other writers are sincere—but they are not Lewis. No. There was something in the whole quality and structure of his thinking, something for which the best label I can find is "presence of mind." And if I were asked to expand on that, I could only say that somehow what he thought about everything was secretly present in what he said about anything.

Since at different times in his life he thought differently about several big things, he also said different things; but that quality, however it ought to be named, transcended all changes of opinion, as it transcended all diversities of topic. And it was there from the start. It is there in *Mere Christianity* as it is there in *A Preface to Paradise Lost* or in *Till We Have Faces*. But it was also there already, unless my memory is playing me tricks, in the refusal to spoil a case by overstating it, in the level gaze and the eagerness behind the level gaze, of a shabbily dressed undergraduate who bicycled in from Headington and met me for tea in the rooms of a mutual friend in Oxford in November 1919.

# Introduction

In the last decade many scholars have turned their attention to the work of Clive Staples Lewis, long a popular Christian writer and a favorite among science fiction and fantasy aficionados. Lewis has thus become the object of many theological treatises and not a few works which examine his fiction. Unfortunately, many of the earliest studies of Lewis have tended to reflect more hagiography than scholarship, more paraphrase than analysis, yielding few insights into source and strength of Lewis's literary achievements. Recently, however, scholars have begun to go beyond surface treatments of Lewis's work and consider more creditably the fuller scope of Lewis's writing career, offering students of Lewis a more critical vantage point from which to assess his work.

The 1980s have given us such significant works as Margaret P. Hannay's masterful overview of the life and career of Lewis; Michael Aeschliman's suggestive study of Lewis's *Abolition of Man* and its indictment of modern scientism; and William Griffin's unique life-and-times biography of Lewis.

Missing, however, in this tumult of interest in Lewis have been volumes which consider in detail his characteristic methods of literary criticism, his defense of reading as a transcendent act, and the extent to which these notions of criticism and reading informed his own fiction. The sheer popularity and quotability of this prolific and talented author have overshadowed his career as a serious and provocative critic and literary theorist—and have precluded, as Owen Barfield says in his preface to this volume, an examination of the relationship between Lewis the scholar and Lewis the imaginative writer.

There have been exceptions, certainly; for instance, Corbin Scott Carnell's early study of Lewis's romanticism illuminated the place of "Sehnsucht," or "longing" in the criticism, fiction, and apologetics of Lewis; Peter Schakel's close reading of Lewis's *Till We Have Faces* helps us fathom Lewis's understanding of reason and imagination; and my own *A Rhetoric of Reading* attempts to place Lewis's critical principles in the context of contemporary literary theory. By and large, however, attention has been diverted away from writing the kind of informed, broadly-based critical scholarship *about* Lewis which is exemplified in his criticism and which earned him the appreciation and begrudging admiration from colleagues during his careers at Oxford and Cambridge. This is unfortunate for several reasons, not least of which is the fact that Lewis has much to contribute to the contemporary debate about the status of texts, the role of readers, and the authority of authors. His potential influence has been preempted by the public notion that Lewis is, perhaps, only a lightweight theological or children's writer who has nothing to say about "serious" critical matters.

*The Taste of the Pineapple* is thus intended to fill a gap in Lewis studies by offering essays that explore and critique the premises with which Lewis the scholar worked and that determine how these premises informed his own imaginative writing. Its ultimate goal is to revitalize interest in Lewis as an important spokesman to a generation of writers, readers and critics who seem to have lost their moorings, conflating reading and criticism with a host of other, ancillary activities. The fifteen essayists in this volume share the conviction that C.S. Lewis was an uncommonly lucid writer whose conception of the literary enterprise—the complementary roles of author, reader and text—are necessary counterbalances to the obscurantism of much academic reading and criticism here at the end of the twentieth century.

Part I, C.S. Lewis and the Critical Enterprise, features essays which attempt to explicate and place in context Lewis's critical practice, extrapolating a theory of criticism from his works that he himself did not stop to codify during his lifetime. Jerry Daniel's title essay, *The Taste of the Pineapple,* takes a close look at Lewis as reader, articulating those reading strategies that animated Lewis's critical practice and explaining how these same qualities found their way into his own craft of fiction. My essay, "Rehabilitating Reading: C.S. Lewis and Contemporary Critical Theory," suggests the part Lewis might play in reconciling some of the conflicting views posited by contemporary deconstructors, reader-response theorists, and fallen new critics about the status of literary texts. The third essay in this section, Robert Meyers's "...the Abstractions Proper to Them," cogently explicates Lewis's most sustained attempt at literary theory, the beguiling *An Experiment in Criticism,* placing it in the context of the institutional theory of art and literature.

Part II, C.S. Lewis: The Practice of Criticism, offers essays which examine the rhetorical strategies employed in Lewis's critical oeuvre, focusing on particular exemplars and discovering both his innovation and his technique. Two essays consider Lewis's early, seminal work, *The Allegory of Love*. Margaret P. Hannay's "Provocative Generalizations: *The Allegory of Love* in Retrospect" discusses the impact of Lewis's first scholarly publication on subsequent Spenser scholarship, while Paul Piehler's essay, "Visions and Revisions: C.S. Lewis's Contributions to the Theory of Allegory," takes a broader view of Lewis's notion of allegory and analyzes its lasting effects on the study of that genre. David H. Stewart's "Style and Substance in C.S. Lewis's Prose" offers a rhetorical analysis of the lucidity and articulateness of Lewis's prose, suggesting the reasons why Lewis is always compelling even when one is inclined to dissent from his opinions. Finally, Paul Leopold examines in exhaustive detail Lewis's "lexicon," i.e., his characteristic diction, and provides significant insights into Lewis's linguistic battle against "verbicide" in the language of his contemporaries.

Part III, C.S. Lewis: The Critic as Imaginative Writer, presents essays which are unique among critical treatments of Lewis's fiction in that they closely consider the relationship of Lewis's critical principles to his own imaginative works and thereby help us read his fiction more evocatively. In "Subcreation and Lewis's Theory of Literature," Margaret L. Carter argues that Lewis's appreciation for and facility in writing fantasy stems in part from his theory of subcreation, that a writer's creation of a secondary, literary world enables readers to see their own worlds more keenly than before; it is this premise, she suggests, which informs the landscape in *Perelandra*. Robert Boenig's essay, "Critical and Fictional Pairing in C.S. Lewis," advances the hypothesis that Lewis's imaginative works may be coupled with counterparts from his critical texts that, in fact, provide the reader with the basis for a kind of natural "source-criticism"; Lewis himself was, of course, a master of this kind of critical praxis. Kath Filmer employs an engaging mythopoeic analysis in her essay, "The Polemic Image: The Role of Metaphor and Symbol in the Fiction of C.S. Lewis," to amplify how central rhetorical, polemical tropes perform as arguments for Lewis's Christian Platonism. Finally in this section, Joe McClatchey's essay, "The Affair of Jane's Dreams: Reading *That Hideous Strength* as Iconographical Art," illustrates a critical method Lewis used in his posthumous book *Spenser's Images of Life*. As Lewis found six forms of iconography verbalized in Spenser's *The Faerie Queene*, Professor McClatchey ably and amply demonstrates their particular relevance for understanding Lewis's rhetorical manuevers in *That Hideous Strength*.

Part IV, C.S. Lewis and His Critical Milieu, offers three essays which consider and place Lewis in the context of his influences, adversaries, and contemporaries. Kathryn Lindskoog and Gracia Fay Ellwood's essay on the centrality of "natural law" in Lewis's view of literature and reality explains the emphasis Lewis placed on objective value in his critical, apologetic, and imaginative work, and how this separates him from those among his contemporaries and present day readers and critics who reject it. Given that Lewis, in effect, inherited Chesterton's mantle as the preeminent British Christian journalist. Alzina Stone Dale's incisive essay, *Conservative Defendants as Critics,* is a particular revelation that illuminates the lives of two writers who never met but who shared a common intellectual and imaginative outlook. The final essay, John Martin's, "Voices of Fire: Eliot, Lewis, Sayers and Chesterton," is included as a tour de force which mirrors the kind of witty, name-dropping, anecdotal, inclusive writing for which Lewis distinguished himself in his *English Literature in the 16th Century*. Professor Martin sees in this quartet of writers a common thread which he elucidates and illustrates with numerous evocative citations from each of their biographies and works, a fitting concluding essay to a volume intended in apart to exemplify the critical practice of Lewis.

In sum, there is about Lewis's work that tantalizing "taste of the pineapple," an elusive, compelling flavor and scent that speaks to us from and about another time, another country, a critical stance which draws us in and yet calls in question all of our favorite and familiar modes of discourse and analysis. This volume is thus sent forth as a message in a bottle toward a scholarly sea cluttered with flattery and annotation, a collaborative effort deliberately focused on those aspects of Lewis's scholarship and fiction which have received slight critical attention but which, ultimately, may be the most enduring and influential contributions of Lewis's career. To the extent that it provides an impetus to other literary scholars to take seriously Lewis's critical practice and literary theory, examining them with greater attention and perspicacity, and to the extent that it helps Lewis's admirers discover this "other Lewis," it will have served its contributors' purpose.

## Works Cited

Aeschliman, Michael D. *The Restitution of Man.* Grand Rapids: Eerdmans, 1983.

Carnell, Corbin Scott. *Bright Shadow of Reality: C.S. Lewis and the Feeling Intellect.* Grand Rapids: Eerdmans, 1974.

Edwards, Bruce L. *A Rhetoric of Reading: C.S. Lewis's Defense of Western Literacy.* Provo, Utah: Center for the Study of Christian Values in Literature, 1986.

Hannay, Margaret P. *C.S. Lewis.* New York: Frederick Ungar, 1981.

Griffin, William. *C.S. Lewis: A Dramatic Life* New York: Macmillan, 1986.

Schakel, Peter. *Reason and Imagination in C.S. Lewis.* Grand Rapids: Eerdmans, 1984.

# Part I:

# C.S. Lewis and the Critical Enterprise

# A Note About Documentation

Throughout this volume, I have sought, as editor, to prepare the documentation of its fourteen manuscripts in accordance with the new Modern Language Association documentation style. I have, however, made exceptions in three of the essays, those by Margaret P. Hannay, David H. Stewart, and Joe McClatchey. Because their often copious notes explain and elucidate—frequently in great bibliographical detail—various aspects of Lewis's work and the critical reactions to it, I have elected to use the older "notes" documentation style for their essays, rather than clutter the text itself with frequent annotations and elaborations which might thereby distract the reader. I hope readers of this volume will find the compromise not too unsettling.

# The Taste of the Pineapple: A Basis for Literary Criticism

*Jerry L. Daniel*

C.S. Lewis has described the impact which A.K. Hamilton Jenkin made on his thinking early in his Oxford career:

> Jenkin seemed to be able to enjoy everything; even ugliness. I learned from him that we should attempt a total surrender to whatever atmosphere was offering itself at the moment; in a squalid town to seek out those very places where its squalor rose to grimness and almost grandeur, on a dismal day to find the most dismal and dripping wood, on a windy day to seek the windiest ridge. There was no Betjemannic irony about it; only a serious, yet gleeful, determination to rub one's nose in the very quiddity of each thing, to rejoice in its being (so magnificently) what it was. (*Surprised by Joy* 199)

This predilection of Jenkin's continued the education already begun by Arthur Greeves. Arthur enjoyed, and taught Lewis to enjoy, all traces of the "homely," the simple and down-to-earth qualities of nature ("ordinary drills of cabbages—what can be better?" [*Surprised* 157]).

Lewis was a poet at heart, and was a very good pupil in the school of Greeves and Jenkin. His love of Northernness—"cold, spacious, severe, pale, and remote," "huge, clear spaces hanging above the Atlantic in the endless twilight of Northern summer" (*Surprised* 17, 73)—demonstrates that even prior to meeting those two young men he was strongly attracted to certain "tastes" or "flavors" in art and literature as well as in nature. And that love continued to grow during boyhood and early manhood. His letters to Arthur contain countless illustrations of his reveling in nature, immersing himself in the very essence of the world around him. Whether describing the cold, clear spaces of the North or a hedge-row beside a lane, his choice of words reveals a soul almost intoxicated with the "pure organic pleasure" of things as they are. With the soul of a poet or a painter he not only saw but communicated what he saw with unusual clarity. All his senses were open to the nature of things. In his own words: "It was the mood of a scene that mattered to me; and in tasting that mood my skin and nose were as busy as my eyes." (*Surprised* 78).

By the time he began writing to Arthur, he would have agreed wholeheartedly with Chesterton's comment: "Plato held, and the child holds, that the most important thing about a ship (let us say) is that it is a ship." And I do not doubt that he would have subscribed to the theory of art that follows:

> Thus, all these pictures are designed to express things in their quiddity. If these old artists draw a ship, everything is sacrificed to expressing the 'shippishness' of the ship. If they draw a tower, its whole object is to be towering. If they draw a flower, its whole object is to be flowering. Their pencils often go wrong as to how the thing looks; their intellects never go wrong as to what the thing is. ("The Grave Digger" 113)

The quality of a landscape, of a conversation, or even of a dream, could be so forcefully present in his mind to call forth detailed and emotive description.[1] The point should not be labored; he had by nature a profound appreciation of the essence of things—an appreciation sharpened and enhanced by the influence of Greeves and Jenkin.

This matter is important to anyone who is concerned to analyze Lewis's approach to literature. It has been mentioned often in books and articles about Lewis, but I doubt that it has been sufficiently stressed, and particularly in regard to literary matters. If it is an overstatement to say that this emphasis on the quiddity of things provides the key, it is at least in order to say that it furnishes one important insight into his approach—whether as a reader, critic, or an imaginative writer. We will now explore several ways in which it does so.

*Lewis the Reader*

Lewis's love of the essence is an obvious factor in his reading. Just as he immersed himself in the quality of the world around him, he immersed himself in the quality of a story or a poem he was reading; and this is equally true of Lewis the boy and Lewis the man.

His descriptions of books and poems are completely revealing. Charles Williams's poetry is praised for its "golden, noonday vitality" (*A Sacred Poem* 275), and again for its "shy, elusive laughter; angelic laughter rather than elfin laughter" (Rev. of *Taliessin* 249). The first volume of Tolkien's trilogy is enjoyed for (among other things) its "silvan leafiness," and its "remote horizons" ("The Gods Return" 1083). In one passage he contrasts the "cool water-colour effects of Morris, his northern bareness," with the "gold and scarlet and all the orgiastic drum-beats of Chesterton" (*The Literary Impact* 23). St. Athanasius' *Study of the Incarnation* is said to be "a sappy and golden book, full of buoyancy and confidence" ("Introduction" *Incarnation* 11). He esteems Arnold's poetry for its sense of "infinite distance,...blended with his own sad lucidity, filled with the charm of strange, remote places" ("De Audiendis"

10). He calls attention to the "exuberant power" of Dryden, and also to "the fine breezy, sunshiny weather of the man's mind" ("Shelley, Dryden and Mr. Eliot" 188, 194) and notes the "lightness and liquidity" of Shelley's *Witch of Atlas* (200). He acclaims the "curious stillness or tranquillity" of Shakespeare's sonnets (*English Lit in the 16th C.* 508), and his entire lecture on *Hero and Leander* is a moving description of the "mythopoeic" quality of Marlowe's portion of the poem as compared with the "graver voice" of Chapman. (*Hero* 25-27). In one passage in *The Allegory of Love* (317), he labels Shakespeare's sonnets as "mellifluous," Shelley as "airy," Keats as "swooningly sensuous," and William Morris as "dreamlike." He sees Milton's Beelzebub as a great romantic figure because of his "dim vastness and his ruined splendour," ("Variation" 165) and the complex and composite *Morte D'Arthur* delights him as a "great cathedral of words" which "stands solidly before us" ("The English prose 'Morte' " 25). In comparing Wace's writing to that of Layamon, he says the former is "bright and clear, not without gaiety," and the latter "sterner, more epic, more serious" ("Introduction" to Layamon" vii-viii) and again, "darker, graver, more wintry" ("The Genesis of a Medieval Book" 26). In his contribution to the *Oxford History of English Literature,* he objects to Shakespeare's *Venus and Adonis* because the atmosphere is smothering—Venus is depicted as a "flushed, panting, perspiring, suffocating, loquacious creature," reminiscent of "certain horrible interviews with voluminous female relatives in one's early childhood (498-99). Joy Davidman's poetry is said to have a "deep bell-like note ("Foreword" 1)

Illustrations could be multiplied almost to infinity; the point being that Lewis read the works of others with a view to the inherent *quality* of the work. Whether prose or verse, all works were "poetry" to him in the sense that the "feel" or "taste" was primary. He sometimes liked, sometimes disliked, but always his response seems to have been based on the quality or taste of the work, rather than, say, on character drawing, or on suspense.

The sort of thing I have in mind is best described by two remarks Lewis makes about the poetry of Charles Williams. In *Arthurian Torso,* he observes:

> Those who dislike it will, I think, confess that it has a very positive quality, a taste which, if you hate, you will find it difficult to get out of the mouth. The world of the poem is a strong, strange, and consistent world. If the poem is rejected you will reject it because you find that world repellent. (198)

And in an *Oxford Magazine* review of *Taliessin through Logres,* he presses even further the image of taste:

If this poem is good at all it is entirely irreplaceable in the sense that no other book whatever comes anywhere near reminding you of it or being even a momentary substitute for it. If you can't get an orange, then a lemon or a grapefruit will give you a taste that has something in common with it. But if you can't get a pineapple, then nothing else will even faintly put you in mind of it. *Taliessin* is like the pineapple. You may like or dislike that taste; but once you have tasted it, you know you can get it from no other book in the whole world. (249-50)

In his preface to D.E. Harding's *The Hierarchy of Heaven and Earth* he uses a different figure to communicate the same idea: "One has breathed a new air, become free of a new country. it may be a country you cannot live in, but you now know why the natives love it" (13). Speaking of the various species invented and described in *The Lord of the Rings,* he asserts that they all "would have been worth creating for their mere flavour even if they had been irrelevant" ("The Dethronement" 1373). In each case the inherent quality is the basis of judgment.

In his essay entitled "On Stories," Lewis gives several illustrations of his method of reading. First, he describes the very different literary response of one of his pupils (4). The young man portrayed his pleasure in a childhood reading of a scene in one of James Fenimore Cooper's books, attributing his pleasure entirely to the suspense of the scene. Lewis felt certain that the young man had missed the point of the experience. Reasoning from his own reading habits, Lewis concluded that the pleasure really lay in Cooper's depiction of the American Indian, the "Redskinnery" of the story, rather than in the mere suspense. The pupil quickly rejected this idea, stating that the "Redskinnery" was a distraction, not a source of pleasure. Two things are clear from this anecdote: first, Lewis read for "feeling" and "atmosphere;" and second, not everyone shares this propensity.

He then relates his pleasure in the closing parts of Haggard's *King Solomon's Mines,* where the "heroes are awaiting death entombed in a rock chamber and surrounded by the mummified kings of that land" (5). He was sorely disappointed in a film version of the story, in which the ending had been altered to include a noisy and dramatic series of eruptions and earthquakes. For Lewis this ruined the story. It changed the atmosphere, the quality of the narrative. "What I lose," he tells us, "is the whole sense of the deathly...—the cold, the silence, and the surrounding faces of the ancient, the crowned and sceptred, dead" (6). Again, the thing that counts is the atmosphere of the story; far more than the excitement, the psychology, the character-drawing, or anything else.

He mentions his lack of response to *The Three Musketeers,* and ascribes this entirely to the "total lack of atmosphere" (7). There is no weather, no country, "except as a storehouse of inns and ambushes." Plenty of excitement, plenty of adventure, but nothing of the sort that

# The Taste of the Pineapple

really mattered to Lewis. Other illustrations are given (cf. 8, 9), but they do not add to the point, except to underscore the absolute consistency of Lewis's approach to literature. He was alive to the mood of the passage before him, drinking gratefully and in a sense uncritically from whatever fountain was available. His favorite was the cold, clear distance of Northernness ("No mountains in literature are as far away as distant mountains in Morris" ["William Morris" 22]), but almost all moods were welcome.

I said that *almost* all moods were welcome. His antipathy to much modern work, that of the "pale young men" and their type, necessitates the qualification. Though he could applaud the "fresh, harsh energy" of modern poetry, ("A Sacred Poem" 275) and could even praise Eliot's poetry for its ability to "convey the sense of stillness, hushed expectancy, vacancy, death" (Rev. of *Taliesen* 248), his overall reaction was thoroughly negative. In *The Personal Heresy* he comments that poems of the twenties "succeeded in communicating moods of boredom and nausea that have only an infinitesimal place in the life of a corrected and full-grown man" (106). This kind of thing was, to Lewis, depraved. Then too, much modern poetry (and prose too, for that matter) is so subjective as to defy consistent interpretation. In his famous Cambridge inaugural, he argues that modern poetry is an entirely new phenomenon—new in that no single correct interpretation can be given for a particular piece. He refrains at the time from negative judgment, but there is little doubt where his sympathies lie.

But to return to the fundamental question, even such an unlikely source as *Studies in Words* reveals evidence as to Lewis's feelings in the matter. He reminds us of Burns's simile of the "red, red rose," used to describe his lover; and of Wordsworth's very different image: "a violet by a mossy stone Half hidden from the eye," then he comments:

> I see the rose-like, overpowering, midsummer sweetness of the one; the reticent, elusive freshness, the beauty easily overlooked in the other. After that my emotions may be left to themselves. The poets have done their part. (317-18)

Then follows a warning to beginning writers to avoid such words as "mysterious," "loathsome," "awe-inspiring," or "voluptuous," the use of which does not at all set the tone desired:

> You must bring it about that we, we readers, not you, exclaim 'how mysterious!' or 'loathsome' or whatever it is. Let me taste for myself, and you'll have no need to *tell* me how I should react to the flavour. (317)[2]

Once again, the taste is the thing. Writing which succeeds is writing which communicates the vision. Merely emotional terms—"mysterious," etc.—only tell *about* a vision; good writing displays the vision itself.

At least twice in Lewis's writings ("On Science Fiction" 70, 71; *The Personal Heresy* 102-03), he lists works whose quality or flavor is such that they give "sensations we never had before, and enlarge our conception of the range of possible experience." He does not equate this kind of writing with "good" work; he merely states that such work provides a new experience. The flavor of the work is the root of the experience

In "On Stories," he argues that a truly literary reader will always approach his reading for the inherent flavor offered, and will therefore return to the same books when again he desires the same flavor. Rereading, then, is an important test: it shows that a reader is not merely seeking excitement or suspense; rather, he is seeking something he received on a prior reading, and which can be had on subsequent readings. Suspense will, of course, disappear; the intrinsic flavor of the book will not. I think it can be said that the essay "On Stories" and the book *Experiment in Criticism* are both appeals for this approach to reading and reviewing books.

This deep love for the essence of a book seems to have pervaded Lewis's entire reading experience. Both the Greeves correspondence and *Surprised By Joy* reveal that he was very concerned with even the bodies of books: "The set up of the page, the feel and smell of the paper, the differing sounds that different papers make as you turn the leaves." (*Surprised* 164). As he describes William Morris's writings to Greeves he says, "The very names of chapters and places make me happy." This sort of enjoyment led him to a concern for pronunciation—after all, the pronunciation of a name is a factor in establishing the flavor of a work.[3] It seems that this attitude toward reading went very deep indeed; it governed his reading experiences through and through.

Matters of style, then, are of secondary consideration, overshadowed by this emphasis on the quality of a book or poem; though, obviously, bad writing style can and does alter the quality. Lewis's well-known love for the works of Rider Haggard does not prevent his complaining of Haggard's poor writing, going so far as to denounce his "*cliches*, jocosities, frothy eloquence" ("Haggard" 1044). For a writer who was himself a remarkable stylist and a philologist, it may seem strange that he would profess to love books in which the style is deficient; but the key is found in the same article: "The significant fact for me is the feeling we have as we close *King Solomon's Mines*, or still more, *She*."(1044). The feeling is the vital part, the heart and core of his enjoyment. Unless stylistic shortcomings are so bad as to destroy the feeling, stylistic shortcomings are unimportant. He expresses similar attitudes toward David Lindsay's *Voyage to Arcturus* and W.H. Hodgson's *The Night Land* ("On Science Fiction: 71; "On Stories" 12). Poor writing is harmful, but only because it smudges the vision the author is trying to impart. Fortunately the vision sometimes comes through, in spite of poor writing.

This focus leads Lewis to his apparently hedonistic view of reading. In a number of places, including his third essay in *The Personal Heresy,* he praises the reader who refuses to read beyond the first few pages of a book except because he likes the flavor of the book (118). This is, of course, an attack on snobbery, the reading of the "right" books to impress the "right" people, but it is more than that. It is a statement of his own reading method, that of opening himself to the experience a particular book has to offer. There is hardly another reason for reading a book.

I would venture to guess, though with some reticence, that Lewis's keen sense of the essence and quality of things influence his philosophic and religious attitudes. In his preface to Harding's *The Hierarchy of Heaven and Earth* (13), he makes some very interesting remarks to the effect that philosophies are similar to works of art in the effects they produce. And in his introduction to Athanasius' *De Incarnatione,* he has this to say:

> In the days when I still hated Christianity, I learned to recognize, like some all too familiar smell, that almost unvarying *something* which met me, now in Puritan Bunyan, now in Anglican Hooker, now in Thomist Dante. It was there (honeyed and floral) in Francois de Sales; it was there (grave and homely) in Spenser and Walton; it was there (grim but manful) in Pascal and Johnson;... The supposed 'Paganism' of the Elizabethans could not keep it out; it lay in wait where a man might have supposed himself safest, in the very centre of *The Faerie Queene* and *the Arcadia.* It was, of course, varied; and yet—after all—so unmistakably the same; recognisable, not to be evaded, the odour which is death to us until we allow it to become life. (8-9)

This is, of course, the development of a New Testament image (2 Cor. 2:14-16), and we have met the idea elsewhere in Lewis, as, for example, in Screwtape's twenty-second *Letter.* I am not suggesting that he accepted Christianity because he liked the "smell" or "flavor." In fact, he did not like it when he first met it. Nor am I suggesting that his views were entirely subjective. Yet it seems fair to say that he was aware of and sensitive to the "flavor" of the belief systems he accepted. He tells us in his essay, "Is Theology Poetry?", that on purely literary grounds he prefers Greek, Irish and Norse mythology to Christianity. This is clearly an honest statement, and is further protection against the charge that he allowed the poetic flavor of Christianity to cloud his critical judgment. It should also be noted that the "smell" referred to in the Athanasius article and in *Screwtape* is not merely the poetry of a belief-system. It includes that, but it also includes the "smell" or "flavor" of Christian living and Christian attitudes, along with innumerable historical accretions, not in themselves a part of the faith, but which are now part of the "flavor." All of this initially repelled, but after Lewis had accepted the faith on other grounds, it no longer repelled. I would conjecture that this unique flavor assisted him in maintaining a practicing faith; helping him to recognize doctrinal and moral heresy; helping him to stay near the center of Christianity.

We have, however, strayed from the matter at hand. The paramount fact is that Lewis, freely and naturally, carried over into his reading the same love of the quiddity of things which he applied to the world of the five senses. Not that he is thereby unique; many persons read with a similar approach. Professor Tolkien, for example, has gone on record that his practice is comparable ("On Fairy Stories" 48); and no doubt many of us could attest to the same. Lewis, however, was extraordinary in the breadth of his reading, and it is a striking fact that he read so much of so many different kinds of literature, all with a consistent desire to taste and to savor. He consumed vast amounts of literature in the sheer joy of relishing the special flavor of each, and in doing so became, almost incidentally, an outstanding literary scholar and critic. We will now see a few ways in which he applied his reading method to his criticism, or perhaps it would be better to say, we will see that his criticism was based largely on his reading method.

### *Lewis the Literary Critic*

It seems evident to me that Lewis's penchant for the quiddity of things is a key concept in his work as a critic, and especially as a critic of critics. We will see that he perceived most modern critics to be busily engaged in *avoiding* the essence of the works they criticized. He felt that most moderns worked on a basis precisely the opposite of his own. They were concerned to analyze a work on almost every ground except that of inherent quality. It seemed to Lewis that many of his contemporaries ignored everything he held dear; they missed the poetry while criticizing the poem; or, rather, they criticized various matters related to the poem, not the poem itself.

Lewis leaves no doubt as to his basic method of criticism; he tells us clearly how he works. In a significant passage he states a principle which he applies to Spenserian analysis, but which is equally valid for all his work:

> On my view it is not enough that an interpretation should fit the text logically; it must also fit it imaginatively and emotionally. Indeed, if we had to choose, I should prefer a logical to an imaginative and emotional incongruity. This principle of mine can be contested: in the meantime, it is the principle I work by. ("Neoplatonism" 112)

This statement is important in that it confirms Lewis's method, but no less in its recognition that not all critics share his method. Just how differently others work will be seen in the following paragraphs where are listed several trends which Lewis deplored in modern criticism.

1. *The anthropological approach.* One way in which some critics avoid the poetry, the essence of a work, is that of excessive attention to anthropological theory. Lewis charges, for example, that Professor R.W. Loomis, in his analysis of medieval romance, "is leaving the literary quality of these romances severely alone and is exclusively interested in the pagan myths from which he believes them to be derived: ("The Anthropological Approach" 302). "Leaving the literary quality severely alone" is the keynote. That, to Lewis, is the root sin of the method. He has no confidence in the anthropological conclusions, but that is beside the point. Even if correct, they are unhelpful, because they take our attention away from the nature of the book or poem being reviewed. Even if a critic can trace some ritual in*Beowulf* to its primitive origin, he has not helped us enjoy the unique quality of *Beowulf*. A strict attention to the text might conceivably enable us to recapture the spirit of the ritual, but it will not work the other way around. Conjectures as to the dim origins of a ritual will not help. "The savage origins are the puzzle; the surviving work of art is the only clue by which we can hope to penetrate the inwardness of the origins." The anthropological approach "always takes us away from the actual poem and the individual poet to seek the sources of their power in something earlier and less known" (305-06).

Thus the anthropological approach merits Lewis's ire in that it violates his cardinal principle: attend to the poem itself. It takes us outside the poem and leaves us there; also, it dismembers the poem, calling undue attention to minor points, and so destroys the "flavor" of the whole, "leaving hardly a rack behind." Lewis admits that it is sometimes necessary to go outside the poem, in order to come inside again, "better equipped" (De Audiendis" 1), but he obviously believes the anthropological approach capable only of taking us outside. "There's life in the fountains," but the fountains are in the poetry—the inner quality of the book, play, or poem—not in the conjectural origins of the bits and pieces.

2. *The personal heresy.* The Lewis-Tillyard controversy published under the title *The Personal Heresy,* sets forth the problem as Lewis sees it. Many critics use the text before them as raw material to supply clues to the psychological state of the author. Stated simply, "the concealed major premiss is plainly the proposition that all poetry is *about* the poet's state of mind" (2). This view leads the critic to neglect the spirit of the text, using it merely as a lens to examine the author. Lewis admits that it is a valid question to ask to what extent, say, a character in a

play resembles the author of the play, but adds that such a query involves a turning away from imaginative experience (p. 8). While we are psychoanalyzing the author, or speculating as to his identity with one of his creations, we are missing the play, or the poem, or the story. We are experiencing something, but not what we were intended to experience. In a characteristic way Lewis summarizes his view:

> Let it be granted that I do approach the poet; at least I do it by sharing his consciousness, not by studying it. I look with his eyes, not at him. He, for the moment, will be precisely what I do not see; for you can see any eyes rather than the pair you see with, and if you want to examine your own glasses you must take them off your own nose. (11)

Remember, too, that for Lewis psychological analysis of any kind is of a mingled yarn, and not necessarily to be trusted. So, once again, we have a two-fold problem: a) the personal heresy takes us away from the essence of the work, and, b) it is very unlikely, even on its own grounds, to produce any information of value.

The personal heresy is, in Lewis's thought, related to the philosophy of subjectivism:

> For the typical modern critic is usually a half-hearted materialist. He accepts, or thinks he accepts, that picture of the world which popularized science gives him. He thinks that everything except the buzzing electrons is subjective fancy; and he therefore believes that all poetry must come out of the poet's head and express (of course) his pure, uncontaminated, undivided 'personality' because outside the poet's head there is nothing but the interplay of blind forces. (28)

This is not, then, merely a literary problem. It is one manifestation of a much broader malady, and as such has a significance for Lewis that transcends things literary.

Perhaps connected with the personal heresy is another critical trend that Lewis despises—that of reconstructing imaginary histories of the process by which a book is written. (Lewis himself sees a connection between the two; cf. p. 120). He notes that much of the time critics do not really criticize at all; that is, they do not spend their time in deciding what makes a work good or bad; rather they waste a lot of ink in speculating how the work was composed. This is, of course, one of the main thrusts of the article, "Modern Theology and Biblical Criticism."[4] He is convinced that imaginary reconstructions are almost always wrong, and that even if correct they are irrelevant. The critic speculating as to how a work was composed is not attending to the work itself. This is, then, simply another method of avoiding the poem.

3. *Character criticism.* This type is treated in a number of places, but the fullest treatment is in that superb essay, "Hamlet: The Prince or the Poem?". Here he calls us back from an almost universal focus

on the character of Hamlet to a poetic consideration of the play itself. "It has a taste of its own, an all-pervading relish which we recognize even in its smallest fragments, and which, once tasted, we recur to. When we want that taste, no other book will do instead" (92-93). He then suggests certain components of that taste by stressing the "cold and darkness and sickening suspense of the ghost scenes" (97), and above all the focus on death. Not merely a concern with dying, but death itself. In a passage of unusual power he captures this element of the play:

> In *Hamlet* we are kept thinking about it [being dead] all the time, whether in terms of the soul's destiny or of the body's. Purgatory, Hell, Heaven, the wounded name, the rights—or wrongs—of Ophelia's burial, and the staying-power of a tanner's corpse; and beyond all this, beyond all Christian and all Pagan maps of the hereafter, comes a curious groping and tapping of thoughts, about 'what dreams may come'. It is this that gives to the whole play its quality of darkness and of misgiving. (99)

For me, at least, this essay forever lays to rest any feeling that character analysis is the main way to approach a play or a book. Character study can be interesting, but so often we strip away all else, leaving "character" standing "like a pistil after the petals go." Lewis elsewhere mentions readers who seem interested only in detailed studies of complex human personalities, and he admits that some forms of literature lend themselves more readily to that procedure ("On Science Fiction" 65; "On Stories" 3). But such is not his approach either to reading, to writing, or to criticism.

4. *Source criticism.* Source hunting seems an intrinsic part of all literary scholarship, and to this Lewis voices no objection. He does, however, object to the kind of criticism which looks only for sources, minimizing or ignoring the quality of the work being reviewed. And he makes a clear distinction between the task of the literary critic and that of the literary historian. Analyzing the work before him is the critic's task; source hunting is the historian's. In his own words:

> As historians, as critics of authors, we may want to know whether some simile in the *Brut* came first from Wace or Layamon; whether some speech in *Troilus* came first from Boccacio or Chaucer. But as readers we are concerned only to receive, as critics of books we are concerned only to diagnose and evaluate, what this simile or speech contributes to the whole 'communicating and doing' of the work before us. ("The Genesis of a Medieval Book" 39).

Lewis also deplores the tendency to forget that a source may be very inferior in quality to the work which springs from it. Very often the sort of critic who thinks only in terms of sources leaves the impression that everything in the later work came from the source; that the author was merely a conduit to carry the source materials. Lewis reminds us that authors are creative, and often provide a radically different finished product.[5] Perhaps there is no power in the tongue of man to alter the trend toward source criticism, but Lewis certainly did his part.

5. *Motif criticism.* The search for motifs is simply another form of the search for sources, and is open to the same objections; subject to the same limitations. It, too, distracts us from the business at hand. Lewis says it well: "The search for 'motifs' forces upon our attention in each text precisely what mattered least to the story-teller and his audience" (Rev. of *The Other World* 93). A motif is, in a sense, artificial. When a writer tells a story of revenge, he is not thinking of the "revenge motif." He is thinking at the moment of a particular offense which in that story calls for revenge. Criticism which centers on motifs may, then, be "an infinite deal of nothing," the least helpful of all.

6. *Authorship criticism.* When dealing with works whose authorship is in doubt, who can resist the obvious temptation? Think how much time has been spent in seminaries and churches haggling over the authorship of the book of Hebrews and of the fourth Gospel! And, of course, it can be an important question; in some instances important to an understanding of the work. Lewis seemed able to keep such matters in perspective; he often dealt with questions of the type, but was able to keep them sufficiently in the background not to obscure the work itself. As early as *The Allegory of Love* he can say of a medieval poem: "The authorship of the poem has been disputed, but the dispute need not concern us" (236). This is the kind of thing he would have said on a boyhood walk with Arthur, and it is the kind of thing he could say from his Cambridge chair.

In fact, all questions which are usually classed under the term "higher criticism" received the same treatment—author, date, purpose, occasion, and such like. He could and did deal with them when necessary, but he preferred not to allow such matters to distract from the nature of the work. That he was capable of technical and detailed criticism is evident to readers of such articles as "Genius and Genius" and "A Note on *Comus*." Even in these articles, however, we run across telling phrases: "the cold, tingling, almost unbreathable, region of the aerial spirits," and "the tendency is one easier, no doubt, to feel than to define" ("A Note on Comus" 175). Never, regardless of the technical difficulty of the enterprise, does he get very far from the quiddity of the text before him. This is the most consistent fact about his work.

Sophisticated commentaries, he felt, are usually harmful in that they interfere with the reader's surrender to the spirit of the text. It is difficult to retain the spirit of a poem while thumbing through a commentary or a glossary. I suppose we would all agree that *The Faerie Queene* is formidable for a modern reader, but, even here, Lewis encourages us to go directly to the text:

> And unfortunately *The Faerie Queene* suffers even more than most great works from being approached through the medium of commentaries and 'literary history'. These all demand from us a sophisticated, self-conscious frame of mind. But then, when we have used all these aids, we discover that the poem itself demands exactly the opposite response. Its primary appeal is to the most naive and innocent tastes. ("Edmund Spenser, 1552-1599" 97).

One type of commentary met his approval: the type which provides ahead of time a background in the culture and language of a period, enabling the reader to prepare himself prior to reading an old work. This kind he himself furnishes in *The Discarded Image* and in his essay, "Imagination and Thought in the Middle Ages."

No critic can, in Lewis's view, function properly as a critic until he has opened his heart to the work being analyzed. No amount of source hunting, anthropological speculation, motif-tracing, or anything else will do the trick. One must receive the work as it is, allowing it to serve the imagination as it will. Just as one cannot profitably discuss the nature of the comic until he first sees the joke and receives it as a joke, so he cannot discuss literature until he has seen and received it as it was intended ("Undergraduate Criticism").

A reviewer's "critical theories" fade into insignificance. On several occasions he calls attention to discrepancies between the actual literary experience and the implicit literary theory of a critic.[6] It is unfortunately true, however, that if a critic holds to his theories too dogmatically they can kill his enjoyment, rendering him incapable of supplying the type of critique Lewis advocated. I once had a friend who for some reason felt that all stories should tell of strange adventures. He refused to admit any value at all in *Huckleberry Finn* on the grounds that it contains nothing strange. I have no idea how he defined the word "strange," but in any case his arbitrary theory destroyed his enjoyment of much excellent literature. How would you like to read a review of *The Grapes of Wrath* written by my friend?

Lewis believed that his method could help us enjoy forms we had hitherto despised. He reasons, for example, that this kind of approach could lead to an enjoyment of allegory—that form so often scorned in modern times. After describing the wrong manner of reading allegory—that of "reading into" it, putting our own concepts in the place of the symbol—he says:

> But that method leads you continually out of the book back into the conception you started from and would have had without reading it. The right process is the exact reverse. We ought not to be thinking, 'This green valley, where the shepherd boy is singing, represents humility'; we ought to be discovering, as we read, that humility is like that green valley. That way, moving always into the book not out of it, from the concept to the image, enriches the concept. And that is what allegory is for ("The Vision" 1007).

For another example, if Bunyan pictures the process of repentance as the crossing of a deep gorge, we tend to say, "He is talking only of repentance"; and we are mildly disappointed. We could derive more pleasure and instruction (and get closer to the meaning of the book) if we said, "So that is what repentance really is; the rigorous scaling of the walls of a deep canyon." In the first instance we empty the symbol of all meaning except that of which we are already aware. In the second, we allow the symbol to suggest new meaning to us, to open our eyes and stimulate our imaginations.

Lewis is not, of course, alone in his contention that essence is of first importance, though he may be almost unique in the strength of his emphasis and in the consistency of his application. There are, though, many other literary scholars on the same side of the fence, and Lewis himself, in "Hamlet, the Prince or the Poem?" (89-93), cites several examples of authors who approach literature more or less as he does.

It is best, according to Lewis, to have first met *The Faerie Queene* in a large illustrated edition, on a wet day, between the ages of twelve and sixteen ("Edmund Spenser," 40). A sentence like that gives us some hint of the profound pleasure such reading must have brought him. When he settled in by the fireside to read Spenser, his mind was at that moment far away from literary theories. In fact he was not thinking of literature at all. Nor even of Spenser. He was thinking of knights and horses and swords and monsters and of all the other beauties and horrors of the tale; also, no doubt, of the moral allegory. To use one of his characteristic analogies, we do not normally look at the sun; rather, we use it as a means by which we see other things. An astronomer might look at it to study it, but this is an exceptional use. A literary critic might look *at* a work of art to study it, but this is not its designed purpose. The critic who follows Lewis's method will find that he has less and less concern for theories and even for "literature" as an abstraction. These "losses" will be compensated by a childlike pleasure in books—not in "literature" but in particular books. Who knows? He may even find himself longing for a wet day and a large illustrated edition of *The Faerie Queene*.

### *Lewis the Imaginative Writer*

Only a few remarks need be made here. Much has been written on this subject; far more than on the earlier points of this paper, and I suspect his approach to imaginative writing is generally better known than is his approach to literary criticism. In a sense, however, they are one and the same. In his imaginative writings he attempted to apply the principles by which he judged the works of others.

Having established that Lewis stressed the essence of a literary work above all else, it is safe to assume that his own novels, stories and poems were written from this viewpoint. And that is exactly what we find. As every Lewis reader knows, he always began by "seeing pictures"—a faun with an umbrella, a huge golden lion, floating islands—and wrote to communicate those pictures. As the story grew the didactic parts grew of themselves, developing from the fabric of the story. In writing as in reading, the quiddity is the thing.

That is why he is so negative toward imaginative writing as self-expression. Self-expression is the personal heresy through the other end of the telescope. He wrote to communicate whatever vision was filling his imagination at the moment, not to reveal his inner self.

Nor did he write to provide mere action and excitement. In one of his letters to Arthur (Greeves, 409-10), he indicates his fear that a strong "narrative lust" may well injure the "taste for other, better,. . .forms of literary pleasure." He realised that the quality of a vision could be hampered by too much action. Would we not agree that what we remember and cherish about Narnia is the golden and enchanting atmosphere? The events fascinate; the Christian symbolism speaks to us; but the essence of Narnia is what counts.

As to his success in communicating the essence of his vision, no defense is needed, for who would deny it? We can taste the strong flavor of Narnia, the brooding darkness of *That Hideous Strength*, and especially the strange mixture of black and gold that is *Till We Have Faces*. For this one reader, at least, even the unsatisfactory fragment, *The Dark Tower*, imparts the vision with flawless clarity. The scene in the room of the Stingingman is forever printed in my mind.

One thing, however, is deserving of special mention, and that is Lewis's ability to impart his vision and elicit response even in his more mundane writings. One would expect an emotional response to his mythical worlds and to his poetry, but I have always been impressed with the emotive power of almost everything he wrote—articles, essays, literary history, literary criticism, autobiography, theology, ethics, controversy—everything! I find myself caught up in the spirit of whatever he is doing, and though I admit to a strong bias in his favor, I do not think that accounts for all of it. After all, the bias had to have a cause.

There are no doubt many and complex facets to his ability to express his vision and to provoke emotion, even in writings in which it would be least expected. But I have noticed one thing—a little thing—but for me it is important. It is what I would call his tendency to "irrelevant description." He constantly throws in small details which have nothing whatever to do with the point he is making, but which contribute handsomely to the effect of the passage. Having argued in his introduction to the Athanasius work that any book, even serious theology, can have a devotional impact, he says: "I believe that many who find that 'nothing happens' when they sit down, or kneel down, to a book of devotion, would find that the heart sings unbidden while they are working their way through a tough bit of theology with a pipe in their teeth and a pencil in their hand" (10). "Pipe in their teeth" is as irrelevant as a set of words can be. It may even be harmful, since it seems to make theological study a masculine and an adult pursuit. But it still has an effect. In his description of the evening on which he discovered MacDonald's *Phantastes,* he says: "Then the train came in. I can still remember the voice of the porter calling out the village names, Saxon and sweet as a nut—'Bookham, Effingham, Horsley train' " (*Surprised* 179). In telling us of Kirk, he adds among the necessary details: "The bitterest, and also funniest, things came out when he had risen abruptly from table (always before the rest of us) and stood ferreting in a villainous old tobacco jar on the mantelpiece for the dottles of former pipes which it was his frugal habit to use again" (*Surprised* 148). In his preface to the *Essays Presented to Charles Williams* he sees Williams's face "through clouds of tobacco smoke and above a pint mug" (x). Examples are easy to come by, and it would be fun, and perhaps instructive, to read Lewis looking for them. What does it matter that a porter happened to be calling the trains, or that Kirk rose from table sooner than the others? In one way it matters not at all; but in another it does. It matters to the poetry. Lewis was so alive to the essence of each situation that it usually comes through quite well in his writing. Such bits of data become part of the message.

Lewis's attitude toward "stock response" is also connected with his desire for the essence of things, and, though not mentioned with great frequency, is an important part of his thought. His best treatment of it is in chapter eight of *A Preface to Paradise Lost.* There he reasons that as a rule our responses are not "stock" enough; we are ambiguous in our response to pride, pleasure, pain, cruelty, death, and everything else; deceived by the current accent on "free play of experience" into thinking it unsophisticated to respond as most people through history have responded. (He tells of a man who criticized an actual view of moonlight on water as being conventional.) He makes his feelings known in his poem, "A Confession," part of which reads:

I'm like that odd man Wordsworth knew, to whom
A primrose was a yellow primrose, one whose doom
Keeps him forever in the list of dunces,
Compelled to live on stock responses. (*Poems* 1)

Lewis felt (and this is a natural result of his belief in objective reality) that literature *ought* to produce stock responses: if a story presents a scene of cruelty, we ought to respond with horror; if a poem describes a mother's love for her child we ought to respond with warm satisfaction. Since he, as an artist, was attempting to impart a vision, he was attempting to elicit a response to that vision; and, believing in absolute values, he preferred to elicit a stock response. "Poetry," he says, "aims at producing something more like vision than it is like action. But vision, in this sense, includes passions. Certain things, if not seen as lovely or detestable, are not being correctly seen at all."

If we need not seek to make our responses original, neither must the author seek to make his vision original. No writer in our time has led a better fight against the fetish of originality.

His imaginative writing, then, exemplifies precisely the same trend as do his reading and his critical writings. In each case he applies that cast of mind which came naturally to him—at least after meeting Arthur Greeves and Hamilton Jenkin. I believe it helped make him an outstanding critic and an outstanding writer. I believe it is one of the things we enjoy when we read Lewis.

As I look back over this essay it surprises me that I have spent all this time on Lewis without concentrating on his religious books. I came to him through his religious writings. The logic of *Mere Christianity* and *The Abolition of Man,* the moral persuasion of *Screwtape,* the painful confrontation with *The Great Divorce* which forced me to examine some of my own pettiness, the quiet nourishment of *Malcolm* and *The Four Loves*—these were the books which captured me. But perhaps it is not really so surprising. When we stop to think about it his religious writing and his literary emphases are very close together. One of his primary values as a religious writer has been to champion the objective; to turn us away from the relativism and subjectivism that undermine all values and the very idea of value itself. He is doing the same thing with literature; forcing us to attend to the great reality of the poetry, the vision, inherent in so many works written by so many different persons in different ages of our history.

## Notes

[1]Cf. the dream related to his father in a letter published in Roger L. Green and Walter Hooper, *C.S. Lewis: A Biography,* 181.

[2]Cf. the letter to a child in America, published in *The Letters of C.S. Lewis,* 270-71.

[3]See, e.g., his comments on the pronunciation of the word "Northwind" in a letter to Arthur Greeves dated May 16, 1916, *They Stand Together,* 98.

[4]Cf. Lewis's review of *The Oxford Book of Christian Verse*, 96-97.

[5]Cf. his introduction to *Selections from Layamon's Brut*, 8-9; also his review of *Sir Thomas Wyatt and Some Collected Studies*, 223.

[6]Cf. Rev. of *The Works of Morris and of Yeats* by Dorothy M. Hoare.

## Works Cited

Chesterton, G.K. "The Grave-Digger." *Lunacy and Letters*. Dorothy Collins, ed. New York: Sheed and Ward, 1958.

Green, Roger L. and Walter Hooper. *C.S. Lewis: A Biography*. New York: Harcourt, 1973.

Lewis, C.S. "The Anthropological Approach." *English and Medieval Studies Presented to J.R.R. Tolkien on the Occasion of His Seventieth Birthday*. Norman Davis and C.L. Wrenn, eds. London: Allen and Unwin, 1962. Rpt. in *Selected Literary Essays*, 301-11.

_____. *The Allegory of Love*. London: Galaxy, 1958.

_____. *Arthurian Torso*. London: Oxford UP, 1948.

_____. "De Audiendis Poetis." *Studies in Medieval and Renaissance Literature*, 1-17.

_____. "The Dethronement of Power." *Time and Tide*, 36 (22 Oct. 1955), 1373.

_____. "Edmund Spenser, 1552-1590." *Major British Writers*, G. B. Harrison, ed. New York: Harcourt, 1954, Rpt. *Studies in Medieval and Renaissance Literature*, 121-45.

_____. *"Edmund Spenser." in Fifteen Poets* (Oxford: Clarendon Press, 1941), 40. Rpt. as "On Reading 'The Faerie Queene'." *Studies in Medieval and Renaissance Literature*, 147-48.

_____. *English Literature in the Sixteenth Century, Excluding Drama*. Oxford: Clarendon, 1954.

_____. "The English Prose 'Morte.'" *Essays on Malory*, J. A. W. Bennett, ed. Oxford: Clarendon, 1963.

_____. Ed. *Essays Presented to Charles Williams*. Grand Rapids: Eerdmans, 1966.

_____. "Foreword." *Smoke on the Mountain* by Joy Davidman. London: Hodder and Stoughton, 1955.

_____. "The Genesis of a Medieval Book." *Studies in Medieval and Renaissance Literature*, 18-40.

_____. "The Gods Return to Earth." *Time and Tide* 35 (14 August 1954), 1083.

_____. "Haggard Rides Again." *Time and Tide*, 41 (3 Sept. 1960), 1044.

_____. "Hamlet: The Prince or the Poem?" *Selected Literary Essays* 88-105.

_____. *Hero and Leander*, Warton Lecture on English Poetry, British Academy (London: Geoffrey Cumberlege, 1952. Rpt. in *Selected Literary Essays*, 58-73.

_____. "Introduction." *The Incarnation of the Word of God*. New York: Macmillan, 1946.

_____. "Introduction." *Selections from Layamon's Brut*, ed. G. L. Brook. Oxford: Clarendon, 1963.

_____. *Letters of C.S. Lewis*, W.H. Lewis, ed. London: Geoffrey Bles, 1966.

_____. *The Literary Impact of the Authorized Version*. London: The Athlone Press, 1950. Rpt. *Selected Literary Essays*, 126-43.

_____. "Neoplatonism in the Poetry of Spenser." *Etudes Anglaises*, 14 (April-June 1951). Rpt. *Studies in Medieval and Renaissance Literature*, 149-64.

——— "A Note on *Comus*." *The Review of English Studies,* 8 (April 1932), 175.

——— *Of Other Worlds.* Walter Hooper, ed. New York: Harcourt, 1966.

——— "On Science Fiction." *Of Other Worlds,* 59-73.

——— "On Stories." *Of Other Worlds,* 3-21.

——— *The Personal Heresy.* Oxford: Oxford UP, 1965.

——— *Poems.* Walter Hooper, ed. New York: Harcourt, 1964.

——— "Preface." The Hierarchy of Heaven and Earth, by D.E. Harding. London: Faber and Faber, 1952.

——— *Rehabilitations and Other Essays.* Oxford: Oxford UP, 1939)

——— Rev. of *The Oxford Book of Christian Verse,* ed. David Cecil, *The Review of English Studies,* 17 (Jan. 1941), 96-97.

——— Rev. of *The Other World* by Howard Rollin Patch, *Medium Aevum* 20 (1951), 93.

——— Rev. of *Sir Thomas Wyatt and Some Collected Studies* by E.K. Chambers, *Medium Aevum,* 3 (Oct. 1934), 223.

——— Rev. of *Taliessin through Logres* by Charles Williams, *The Oxford Magazine,* 64 (14 March 1946), 248-50.

——— Rev. of *The Works of Morris and of Yeats in Relation to Early Saga Literature* by Dorothy M. Hoare, *The Times Literary Supplement* (29 May 1937), 409.

——— "A Sacred Poem," *Theology,* 38 (April 1939), 275.

——— *Selected Literary Essays.* Cambridge: Cambridge UP, 1969.

——— "Shelley, Dryden, and Mr. Eliot." *Rehabilitations.* Rpt. *Selected Literary Essays,* 187-208.

——— *Studies in Medieval and Renaissance Literature* Cambridge: Cambridge UP, 1966.

——— *Studies in Words,* 2d ed. Cambridge: Cambridge UP, 1967.

——— *Surprised by Joy.* New York: Harcourt, 1955.

——— *They Stand Together: The Letters of C.S. Lewis to Arthur Greeves.* Walter Hooper, ed. New York: Macmillan, 1979.

——— "Undergraduate Criticism." *Broadsheet,* 8 (9 Mar. 1960), no page number.

——— "Variation in Shakespeare and Others." *Rehabilitations.* Rpt. *Selected Literary Essays,* 74-87.

——— "The Vision of John Bunyan." *The Listener,* 68 (13 Dec. 1962), 1007.

——— "William Morris." *Rehabilitations.* Rpt. *Selected Literary Essays,* 219-231.

Tolkien, J.R.R. "On Fairy-Stories" *Essays Presented to Charles Williams,* C.S. Lewis, ed. Grand Rapids: Eerdmans, 1966, 38-89.

# Rehabilitating Reading: C.S. Lewis and Contemporary Critical Theory

*Bruce L. Edwards*

In critiquing certain philosophical movements of his time, C.S. Lewis once said this:

> It is a disastrous discovery, as Emerson says somewhere, that we exist. I mean, it is disastrous when instead of merely attending to a rose we are forced to think of ourselves looking at the rose with a certain type of mind and a certain type of eyes. It is disastrous because if you are not very careful, the colour of the rose gets attributed to our optic nerves and its scent to our noses, and in the end there is no rose left (*God in the Dock* 271).

One might add that it has become equally disastrous that we have discovered "reading." For we live in a period of fashionably arcane literary inquiry, which by turns has declared the death of the author, affirmed the authority of readers over the stability of intended meaning, and interrogated the text with such ruthlessness that "in the end, there is no" text left. Both ordinary and extraordinary readers wonder in their reading whether they have actually understood something or have only understood their understanding.

My thesis is that the critical principles of C.S. Lewis represent a balance of concerns in the reading process which potentially provides a salutary alternative to the current cacophony of warring critical camps. In this paper I wish to juxtapose what I will style as Lewis's "rehabilitative poetics" with the view of reading emerging in one particular strain of contemporary theory, deconstruction. In so doing, I will survey Lewis's understanding of the relationships between/among readers, texts, and authors. My aim is not a refutation of deconstruction as such, as much as a meditation upon what will have been lost if its attendent epistemology were to prevail in our definition of reading.

## *I*

Deconstructive textual inquiry serves well as an exemplar of the how traditional Western epistemology is being challenged at the end of the twentieth century. And here I wish to distinguish between two different phenomena within the deconstructive camp. In its most innocent form, deconstruction is simply an attempt to deal with the finiteness of human knowledge, the subjective element of perception. It reminds us of the contingent nature of what we consider knowledge and challenges our easy equation of words with things-in-themselves. As such it serves the discerning critic as a fresh reading strategy with which to sift the text for internal incongruity, contradiction, and ambiguity, while interpreting the text against the backdrop of its evoked or implicit worldview. Above all, deconstruction tells us that reality is, indeed, very deep.

In this it much resembles New Critical explication, and indeed, some deconstructive practitioners, wishing to disarm their sometimes hostile opponents, align their descriptions of deconstruction with this notion:

> [D]econstruction is a currently fashionable or notorious name for good reading as such. All good readers are and always have been deconstructionists" (Miller 43)

> [Deconstruction is] the careful teasing out of warring forces of signification within the text. (Johnson 5)

But among devotees, deconstruction is not merely a tool of inquiry to be employed when facing a particularly difficult or demanding text. It is, in fact, a competing epistemology or *Weltanschauung* to traditional Western realism, rejecting the notion that words can bear faithful witness to reality and regarding all "interpretation" always-already as inseparable from and equivalent to reading. We cannot help but "deconstruct" a text, for the text and its author have no independent status or authority to demand that a reader "understand" them in any particular manner.

The underlying premises of this more radical strain of deconstructive inquiry embody what Vincent Leitch has called a "counter-historiography." In its most extreme form, deconstructive dogma regards such concepts as objectivity and referentiality as elements of cultural fascism and the critics who hold these concepts as agents of a police state seeking to impose their personal order on experience to restrain the joyful freeplay of language that might liberate an otherwise oppressed populus of readers. The net effect is, in Gerald Graff's words, is that "to write" and "to read" become intransitive verbs; readership collapses into authorship; and the text, long the most stable and reliable component in the study of literature, relinquishes its ability to *mean* or *be*. In its rejection of the referential power of language, deconstruction thus privileges the present, this moment, in the act of reading; the past is dead, and the future is always now.

*II*

Against this radically skeptical notion of reading and textuality, I place the stance of C.S. Lewis, a man who regarded himself as a dinosaur, anachronistic even in his own culture more than thirty years ago. Lewis possessed an uncanny ability to uncover the hidden assumptions and veiled agendas submerged in otherwise innocuous texts, and his most sustained critique of western thought, *The Abolition of Man,* began with a dissection of a wartime composition text in which he documented with special clarity the loss of objective value in the public contemplation of morality and the arts.

At the heart of his criticism, as well as his apologetics and fiction, is a stance he would call *rehabilitative.* This rehabilitative stance manifested a reverence for the past, a principled skepticism of one's own period's mores and dogma, and a profound propensity for recovering and preserving lost values and ideals.

As an approach to texts, rehabilitation can be defined in this way: Lewis believed that an author's text deserved to speak out of and was capable of speaking out of its own time and culture to a contemporary readership, enabling readers to inhabit the world evoked by and through the author. In the words of Lewis:

> We want to know—therefore, as far as may be, we want to live through for ourselves—the experience of men long dead. What a poem may "mean" to moderns and to them only, however delightful, is from this point of view, merely a stain on the lens. We must clean the lens and remove the stain so that the real past can be seen better (*Studies in Medieval and Renaissance Literature* 2).

Lewis's criticism is replete with attempts to retrieve and rejuvenate authors and whole genres of literature which had been way-laid, forgotten or ignored by an unappreciative generation of readers and critics.

Peter Schakel is nevertheless right, I believe, in arguing that Lewis's approach to texts was in flux during his career, evolving over a long period of time as he struggled to balance textual objectivity and readerly subjectivity, to marry reason and imagination, in the reading act. The young Lewis, for instance, had promoted a most vigorous objectivist stance in his exchange with Tillyard, "The Personal Heresy," placing, as Schakel explains,

> The emphasis...on the object, and on reading as a quasi-mechanical process of absorbing the object presented by the author. The personalities of author and reader were to be disengaged, in good reading, so that private images or overtones would not distort the universality of the things or ideas the author was depicting (164).

If one pays attention, one may observe here something very close to a definition of the New Critical approach to the text. But Lewis was no New Critic, even at the time he debated Tillyard. His intention simply was to circumvent the critic who would identify the poem with the poet in some crude biographical correspondence theory. The mature Lewis, writing in *An Experiment in Criticism,* conceded the subjective element in reading, but refused to surrender the realism, or objectivity, which would permit a reader to engage the world an author had evoked.

While Lewis believed in the integrity of the text, he recognized the profitability of consulting—as available—cultural context and authorial intention, to inform his reading. He advocated this without discounting the response of the reader as crucial to the meaning of a literary text. Lewis's *The Discarded Image* is an excellent example of the kind of scholarship which illuminates and preserves the "real poem," without displacing it or substituting one of one's own making. Lewis proposes in the introduction to that volume that, in reading poetry out of one's own time, the reader acquire beforehand a "tolerable (though very incomplete) outfit" which, taken alone in the reading, might lead into, instead of out of, the text:

> To be always looking at the map when there is a fine prospect before you shatters the "wise passiveness" in which landscape ought to be enjoyed. But to consult a map before we set out has no such ill effect (vii).

This "map," which Lewis elsewhere calls "the insulating power of context," represents an unobtrusive adjunct to the text which sets the text within its historical and intentional context, making it possible for the reader still to put the text first, without distraction.

In *An Experiment in Criticism,* Lewis thus urged a careful distinction between what he called "use" and "reception" in reading

> We [can be] so busy doing things with the work that we give it too little chance to work on us. Thus increasingly we meet only ourselves.... But one of the chief operations of art is to remove our gaze from that mirrored face, to deliver us from that solitude. [I] suggest we should be much less concerned with altering our own opinions—though this of course is sometimes their effect—than with entering fully into the opinions, and therefore also the attitudes, feelings, and total experience, of other men" (85).

"Reception" of the text allowed for, nay, encouraged the reader to minimize his own consciousness in order to inhabit the world evoked by the writer. The reader, Lewis opined, should take no delight in merely imposing his culture on another's, for he understood that true liberation lay not in supplanting the author and substituting one's own "text," but in deliberately leaving behind the self, to become another self. "Use," on the other hand, appropriated texts for its own designs, employing them for the specific purpose the reader had in selecting the text. Lewis further explains:

> When we 'receive' it we exert our senses and imagination and various other powers according to a pattern invented by the artist. When we 'use' it we treat it as assistance for our own activities. The one, to use an old fashioned image, is like being taken for a bicycle ride by a man who may know roads we have never yet explored. The other is like adding one of those little motor attachments to our own bicycle and then going for one of our familiar rides... 'Using' is inferior to 'reception' because art, if used rather than received, merely facilitates, brightens, relieves, or palliates our life, and does not add to it' (88).

A composite model of Lewis's understanding of the relationships between reader-writer-text, might go like this:

> The author creates a text out of the language and context of her cultural community, a text which reflects, when successful, her *intention*. The author may inadvertantly *mean* more or less than she intended, i.e., more (or less) than she *desired*, but in either event the reader may receive the text as a purposeful expression from the author's mind. The reader brings to the text his own set of expectations and viewpoints which may be confirmed or questioned or supplanted in the course of reading. Nevertheless, the reader's first task is always to read the text which the author has actually written, playing the role of the reader made implicit by the text itself.
>
> The text is both a *Logos* (something said) and a *Poiema* (something made). This distinction allows a reader to respond favorably to a text without necessarily accepting its implicit worldview or message, and likewise, appreciate a text's outlook or sentiment without believing it is a well-made artifact. The text thus exists as an objective entity apart from the author or reader's consciousness and as such may delight, teach or move the recipient. Though a text's "public meaning" or significance may change from age to age or from culture to culture, a text's original ontological meaning remains stable and is recoverable by historical and philological study.

This conception of the literary enterprise is, of course, quite out of fashion today. Gerald Graff well frames the questions critics sympathetic to Lewis must face when he suggests that

> Conceptions of literature and the humanities both reflect and shape our conceptions of humanness and our views of man in society. Most theories of literature are more or less concealed theories of the nature of man and of the good society. In this sense, literary thinking is inseparable from moral and social thinking (1).

By this measure, Western culture is indeed in dire straits; for in the past two decades critics have encouraged, indeed celebrated the imperialism of readers over the against the authority of authors, leaving us with texts which may mean or be at the whim of the reader, or, to put it another way, may only be *used* and never *received* by the reader.

If I follow contemporary currents correctly, what animates late twentieth-century criticism is not the hope of inhabiting another writer's world or the discovery or challenge of alternative worldviews but a principled narcissism. Trapped in the prison-house of language, we are also doomed to the prison-house of personhood; we discover that as readers we are at best unwilling, and at worst incapable, of transcending the narrow confines of culture, gender, religion, education, and race which have nurtured us; we may see and hear only what we want to see and hear.

The contemporary myth, properly interpreted, seems to be that we are liberated from one formalism only to become captive of another: our new modes of criticism reveal that there is nothing to be revealed; there is no longer a center, no ground of being, no reference point outside of the text or outside of me to which I can pledge my allegiance, or by which I can navigate my way through the labyrinth of human experience. What began as a desperate flight from debilitating realism has become a blithe trek into a literary solipsism.

This is, of course, the antithesis of Lewis's view of reading, and that of a majority Western readers up until the last decade or so. With the merging of subject/object in the reading act—and, indeed, any perceptual act—man devolves increasingly into an "himself," unperturbed by outside values and judgments. His life itself, his thoughts, his muffled entanglements with other human beings, his reading all loom as "incessant autobiography." Here is a creature intended to become a *person,* who cannot "come out" of himself-as-subject to the objective world where minds may meet.

For Lewis, the loss leads not only to a rather impoverished view of literature—the reader finds only mirrors of his own consciousness, a litmus paper of his own emotions and sentiments, confirming, reasserting, but never challenging or displacing them—but is debilitating and catastrophic for rationality itself. The way out of this dilemma for Lewis is a distinction between what he called "contemplation" and "enjoyment," terms drawn from Samuel Alexander's *Space, Time and Deity,* a book which Lewis read prior to his conversion to Christianity and which, by his own admission, profoundly affected his way of viewing the world. Lewis explains his terms this way:

> "Enjoyment" has nothing to do with pleasure, nor "contemplation" with the contemplative life. When you see a table you "enjoy" the act of seeing and "contemplate" the table. Later, if you took up Optics and thought about seeing itself, you would be contemplating the seeing and enjoying the thought (*Surprised by Joy* 217).

The enjoyment is the process or *doing* of an activity; the contemplation is the *apprehending* of the object of the activity:

> We do not "think a thought" in the same sense in which we "think that Herodotus is unreliable." When we think a thought, "thought" is a cognate accusative (like "blow" in "strike a blow"). We enjoy the thought (that Herodotus is unreliable) and, in so doing, contemplate the unreliability of Herodotus (*Surprised* 217-18).

Lewis regarded this distinction "as an indispensable tool of thought" because it allowed for the separation of seer from object of sight, knower from object of knowledge, thinker from object of thinking and so on. To "see" a table was to be distinct from it, perceiving it and registering it as an "outside" entity; on the other hand, to shift from the seeing of the table to one's act of seeing it—"to take one's eyes out to look at them"—is to lose the object itself:

> In other words the enjoyment and the contemplation of our inner activities are incompatible. You cannot hope and also think about hoping at the same moment; for in hope we look to hope's object and we interrupt this by (so to speak) turning around to look at the hope itself (*Surprised* 218).

As the reader approaches the text and reads, he is "enjoying" the reading and "contemplating" the text: the *text* is the object of his "enjoyment." However, as soon as the reader's attention shifts from the text to the act of reading—in Lewis's terminology, from contemplating the text to contemplating "reading"—the *object* of reading, the text, drops from view. The reader who attends to his own reading may mistake the "sediment" of his own introspective look at reading for the text itself.

Lewis would not deny, of course, that one might choose to attend to one's reading as a process and examine it; he is simply making the proviso that attention to the *process* of reading is not the same thing as reading a text. On the surface this may sound like a restatement of the New Critic's "affective fallacy," the "confusion of the poem with its results (what it *is* and what it *does*)," but that is not Lewis's point here. Instead, Lewis would distinguish two different kinds of *acts*: reading-as-such and the examination of *what* reading is. The former involves one intellect engaging another's textual discourse. The latter involves one intellect examining *itself* in the act of reading. The former has an object outside of the intellect which engages it; the latter does not.

Reader-oriented critics like Stanley Fish as well as deconstructionists like J. Hillis Miller confound the act of reading by trying to "contemplate the enjoyed," by merging criticism with reading. If reading is *always-already* an "interpretation," and the author's intended text cannot be confronted, then the question must arise, "What is it an interpretation of?" Lewis, of course, would respond that by confusing the contemplation of the text with the contemplation of reading, deconstructive critics lose the text:

> You cannot go on "explaining away" for ever; you will find that you have explained away explanation itself. You cannot go on "seeing through" things for ever. The whole point of seeing through something is to see something through it. It is good that windows should be transparent, because the street or garden beyond it is opaque. How if you saw through the garden too? It is no use trying to "see through" first principles. If you see through everything, then everything is transparent. But a wholly transparent world is an invisible world. To "see through" all things is the same as not to see (*The Abolition of Man* 91).

By "explaining away" the reading of a text as an "interpretation," one claims that she is, in effect, "seeing through" to what already "really is." The problem here is not the "Affective Fallacy," but that of failing to distinguish between one's apprehension of the reading *process* and the actual *reading* of a text; not a "confusing of the poem with its results," but a failure to *see* the poem at all.

In the parlance of the New Critic, Lewis believed a poem could both *mean* and *be,* and that a poem may in some sense include its effects. However, it was only because of this "indispensible tool of thought," the distinction between enjoyment and contemplation, between object and subject, that a reader could be in a position to discern the poem from its effects. What is lost, among contemporary theorists, in the experience of reading is that sense that one may leave his cozy world of commonplaces and for a time rest in the imagination of another, and thus chastened or rehabilitated, less a prisoner of one's own time, one's own commitments, one's autobiography.

In an age which is generally ahistorical—and anti-historical when it is not—in an age in which all history is thought to be revisionism, in an age in which the past is regarded as merely the mirror of the present or the collective superstitions of a backward era—in other words, in an age of "chronological snobbery" gone mad—a reader and thinker the stature of Lewis will emerge as the sanest and most innovative of men.

The unspoken premise behind this Lewisian stance is that through writing, an author may step out of himself and that through reading a reader may do the same, enabling both to be "rehabilitated," to understand their own personhood, to become something other. If reading a text is to have any meaning, if texuality is to be rehabilitated in our time, it will be on the basis which Lewis articulated in his work.

I can think of no better way to conclude this paper than to quote at length Lewis's eloquent defense of reading as an act of transcendence, found in the closing pages of *An Experiment in Criticism:*

Those of us who have been true readers all our life seldom fully realise the enormous extension of our being which we owe to authors. We realise it best when we talk with an unliterary friend. He may be full of goodness and good sense but he inhabits a tiny world. In it, we should be suffocated. The man who is contented to be only himself, and therefore less a self, is in prison. My own eyes are not enough for me, I will see through the eyes of others. Reality, even seen through the eyes of many is not enough. I will see what others have invented. Even the eyes of all humanity are not enough. I regret that the brutes cannot write books. Very gladly would I learn what face things present to a mouse or a bee; more gladly still would I perceive the olfactory world charged with all the information and emotion it carries for a dog.

Literary experience heals the wound, without undermining the privilege, of individuality. There are mass emotions which heal the wound; but they destroy the privilege. In them, our separate selves are pooled and we sink back into sub-individuality. But in reading great literature, I become a thousand men and yet remain myself. Like the night sky in the Greek poem, I see with a myriad eyes, but it is still I who see. Here, as in worship, in love, in moral action, and in knowing, I transcend myself; and am never more myself than when I do (140-141).

## Works Cited

Graff, Gerald. *Literature Against Itself.* Chicago: U of Chicago P, 1979.

Johnson, Barbara. *The Critical Difference: Essays in the Contemporary Rhetoric of Reading.* Baltimore: Johns Hopkins UP, 1980.

Lewis, Clive Staples. *The Abolition of Man.* New York: Macmillan, 1947.

______. *An Experiment in Criticism.* Cambridge: Cambridge UP, 1961.

______. *The Discarded Image.* Cambridge: Cambridge UP, 1964.

______. *God in the Dock.* Grand Rapids: Eerdmans, 1970.

______. *Studies in medieval and Renaissance Literature.* Cambridge: Cambridge UP, 1975.

______. *Surprised by Joy.* New York: Harcourt, 1955.

Miller, J. Hillis, "Composition and Decomposition," in Winifred Horner, ed., *Composition and Literature: Bridging the Gap.* Chicago: U of Chicago P, 1983.

Schakel, Peter J. *Reason and Imagination in C.S. Lewis,* Grand Rapids: Eerdmans, 1984.

# "...the Abstractions Proper to Them": C.S. Lewis and Institutional Theory of Literature

*Robert B. Meyers*

Initial reactions to C.S. Lewis's *Experiment in Criticism* strongly imply that the reviewers did not quite know what to make of the critical positions adopted in the book. One critic, for example, suggests his final perplexity harmlessly by labelling the book "mischievous" (Bell 1966). Another straddles the fence by calling it a "compound of brilliance and nonsense" (Logan 563). Bernard Bergonzi typifies the early disinclination to deal fully with the book in his concluding assessment: "one would, I think, be foolish to swallow all of his vigorous, unfair, provocative book; but one would be more foolish to ignore it" (710). As always, though, the reviewers had little difficulty appreciating Lewis's clear and elegant prose style.

Reluctant as I am to do so, I must agree with the reviewers who found the book perplexing. There is much that is oblique and troublesome about its argumentative progress. After all, it contains two chapters ("On Myth" and "Poetry") which are sufficiently digressive as to seem downright superfluous. For the most part, the book develops negatively, stressing what reading—and later literature itself—is not. The arguments seem to develop in an accretive manner: a contention is made casually as if quite clear at point A, then reappears at B to be developed further because it was really not so clear in the first place. The very generality at which Lewis argues his case also poses something of a problem. Some of the reviewers did speculate on the "context" of the argument by suggesting whose work Lewis actually was addressing—F.R. Leavis seemed the most popular candidate. Lewis's very strategy of proceeding at a most general level, though, suggests that setting the argumentative context by naming names is perhaps not the correct route. Nevertheless, general or not, the questions remain: what is the argumentative context which Lewis implies, and why did readers find it so confusing?

In this paper, I want to discuss Lewis's intriguing "experiment" from the perspective that it makes most sense if taken as an institutional theory. I shall take a few paragraphs here to give a broad indication of the perspective adopted in such a theory, but I shall elaborate on its basic assumptions more closely as I discuss the particulars of Lewis's book. Perhaps it is best to begin by observing that the institutional view of literature arises because of the perennial difficulties experienced in the efforts made to define literature. No definition seems ever to satisfactorily encompass everything that ordinarily passes for literature. The romantic/expressionist claim, for example, that great souls make literature has few adherents—especially in its strong sense—in a democratic age. The material approach—dividing language into poetic and non-poetic qualities—has proven a notoriously hopeless task. Yet the concept of literature exists. Members of any community have no difficulty in saying what is and is not a literary work. And individuals have no difficulty because they have been trained to know which works to treat specially as literature and how to treat them. Vague as this account is in its present form, it is at least clear that this perspective makes the strongest possible link between the concept of literature and the community which supports it. In this theory, in fact, no special set of features constitutes the literary work. A literary work is, instead, any verbal artifact that the community treats in a certain way.

This drastically simplified version of the institutional approach immediately raises two questions in related areas: 1) what special sort of treatment do readers extend to works considered literary rather than non-literary? and 2) how (and by whom) is the literary audience constituted? Are all readers equally important, for example?

In providing a general answer to the first question, theorists such as Barbara Hernnstein Smith and John M. Ellis distinguish between the pragmatic and aesthetic uses of language. To follow Smith's terminology, there is "natural" discourse and "fictive" discourse. Natural discourse in any utterance, "trivial or sublime, ill-wrought or eloquent, true or false, scientific or passionate—that can be taken as someone's saying something, somewhere, sometime, that is, as the verbal acts of real persons on particular occasions in particular sets of circumstances" (Smith 15). Such discourse constitutes an historical event. Literary works, on the other hand,

> are not natural utterances, not historically unique verbal acts or events; indeed, a poem is not an event at all, and cannot be said to have 'occurred' in the usual sense. When we read the text of a poem or hear it read aloud, our response to it is governed by quite special conventions and it is understanding that these conventions are operating that distinguishes the poem as a verbal artwork from natural discourse. (Smith 24)

Thus, only the proverbial country bumpkin attempts to stop a murder being enacted on stage in the course of a play. The stock illustration, however, far from exhausts the consequences of the work's essentially fictive status to the literary audience. The interpretive ramifications are quite far reaching.

Perhaps the most startling interpretive consequence of the institutional view occurs in connection with what Ellis calls the work's "context of origin" (44). While natural discourse *must* be interpreted with reference to its context of origin—who said the words, for what reasons, in what circumstances—the application of these considerations to fictive works, according to Ellis, virtually undoes the work as literature. Ellis makes this point strongly in the course of a claim that the relevant context in terms of which to understand a work is *not* the writer's biography:

> The process of a text becoming a literary text involves three stages: its originating in the context of its creator; its then being offered for use as literature, and its finally being accepted as such. The biographical approach returns the text to its former status and reverses the process of becoming a literary text. (113)

The agreement of the community to value it and not the authority of the writer makes a text a literary text. In part, the community values the work for its interpretive potential, not the narrow meaning willed by the author. Since, then, a literary text consists, by definition, entirely of a linguistic structure (as opposed to a natural utterance, which consists of a linquistic event *plus* its historical context) Smith notes that the reader of a literary text plays a necessary and active role in its interpretation. The "characteristic effect" of a poem, she says, is "to invite and enable the reader to create a plausible context for it" (142). This inclination toward interpretive openness, again, is one of the appeals of literary experience.

Lewis makes a fairly obvious contact with the institutional theory on these questions of interpretation in the controversy that he waged with E.M.W. Tillyard concerning the "personal heresy."[2] There, Lewis essentially complained that getting in contact with the author at any level is not the aim of literary experience. Put another way, his position strongly opposed defining literature in terms of its context of origin—the very stance that, in the institutional theory, reduces the text to a mere private message.

I am not, of course, claiming that Lewis ever heard the term, "institutional theory." However his fame as a thinker and clear writer rests in no small part on his capacities to observe lucidly with simple common sense, so it is hardly surprising that he could develop a theory that attends closely to the social practice of literature. I am suggesting that such an examination highlights some of the assumptions in his argument that otherwise are only lightly developed or are barely visible at all. The argumentative structure of *Experiment,* which gave the first readers some difficulty, can be made to show through more clearly on several crucial points.

*II*

From one point of view, Lewis's "experiment" could be taken merely as a proposal to remove some of the acrimony and combativeness from evaluative discussions of literature. If, as he suggests, no one actually has a taste for the bad and if the critic's negative reaction to a work is tempered by a genuine awareness that he may not have responded to the work properly, this way of proceeding leaves the critic with practically no targets for his critical aggression. Such an outcome might follow from what Lewis proposes, but his book is no mere plea for better literacy manners. Despite his apparently tame purpose—to examine how readers read books—the logic informing Lewis's scheme appears to be practically revolutionary. The point of the "experiment" is to effect a change in the fundamental logic of literary judgments. Implicitly, then, he rejects at least two other models, namely the evaluation of works against a valorizing definition (one which prefers some set of features over others) and evaluation of the work by virtue of some special connection it has to its author (evidenced in its sincerity, for example). Lewis, to repeat the point just made, had, in "The Personal Heresy," rejected this latter position. In the whole of *Experiment*, there is but one perfunctory paragraph about the author as a man of greatness. But while *Experiment* hardly attends to the author/work connection at all, a good part of it can only be intelligibly construed as a rejection of the notion that literature can be defined by some special set of privileged features. In taking this position, Lewis aligns himself with the institutional theory's stance that the project of looking for real definitions of literature is a hopeless task. I would argue, though, that the line Lewis pursues is a bit roundabout and constitutes a sort of "special case." That is, Lewis deals with just one particular real definition, realism. Furthermore, he discusses realistic literature less in terms of features that works actually have than in terms of the expectations of readers who, not entirely consciously, have assimilated the "doctrine" of realism. Before he gets to that point, though, he adopts the ultimate institutional stance that literature is fundamentally a practice involving two primary elements: the work that has been offered as literature and the reader who reads it. Quite obviously, any fully historical account of the literary world at any point in time would require a full account of the reader/work transaction plus the answer to a number of other questions: how do works in this era come to be? how do they get published or circulated? by whose authority? by whom are they further judged? and so on. At any point in time, the literary world always includes a complex array of readers, ranging from persons who just happen to read the work, to editors, reviewers, teachers of literature—"official" readers, as it were, whose weight in accepting a work and maintaining it in the literary canon varies immensely. No matter how this system is structured at any given historical moment, though, it is clear that everyone who reads a particular work does not have equal say in its enfranchisement into the canon. Lewis retains, even foregrounds, the hierarchical assumption about the readership that is fundamental to the actual practice of the literary world, but he begins by largely sidestepping particulars to get to the essential factor: literature consists of a transaction that occurs between the *literary* reader and the offered work. The vital evaluative dimension of the literary world is retained in his concept of the *literary* reader. Literature happens, exists only in this transaction.

Lewis's extensive interest in mapping the literary audience into its various subdivisions follows directly from these initial assumptions. He begins *Experiment* by positing a hierarchical continuum of readers, extending from the Few (the literary) to the Many (the unliterary), considering first the larger social behavior of the two groups and then moving to their reading habits and behavior. He points out, for example, that although some of the unliterary read frequently, their reading is always undertaken as a last resort for want of something better to do. Nor do they ever bother to read anything twice. In contrast, the literary seek constantly to read. Their reading experiences are sometimes "so momentous that only experiences of love, religion, or bereavement can furnish a standard of comparison"(3). Because their reading is so important to them, what they read is constantly and prominently present to mind for them. "Scenes and characters from books provide them with a sort of iconography by which they interpret their own experience" (3). A crucial consideration in his classification, evidently, is the general importance of the practice of literature to the whole life of the reader in question.

While this larger behavior is important, Lewis's primary object is the *quality* of the literary transaction, and so he is concerned to explore how these two groups read. He pursues this task through four whole chapters which emphasize the unliterary: "False Characterizations," "How the Few and the Many Use Pictures and Music," "The Reading of the Unliterary," and "The Meanings of 'Fantasy.' " I will not discuss all the complex matters he considers in these chapters. Lewis speaks in behalf of his own immediate interests quite adequately. Yet through all his classification and qualification, a close examination shows, I think, that he dissects the reading of the unliterary through three lines of inquiry: 1) why do they read; 2) what reading dispositions are thereby cultivated; and 3) what kinds of literary works best satisfy these dispositions. In his actual discussion, however, motivation (why do they read) comes last, when he introduces "Castle-building," by which he means daydreaming "indulged in moderately and briefly as a temporary holiday or recreation, duly subordinated to more effective outgoing activities" (51). He distinguishes two kinds—"Egoistic" and "Disinterested." In the former, "the day-dreamer is himself always the hero" (52). In the Disinterested type, the daydreamer may not even be present; he simply imagines invented landscapes and the like. The cooperative play of children marks an even further development of this spectrum:

> [Children] may feign a whole world and people it and remain outside it. But when this stage is reached, something more than mere reverie has come into action; construction, invention, in a word, fiction is proceeding. (53)

This continuum, significantly, puts fiction at the opposite pole from any appropriation of the imagination by the ego. The disposition to seize the work for the narrowest kind of manipulation by the reader's ego defines the lowest order of the unliterary.

Since the unliterary read for simple ego gratification, they tend to be incomplete, even sloppy readers, inasmuch as literary works typically contain elements that do not readily lend themselves to such handling by the ego. The point is first made in a parallel argument concerning the viewing of the artistically unsophisticated and the listening of the unmusical. Simplistic viewers "use" the picture "as a self starter for certain imaginative and emotional activities of [their] own" by attending only to "a hasty and unconscious selection of elements in the picture" (16). Lewis foregrounds this inattentiveness when he discusses the unliterary and their responses to style. Inattentiveness renders style either invisible or positively intrusive for the unliterary.

> But the unliterary reader never intends to give words more than the bare minimum of attention necessary for extracting the event. Most of the things which good writing gives or bad writing fails to give are things he does not want and has no use for. (32)

The inattentiveness, again, is compelled by the narrow egocentricity of the unliterary's purpose—merely to provide a framework for daydreaming.

Why they read and how they read accounts for what the unliterary bother to read—narratives particularly swift-moving narratives. The interest in "what happened" ("the Event," Lewis calls it) is further distinguished into three types:

1) The exciting narrative that continually arouses and titilates anxiety.
2) Narratives that arouse, prolong, exasperate and finally satisfy inquisitiveness.
3) Narratives which allow vicarious participation on the reader's part.

Having an interest in these facets of literature is, in itself, not suspect. These elements and the vicarious feelings they can generate are a legitimate part of the experience of readers at all levels. "The unliterary," Lewis explains, "are unliterary not because they enjoy stories in these ways, but because they enjoy them in no other" (38). The lowest kind of reader—the Egoistic Castle-builder—has so small a capacity for enjoying the full range of literary possibility that he voluntarily confines himself to works that most narrowly employ even the narrative dimension: "success stories, certain love stories, and certain stories of high life" (54) are all that these readers seek out because such stuff demands so little of them.

Thus through the first chapters of *Experiment,* Lewis ranges back and forth through his three implied questions: why, how and what? and provides commentary quite directly relevant to the institutional theory. In effect, his various classifications of the audience are grounded in impediments within the reader himself to establishing full contact with an offered work. As he describes them, the crimes of the unliterary tend to be crimes of neglect. The unliterary, for reasons having nothing to do with the work but rather having to do with themselves, distort the work by actually neglecting parts of it. Since not all of it is actually apprehended, the transaction which is literature (rather than some other activity) never takes place. yet even Lewis's unliterary can fully receive some small range of works. Lewis does mention works written in such a way as not to invite much stylistic scrutiny, etc. The rest they distort or, more likely, simply avoid.

## *III*

While the very shift to the transaction model of literature is itself a decisive step, what Lewis actually discovers about the unliterary is not very monumental. It seems no great feat of analysis to come to the conclusion that the proper reading of a work demands that the reader attend to all of it, not just some of it. At this point, however, Lewis turns away from the reading habits of the unliterary to a consideration of realism. At first sight, this shift seems to suggest an entire change of strategy, from an examination of how readers read to what features realistic works typically have. The shift, though, is misleading, for what really concerns him are the reading expectations associated with realism, and while he continues to pay some attention to the impact of such expectations on the unliterary reader, his main interest is the misreading which such expectations induce in the literary reader, a line of inquiry that culminates in Chapter VIII, "On Misreading by the Literary."

In one sense, Lewis seems to be contradicting himself. If a capacity for whole receptivity makes the reader a literary reader, how can anyone who misreads qualify to be called a literary reader in the first place?

Is not one who misreads unliterary by definition? Lewis himself neither acknowledges nor addresses this difficulty.

The key to resolving it consists in recasting one's assessment of Lewis's overall argumentative purpose in writing the book. At the outset, proceeding in a most general fashion, he seemed to have posited an ideal, ahistorical category with his "Few." However, the "Few" shrinks dramatically inasmuch as Lewis, somewhat surprisingly, keeps disqualifying readers whom one might expect to populate the select category. He finds whole subdivisions of readers—the "devotee of culture," the "status seeker," the "Style-mongers," and still others—who, for various reasons, he cannot happily include among the "Few." Some of these groups, furthermore, do not consist of permanent "types" that one might expect to find in the readership of any literary community, no matter what the period. On the contrary, some of them—the "professional" and the "Literary Puritan" in particular—seem narrowly historical. I shall consider the implications of this subtle historical intrusion presently. Meanwhile, the reservations that have Lewis producing so many qualifications in his ideal class suggest that perhaps the "Few" really ought to be divided into two groups. I propose calling them the High Literary and the Middle Literary, using the former name for the original "Few" and the latter for the various subdivisions of the "literary" under suspicion. Despite the various defects the Middle Literary suffer, Lewis obviously is not prepared to expel them from grace altogether. Notwithstanding limitations, the Middle Literary, he recognizes, do have a wide capacity for the appreciation of literature. Nevertheless, the incapacities of the Middle Literary, I think, are the very reason that Lewis has to propose his "experiment," in the first place, and these incapacities are inextricably linked to the "doctrine" of realism.

Lewis takes for granted a broad division of Western literary culture into two periods: the present, in which the concept of realism is implicitly exalted, and all previous times, in which it was not. Converting his analysis into institutional terms, I am claiming that he perceives the taste for realism as virtually the same as *having* a definition of literature in terms of preferred features, techniques, etc. Such a definition, or the expectations it engenders, excludes very much of what the literary of earlier periods once counted as literature. Lewis, I contend, is mightily, even primarily, devoted to resisting the demotion of works in great ranges of Western literature from their status as literature in behalf of what, in his view, amounts to a local prejudice. It is a demotion he evidently fears will happen by neglect The works simply will not be read.

These basic concerns explain, I believe, the concern found in the latter half of *Experiment* to expose the logical weaknesses of the critical theories the Middle Literary construct. In particular, he singles out the theory of Tragedy. But his analysis of that theory occurs in chapter VIII whose title indicates that misreading, not mistheorizing, is the object of attention. It might then be expected that Lewis would argue, for example, that just as the Egoistic Castle-builder "uses" the work as a starter for an ego trip, so too, at a more complex level, the adherents of the "Tragic view" (as he calls the philosophy derivable from the theory of tragedy) "use" specific tragic works, which would seem to mean that, like the unliterary, they somehow attend only to the elements that suit some extraneous requirement. Yet in the context under discussion, Lewis's analysis suggests that, if anything, the Middle Literary read tragedy too well. Tragedy makes its impression so forcibly that the Middle Literary mistakenly allow the "tragic sense" thus generated from *within* the reading experience to be applied beyond that experience to life itself where, Lewis strongly maintains, its application is illegitimate. Here though, what is being "used" is not a particular work *in the act* of some reader reading it; the "use' occurs *after* the experience of reading when the reader draws from it a philosophy which it cannot legitimately provide.

The "doctrine" of tragedy, Lewis claims, rests on two propositions which works supposedly imbued with the "tragic sense" communicate: first, that a tragic flaw is the cause of the miseries the principle character suffers, and second, that these sufferings "reveal a certain splendor in man, or even in the universe" (77). He dismantles the position in two steps. First, he shows that it is bad philosophy because it leaves out so much of what actually constitutes real suffering. Second, he points out that the suffering tragedies do reflect is included for purposes of affective impact, not to give a whole account of suffering. Put another way, Lewis has recourse to a traditional concept, the principle of artistic selection, to criticize the theory of Tragedy, but he revives the concept and breathes fresh life into it by underscoring its double-sidedness. Selection involves special consideration concerning what goes into the work, but it involves equally careful consideration to what is left out.

In his assault on the notion of tragedy, Lewis begins by showing the shallowness of the "tragic view" by emphasizing, with great vigor, what it leaves out:

> Flaws in character do cause suffering; but bombs and bayonets, cancer and polio, dictators and roadhogs, fluctuations in the value of money or in unemployment, and mere meaningless coincidence, cause a great deal more. Tribulation falls on the integrated and well adjusted and prudent as readily as on anyone else. (77-78)

The literary fail to note that the tragedian "dare[s] not present the totality of suffering" because "it would ruin his play" (78). What the play does contain is never the complete picture; very much must be *excluded*. Thus, the whole of suffering "in its uncouth mixture of agony and littleness" would make a play "merely dull and depressing" (78) rather than tragic. The tragedian must, therefore, exclude much of what really is part of suffering and select for inclusion "the exceptional," not the specially "real."

After this discussion of the negative dimension of selection (what must be excluded), he takes up the tack more normally pursued: selection as inclusion. In doing so, he particularly addresses the second proposition, that tragic suffering leads to a sense of splendor. Lewis presses especially hard here since this impression lies at the heart of whatever moral truth tragedy is supposed to convey. The impression emerges, furthermore, precisely from the circumstance that the events selectively portrayed are organized artificially into a plot, and the events in a plot, unlike the events in real life, can end at an artificial yet convenient point.

> Nor do real miseries end with a curtain and a roll of drums 'in a calm of mind, all passion spent.' The dying seldom make magnificent last speeches. And we who watch them die do not, I think, behave very much like the minor characters in a tragic death-scene. For unfortunately the play is not over. WE have no *exeunt omnes*. The real tragedy does not end; it proceeds to ringing up undertakers, paying bills, getting a death certificate, finding and proving a will, answering letters of condolence. There is no grandeur and no finality. Real sorrow ends neither with a bang nor a whimper... Sometimes it remains for life, a puddle in the mind which grows always wider, shallower, and more unwholesome. Sometimes it just peters out, as other moods do. (78)

Thus, after noting that tragic events are organized in a plot and follow certain conventions, Lewis is again off enumerating what a tragedy must *exclude*. Tragic grandeur cannot emerge from the "ugly, slow, bathetic, unimpressive" movement of real time because tragic grandeur is an affect that depends totally on literature's capacity to leave out what dilutes the desired affect and to include and even intensify whatever supports it.

His consciousness of selection as exclusion as well as inclusion reaches its highest pitch, however, in a merely parenthetical three paragraph discussion which immediately follows his assault on tragedy as a philosophical outlook. He conjectures that this way of misconstruing tragedy perhaps accounts for the "belief that tragedy is 'truer to life' than comedy" (80). Several sentences later, he adds still another misperception concerning a literary genre: "the same people who think comedy less true than tragedy often regard broad farce as realistic" (80). What follows in the two remaining paragraphs is a brief but powerful refutation of these misguided claims which, in effect, constitute his strongest criticism of the Middle Literary's very capacity to theorize about literature. The argument contains the seeds of an explanation as to why they sometimes misread and especially *how* they misread. He proceeds by means of an approach that sharply contrasts with the approach adopted by the advocates of the "realism" definition. That approach makes "truth to life" the paramount consideration in all literary works and thereby, either explicitly or implicitly, ranks works according to the degree to which they exhibit either realistic surface features (which Lewis calls "realism of presentation) or a realistic world view (his "realism of content").

The logic implicit in Lewis's approach is quite different. First, he obviously relies on his cultural knowledge that the three forms exist as part of Western literary culture and even have names assigned them—tragedy, comedy, and farce. He also relies on his literary experience that all three forms produce different literary experiences. All three, he knows, refer verbally to the lived world. He rejects, however, the proposal that what accounts for the differences perceived in experiencing them has anything to do with the "amount," as it were, of reality present, which seems to be the case for the "realism" advocates. To account for the differences in the three forms, therefore, he does not look for some single feature or combination of features that one form can be shown to have in greater abundance than the next, and so on. Instead, he traces the differences in the forms to the differences in their selection assumptions. Each genre generates the experience peculiar to it by typically including references to certain facets of life and simultaneously excluding references to certain other facets of life. "All three forms," he puts it, "make the abstractions proper to them" (81). The "world" of farce (represented by Chaucer's *The Miller's Tale*),

> is hardly less ideal than that of pastoral. It is a paradise of jokes where the wildest coincidences are accepted and where all works together to produce laughter. Real life seldom succeeds in being, and never remains for more than a few minutes, nearly as funny as a well-invented farce. That is why the people feel that they cannot acknowledge the comicality of a real situation more emphatically than by saying 'It's as good as a play.' " (81)

Jokes and coincidences occur in life, but punctuated by long stretches of everything else that can also happen. Farce, on the other hand, is a "world" in which jokes and coincidences occur in such abundance that Lewis can rightly call it a "paradise" of such things. The point is that farce not only typically makes certain kinds of inclusions but also intensifies the presence of these inclusions. As Dryden once put it when defending the use of rhymed verse in drama, literature imitates nature, but "nature wrought up to a higher pitch."

After making his positive characterization of farce (stressing what it "imitates" and the intensification of this "imitation"), Lewis analyzes all three genres from the perspective of exclusion:

> Tragedies omit the clumsy and apparently meaningless bludgeoning of much real misfortune and the prosaic littleness which usually rob real sorrows of their dignity. Comedies ignore the possibility that the marriage of lovers does not always lead to permanent, nor ever to perfect happiness. Farce excludes pity for its butts in situations where, if they were real, they would deserve it. None of the three kinds is making a statement about life in general They are all constructions: things made out of the stuff of life; additions to life rather than comments on it. (81)

Farce, to stress the point as Lewis does not, *cannot* come into being except by eliminating pity for the objects of its raucous joking. If the reader of a farce commiserates where he is not invited to commiserate—indeed where he cannot commiserate—then he virtually dismantles the construct and thereby dissolves the "world" of farce. Farce, in other words, not only passively excludes facets of reality simply by not bothering to include reference to them; it also positively erases a moral or ethical element (pity) that ordinarily ought to be present: "if they [the victims of the jokes] were real, they would deserve it [our pity]."

I have drawn attention to what seem to me to be the basic assumptions of the case that Lewis brings to a head in this parenthetical argument. I have also made explicit the contrast his argumentative assumptions make to the thinking which underpins the arguments of his perceived adversaries throughout much of the middle of the book—the advocates of realism. Still another case, it seems to me, follows from all this, having to do with *how* the literary misread and, once again, I do not think that Lewis actually asserts it. Lewis does, of course, acknowledge that the reader can fail to take textual instructions any time he feels so disposed. Through the first part of *Experiment,* Lewis shows that the unliterary read sloppily by not attending to all that is there. Whatever response such slovenly attention evokes cannot, therefore, be the full response that the work invites and allows. In reading this way, though, the unliterary fail to respond to the positive demands of the selection process: they do not notice what actually has been included, the emphasis with which it has been included, and so on. The Middle Literary, on the other hand, make a corresponding but more complex error of inattention with respect to the negative demands of selection. Such a reader might, at any point, not honor the required exclusions and put back with misguided imagination what has been deliberately taken out. Following Lewis's lead, I would say that works in the comic and farcical range are especially susceptible to this *reading* mistake.

Such an argument would seem to provide Lewis with an analytical explanation for the behavior of the young man, recalled early in *Experiment,* who accompanied him from Mill Lane to Magdalene, Lewis says, "protesting my vulgar, my wounding, my irreverent suggestions that *The Millers Tale* [the very farce to which Lewis refers in the three-paragraph case under discussion] was written to make people laugh"

(12). The young man is just one example of a class Lewis calls the "literary Puritans," all of whom seem not to be able to bring into imaginary existence the sort of world that comic works enable. In Chapter II, where he originally notes this class, he does not, however, explain *how* it comes to pass that such a difficulty could occur. He merely cites the literary Puritans as the strongest contrast he can imagine to the receptive reader, whom he considers the "proper" serious reader:

> Now the true reader reads every work seriously in the sense that he reads it wholeheartedly, makes himself as receptive as he can. But for that reason he cannot possibly read every work solemnly or gravely. For he will read 'in the same spirit as the author writ'. What is meant lightly he will take lightly; what is meant gravely, gravely. (11)

Inasmuch as the literary Puritans read solemnly where they should read lightly and thus positively miss the kind of experience the comic work is designed to generate, they truly misread. How they misread—by putting back into the work something that had to be taken out in order to render a comic world—was discussed above. Lewis, again, provides the seeds of this analysis, but he does not specifically articulate it. Nor, in fact, does he show in Chapter VIII any instance of the literary misreading. Instead, he does show that they theorize badly.

## *IV*

I said earlier that Lewis's motive for writing *Experiment* might well have been to correct the various difficulties the Middle Literary suffer concerning literature as an idea. Despite this group's considerable capacities for receptivity (the hallmark of the truly literary reader), their theorizing is practically ruinous. Thus, while many of them readily can read individual tragedies, they are prone to concoct sadly deficient recuperative theories about the genre as a whole which posit notions like the "Tragic view." The aim seems to be to capture the genre within the "doctrine" of realism by crediting the genre with an especially philosophical "realism of content." The discussion of comic and farcical works just presented suggests that the inclination toward recuperative theories there flatly encourages the misreading of those forms. To foist "realism of content" on these works by discovering philosophical messages in them requires disregarding the most basic reading instructions generated by such works, which results in their blatant "use" rather than their proper reception. Yet Lewis does more than just point to the areas of difficulty in the literary theory of the Middle Literary; he strews hints throughout *Experiment* pointing to the operation of broader social factors which have the Middle Literary so far astray from the foundation of literature in society—the reader/work transaction—that he has to propose its rediscovery in the guise of an "experiment."

Ironically, Lewis singles out as enormously contributing to the problem the "increasing importance of'English Literature' as an academic discipline" (86).

Making clear the force of the case that Lewis gathers against the academic study of literature requires going back to a puzzlement I noted earlier concerning his progressive diminution of the "Few," his initial characterization of the literary. I gathered his exclusions into the Middle Literary, recognizing that while Lewis has reservations about these readers, he has no intention of putting them altogether beyond the pale. It is most important to note, I would say, that several of the categories Lewis invents to reflect his misgivings concerning their members only exist at all because English literature as an academic subject exists. His quarrel with the academic study of literature is, however, scattered throughout his book, but when it does surface, it usually surfaces with polemical force. The majority of his more colorful outbursts are directed against some facet of this academic phenomenon. Scattered as they are, they fall into three main categories.

First, Lewis deplores the development of professionalism in literary studies and all that that implies. Most generally, he sees such a development as the source of a variety of distractions to the reader/work transaction. He finds it "disquieting" that "those who might be expected *ex officio* to have a profound and permanent appreciation of literature may in reality have nothing of the sort" (6). He then proceeds to a brief, withering account of the plight of the American literary scholar/ professional:

> I am thinking of unfortunate scholars in foreign universities who cannot 'hold down their jobs' unless they repeatedly publish articles each of which must say, or seem to say, something new about some literary work. (6-7)

For such persons, the work is "raw material" that has to be converted into something capable of notice to an economic system, not a literary system. Given that a major purpose of *Experiment* is to discuss impediments to proper literary reception, it is hardly surprising that Lewis is unusually dismayed concerning this particular feature of "English literature as a subject."

Second, Lewis comments negatively on a kind of exploitation that attends making English literature an academic pursuit. Many of the people lured to such study are constitutionally unsuited for it. His literary Puritans especially exemplify the problem. Drawn to the study by the belief that it is "meritorious," these young people see literature as "therapy." Persons of so serious a stamp, incapable of the capacity for pleasure that literary appreciation presupposes, readily succumb to the temptations posed by the "doctrine" of realism to process works into philosophical, sociological, or ethical documents. Not only economic inducements, but personality dispositions, distract these persons from the posture of receptivity necessary actually to allow literary experience to take place. As I showed earlier, the extreme members of the academic establishment who suffer those difficulties are the only persons who Lewis hints are actual misreaders—persons who get the experience all wrong in the very act of reading. In what must have been the bitterest of ironies to Lewis, the study of English actually recruits for inclusion into the ranks of the literary establishment persons totally deficient in the temperamental capacities required of the High Literary.

Finally, making English literature a subject seems to have provided the occasion for the proliferation of "evaluative criticism," an aberration so pernicious that Lewis, in the final two paragraphs of the last chapter ("The Experiment") proposes banishing the stuff for at least ten years. This point is difficult, I think, since it throws the last chapter into considerable confusion. It is simply not clear what Lewis means by "evaluative criticism."

In his final paragraph (not counting the "Epilogue"), Lewis contends that the greatest danger to the new generations of readers, for whom literature and the study of English literature are mixed together, is "criticism." Young people, he complains, are "drenched, dizzied, and bedevilled by criticism to a point at which primary literary experience is no longer possible" (129). Students of literature nowadays read more Shakespearian criticism than they read Shakespearian plays:

> Less and less do we meet the individual response. The all-important conjunction (Reader Meets Text) never seems to have been allowed to occur itself and develop spontaneously. (128-29)

Twice in this context Lewis calls this criticism "evaluative criticism," but it is clear that he does not simply mean criticism passionately devoted to "ranking." This is considerably confusing since, through much of *Experiment*, it does seem as if the "ranking" passion is precisely his target. He starts the book with this intent:

> In this essay I propose to try an experiment. Literary criticism is traditionally employed in judging books. (1)

And he begins chapter XI ("The Experiment") referring to criticism as a "ranking" game, along with its typical concomitants, taste, judgment, and so on. He expresses an impatience with the process not unlike that expressed by Northrop Frye in the famous "Polemical Introduction" to the *Anatomy of Criticism*. To Frye's "stock exchange" metaphor describing the rise and fall of literary reputations, Lewis adds the complaint that persons so devoted to condemning, damning, and excluding often even fail to read the works so judged. In this context,

Lewis even acknowledges that much of his argument could be construed as an elaborate way of saving from condemnation whole genres, like fantasy, for which he has an especial fondness:

> Inevitably all this will seem to some an elaborate device for protecting bad books from the castigation they richly deserve. It may even be thought I have an eye to my own darlings or those of my friends. I can't help that. I want to convince people that adverse judgments are always the most hazardous, because I believe this is the truth. (116)

One can easily take Lewis at his word. Whatever motivates his argument, he still makes a persuasive case against the exclusion of any work in terms of preconceived characteristics. He follows the same logic developed earlier: a definition of literature (in terms of realism) cannot void the status of works already in the canon. Here, he simply notes that the same definitional prejudice ought to be eliminated with respect to works newly made: works of literature cannot be defined in advance. Nor can the word of some arbitrary authority (who may not even have read the work) prejudice the possibility that a given work is a suitable candidate for literary use. Only the unprejudiced reception of a work by a literary reader constitutes the genuine test of suitability for literary use. If even one literary reader cherishes a particular work, that fact in itself speaks strongly in that work's favor. All through this section, though, Lewis is quite clear; "evaluative criticism" has its "ranking" sense.

After this point, however, following some remarks on Arnold's sense of "criticism"—which Lewis says, finally, is to "see the object in itself as it really is"—he undertakes a personal reflection of what criticism he has found over his lifetime to be of any particular use:

> This drives me to a question which I never asked myself until a few years ago. Can I say with certainty that any *evaluative criticism* has ever actually helped me to understand and appreciate any great work of literature or any part of one? (121, my emphasis)

He mentions four kinds of "criticism," only two of which can be said to be evaluative at all: the works of "emotive" critics and the works of "great" critics, like Aristotle, Dryden, Johnson, etc. The first two groups—the Dryasdusts (by whom he means editors, lexicographers, and so on) and the literary historians—would seem to lend descriptive aid to the reader, and so their work would not be appropriately called "evaluative criticism." By the same token, it seems quite possible to think of the memorable work of Aristotle, Dryden, and Johnson as critical theory, not "evaluative criticism." In any event, Lewis goes on to make the unexceptionable point that to appreciate any of these theories you first have to know the class of objects to which the theories refer; otherwise, such "criticism" itself is simply unintelligible. His point: literary experience necessarily precedes critical theory, and so literary experience aids critical theory, not the other way around.

Next, he moves to a discussion of the "Vigilant school of critics" (probably Leavis and friends) for a few pages, and finally he makes the proposal with which this discussion of "evaluative criticism" began; that is, in the last paragraph of the book, he proposes banning "evaluative criticism" from the republic of letters for at least ten years:

> Such a surfeit of criticism is so dangerous that it demands immediate treatment. Surfeit, we have been told, is the father of fast. I suggest that a ten or twenty year's abstinence both from the reading and the writing of *evaluative criticism* might do us all a great deal of good. (129, my emphasis)

Again, he has in mind here an "evaluative criticism" so abundantly present that students of literature get crushed beneath mountains of it; the primary works are forgotten in the meanwhile; and the primary literary transaction ("Reader Meets Text") does not occur.

What must be banned because it produces a state of affairs that "seems. . . a far greater threat to our culture than any of those from which the Vigilants would protect us" (129) surely cannot be the reading of the fourth category of criticism that Lewis dismisses as not particularly helpful just paragraphs earlier—the critical theories of Aristotle, Dryden, Johnson, and so on. The three named produce theories of literature rather compatible with what Lewis himself espouses. Certainly, none of them falls prey to the "doctrine" of realism that Lewis battles throughout much of *Experiment*. Similarly, Lewis is not simply referring to the sort of "ranking" with which he begins his last chapter. The arguments there seem directed at those who would deny inclusion into the ranks of respectable literature literary works—or even whole genres—which presently enjoy no such status. These fellows stand in the way of certain legitimate works, but they are hardly a threat to our very culture. Finally, he seems not to mean by "evaluative criticism" the work of the Vigilant school. As his comment just quoted above suggests, the danger posed by "evaluative criticism" is something outside that school, something that the Vigilant school has not even noticed, so busy is it waging battles with false enemies.

To discover what Lewis does mean requires, I suggest, reviewing his stance on the more generally formulated category, "talk about literature," as it is scattered through *Experiment*. He is of two minds on the subject and discusses talk about literature sometimes as if it were helpful and sometimes as if it were harmful. In his last chapter, he considers the helpful possibility when he confronts the difficulty that his "experiment" forces the issue of judgment from books themselves, which one can at least hold in one's hands, to the act of reading these books, an elusive object at best. To satisfy the difficulty, Lewis returns to several points he made early in the book concerning the general behavior of the literary and the unliterary. The unliterary, since they bother so little with books, rarely talk about them. The literary, on the other hand, do talk about them, and one will be able to ascertain, by this talk, *how* the books were read. When, on the other hand, he castigates the academic study of literature, Lewis considers the harmful possibilities of talk about literature. At the end of chapter VIII, he pronounces that the "sort of misreading" he has been condemning in the chapter is "encouraged by the increasing importance of 'English literature' as an academic discipline." But he presents the "misreading" as intimately connected with a kind of talk:

> Forced to talk incessantly about books, what can they do but try to make books into the sort of things they can talk about? Hence literature becomes for them a religion, a philosophy, a school of ethics, a psychotherapy, a sociology—anything rather than a collection of works of art. Lighter works—*divertissements*—are either disparaged or misrepresented as being really far more serious than they look. (86)

At its broadest level, the kind of criticism found objectionable in these remarks is thematic criticism—criticism that discovers, to use an American example, that Melville's "Bartleby" is really about transcendentalist philosophy, Thoreau, Christ, alienated workers, disaffected writers, nihilism, and very much more. Such efforts convert all works in any genre into intellectual allegory and run directly against the grain of all that Lewis thinks vital to the proper reception of the literary work as literary work. The qualities of a work as a literary construct must be largely ignored in favor of simply using it as a source for intellectual topics—a function any verbal configuration could be made to perform to produce a limitless procession of "readings." Even persons originally uncontaminated by a disposition to so "use" literary works might eventually suffer corruption if, as part of a habitual curricular ritual, they must practice such activity daily. Academe, in other words, encourages the development of such criticism and constitutes a vehicle for its dissemination. This state of affairs might well pose a danger to the very existence of literary culture, but it is based on *interpretive* criticism, not evaluative criticism.

In a discussion of the institutional theory titled "The Republic of Art," T.J. Diffey remarks that users of the concept of a work of art divide into two groups: "first those who respect the institutional facts or the *status quo*, and secondly those who do not" (148). Some of the most interesting development of the institutional theory undertaken by philosophers has been directed not at the conservatives, who look to art as posterity has handed it to them, but at the *avant garde*, those producing work that challenges traditional notions of art. Arthur Danto, for example, has written provocatively on the contemporary "artworld"

(1964) and George Dickie uses as central examples to demonstrate the institutional nature of art works like the famous urninal that Duchamp entered in an art show under the title, "Fountain" (1974). Writers facing the frontiers take as their problem the chaos that seems to reign in the contemporary art situation to wonder how new and old forms are made art—by a christening process? who does the christening? and so on.

In this regard, Lewis's *Experiment* is positively misleading. Although the "experiment" he proposes would see to be concerned with the making of art in the present century, Lewis's main concern is not the cutting edge. Indeed, chapter X, "On Poetry," shows him fairly throwing up his hands at the notion of what literature is becoming in this century and how it is getting there. For the most part, he looks unashamedly backward, grounding his views solidly in the cultural fact that there is a literary tradition and that the works included in it are available for literary use by any member of the contemporary community who can use them in this way. Nowhere does he entertain even for a moment the notion that contemporary readers have perhaps outgrown this body of literature and that, as in science, progress has occurred in literature which renders obsolete older literary forms. Indeed, while he affirms the absolute necessity of openness and receptivity of art as received through tradition, he shows clear signs in chapter IX that he was not prepared to practice his own preachings with regard to experiments in the making of new literary forms.

In the last analysis, then, Lewis's book does not suggest much of an "experiment" at all. Rather, as I maintained earlier, the book mainly provides an argument against a narrow but popular literary definition which has the potential to decimate the ranks of the literary works handed down by posterity. Lewis's major accomplishment in *Experiment* is to show how firmly entrenched that definition is, especially among the backsliding Middle Literary. Further, as I just tried to show, the book also lays the groundwork for the troublesome possibility that the growth of the academic study of literature supports rather than defeats this unfortunate situation. Thus, rather than having proposed an original "experiment," it seems that Lewis has rediscovered the basic relationship upon which the social practice of literature stands—the interaction f the received work with the literary reader. Despite a good deal of partial or misleading analysis, *Experiment* does substantially relocate the perspective from which to ask vital questions about literature, particularly literature as it is received from posterity. As such, Lewis's book constitutes an unexpected contribution to a critical dialogue that is very much alive today.

## Notes

[1]The theorist most clearly associated with the name "institutional theory" is philosopher George Dickie. See "What is Art?: An Institutional Analysis," in *Art and the Aesthetic,* (Ithaca and London: Cornell UP, 1974), pp. 19-52.

[2]The essays in which Lewis and Tillyard exchanged views were collected and published as *The Personal Heresy: A Controversy* (London: Oxford UP, 1939). The first essay, in which Lewis originally stated his position, is also called "The Personal Heresy."

## Works Cited

Bell, Alan. "Brave Unknown Air War." *Age* 6 April 1966.

Bergonzi, Bernard. "Open to Books." *Spectator* 17 Nov. 1961: 710.

Danto, Arthur. "The Artworld." *Journal of Philosophy* 61 (1964).

Dickie, George. "What is Art?: An Institutional Analysis." *Art and the Aesthetic.* Ithaca and London: Cornell UP, 1974.

Diffey, T.J. *British Journal of Aesthetics* April 1969: 148.

Ellis, John M. *The Theory of Literary Criticism.* Berkeley and Los Angeles: U of California P, 1974.

Lewis, C.S. *The Personal Heresy: A Controversy* with E.M W. Tillyard. London: Oxford UP, 1939.

Logan, Terence P. "Book Review." *Modern Language Journal* Dec. 1960: 563.

Smith, Barbara Hernnstein. *On the Margins of Discourse.* Chicago and London: U of Chicago P, 1978.

"What is Art?: An Institutional Analysis." *Art and the Aesthetic.* Ithaca and London: Cornell UP, 1974.

# Part II:

# C.S. Lewis: The Practice of Criticism

# Provocative Generalizations: *The Allegory of Love* in Retrospect

*Margaret P. Hannay*

Fifty years ago, *The Allegory of Love* appeared and immediately rehabilitated the genre of allegory. Tracing the convergence of the literary form of allegory and the social phenomenon of courtly love in the allegorical love poem, C. S. Lewis argued that the tradition finds fulfillment in the replacement of courtly love by marriage in Spenser's epic *The Faerie Queene*. Helen Gardner, in her moving obituary for Lewis, recalled her first reading of *Allegory* as a momentous occasion:

> I still remember vividly a night in 1936 when, unable to go to the theatre because I had a cold, I went to bed with *The Allegory of Love* and read it without a pause into the small hours. I recognized, and still recognize, in this book a masterpiece of literary history, the work of a truly original mind. Whether one agreed or disagreed, in detail or at large, after reading this book one's imaginative map of the past could never be the same again.[1]

Since then the New Criticism of his day has become the old criticism of ours, and most traditional readings have been deconstructed; but the bold pronouncements of *The Allegory of Love* have continued to delight and to infuriate scholars.[2] Lewis was a provocative critic, making sweeping generalizations which clarified broad trends in literary history, but generalizations which, by definition, could not be entirely true. Nowhere is this more evident than in his brilliant final chapter on Spenser.

As an Oxford undergraduate newly returned from the trenches of France, Lewis was first entranced by the incarnation of moral allegory in the world of faerie. His friend Nevill Coghill remembers the zest with which he repudiated

> the Hazlitt view that if you leave the allegory alone it will not bite you [and] championed [Spenser's] ethical attitudes as well as their fairy-tale terms, with a rich joy in the defeat of dragons, giants, sorcerers, and sorceresses by the forces of virtue.[3]

This same emphasis on moral allegory later formed that influential conclusion of *The Allegory of Love,* written to refute what he saw as five current misunderstandings of Spenser: an over-emphasis on political allusions, which are a defect in the poem; an over-emphasis on language, when Spenser should be read for his matter; a misapprehension of the allegorical nature of the work, a core surrounded by "romance of types and pure fantasy"; a misrepresentation of Spenser "as a man who preached Protestantism while his imagination remained on the side of Rome"; a misrepresentation of Spenser as "a poet entirely dominated by the senses who believed himself to be an austere moralist."[4]

The first four misunderstandings were quickly disposed of. Although contemporary criticism has once again begun to address political readings and the nature of Spenser's language, it has done so with post-structuralist sophistication.[5] By dismissing the rather simplistic historicism of his day and the facile attention to the "prettiness" of Spenser's language, Lewis led the way in focusing on what is still usually perceived to be the essence of *The Faerie Queene,* its moral allegory. His work also served as a catalyst in provoking discussion of such issues in Spenser criticism as courtly love, neo-Platonism, closure, reader response, and iconography, making any complete study of his impact on Spenser criticism beyond the scope of this paper;[6] however, an analysis of the controversy he started over the Bower of Bliss will serve to illustrate his impact on current Spenser studies. Even in the 1980s a Spenser critic cannot approach the Bower without a bow to Lewis.[7]

The Bower of Bliss is the culminating temptation of Guyon, the knight of temperance in Book II of *The Faerie Queene;* repudiating its charms, Guyon lays waste the Bower and takes its proprietress, Acrasia, captive. The central question raised by the episode is, why did Guyon destroy the Bower with such vehemence? In the Renaissance the answer was obvious: Acrasia was a Circe figure who would lure men to bestiality. When Milton argued against "a fugitive and cloistered virtue" in *Areopagitica,* he turned to Spenser for illustration. "Describing temperance under the person of Guion," Spenser brings him "through the cave of Mammon and the Bower of Bliss, that he might see and know and yet abstain."[8] A less attractive Bower, a less sensuous Acrasia, would not have been a true test of temperance.

Romantic critics disagreed, finding in Acrasia, as in Milton's Satan, proof that the poet's heart warred with his moral.[9] Through the early twentieth century such opinions were standard. For example, in the *Poems of Spenser* (1902) William Butler Yeats declared that Spenser should not have

> occupied himself with moral and religious questions at all. He should have been content to be...a Master of the Revels to mankind.... He had no deep moral or religious life.... His morality is official and impersonal—a system of life which it was his duty to report.[10]

In 1930, while Lewis was working on *The Allegory of Love,* an article in the *Times Literary Supplement* articulated the prevalent view that

> we have only to read...the passages of most sustained and various beauty in *The Faerie Queen*— the adventure of Sir Guyon in the Garden of Acrasia—to be certain that Spenser's heart was not in his morality. When it came to a struggle between his morality and his sense of beauty, his sense of beauty, very properly, triumphed.[11]

This "charge of actual sensuality and theoretical austerity" usually centered in the claim that the Bower of Bliss was not sufficiently distinguished from the Garden of Adonis. To answer that objection, Lewis made three generalizations which have provoked Spenser critics for these fifty years: that the Bower is created by art and the Garden by nature; that art in *The Faerie Queene* is usually bad; and that the Bower shows sterility and the Garden fecundity.

*Art versus Nature*

Although the art/nature contrast is a familiar Renaissance trope, the application of that trope to Bower and Garden was original with Lewis.[12] His impetus was undoubtedly Janet Spens's study (1934), which declared that it is virtually impossible to distinguish Bower and Garden; in fact, Spenser "cared more for the artificial than for nature, because in the artifact the sensuous element is more visibly held in solution by the concept."[13]

To disprove this contention, Lewis points to the first description of the Bower, when Atin finds Cymochles asleep: "And over him art, striving to compare/With nature, did an Arber Greene dispred."[14] When the Bower appears again, it is

> ...goodly beautifide
> With all the ornaments of Floraes pride,
> Wherewith her mother Art, as halfe in scorne
> Of niggard Nature, like a pompous bride
> Did decke her, and too lauishly adorne (II.xii.50)

After citing the passage, "The art which all that wrought appeared in no place," Lewis contrasts Bower and Garden. The Bower is made by art; the Garden is "So faire a place, as Nature can deuize" (III.vi.29). The arbour of the Bower is artificial; that of the Garden "not by art/ But of the trees owne inclination made" (IIIvi.44). The ivy in the bower is gold; that in the Garden is real. Finally, the gate of the Bower depicts false love and the Garden has faithful lovers. In sum, "the one is artifice, sterility, death: the other, nature, fecundity, life" (326). The similarity is that of the pretense to the real.

This section of *The Allegory of Love* immediately provoked critics to argue with Lewis or to build upon his distinction. Most of the commentaries use the same methodology as Lewis, basing the argument on a close reading of the text rather than bringing in historical, political, theological or linguistic considerations. G. Wilson Knight (1939) closely followed Lewis's distinction as did A.S.P. Woodhouse in his "Nature and Grace in *The Faerie Queene*" (1949). Agreeing with Lewis's generalization that the art of the Bower is usually false, intended to deceive, he points to an important exception, the bird song. Thus the Bower is natural in part, but its role is "rescued and rehabilitated in Book III, in...the Garden of Adonis."[15] Nor is the Garden devoid of art, in the sense of human ideals; this is indicated by the obvious deficiencies in Amoret's education in the Garden (364).

N.S. Brooke (1949) raised ten objections to the art/nature distinction. The most important of these, which Lewis himself admitted in *Spenser's Images of Life,* is that the Temple of Venus is superior to the Garden because art and nature cooperate.[16] Brooke also examines the implications of Lewis's statement that the Garden is not artificial in a bad sense. If it is not, he has tacitly admitted that artifice can be good or at least neutral, undercutting his earlier antithesis.[17]

To maintain this art/nature generalization, Lewis had dismissed stanza 59—the primary exception—in an aside: "Let us suppose, however, that the reader is still unconvinced: let us even help him by pointing out stanza 59 where the antithesis is blurred. But..." (325). Such an admission may be charming, but it should not be allowed to obscure the data:

> One would haue thought...
> That nature had for wantonesse ensude
> Art, and that Art at nature did repine;
> So striuing each th'other to vndermine.
> Each did the others worke more beautifie. (II.xii.59)

Using this stanza, Millar MacLure added another important corrective to Lewis. Agreeing that the Bower of Bliss pretends to be what it is not, he demonstrated that art is not exactly opposed to Nature so much as in competitive alliance with it.[18] When nature "for wantonesse," is struggling with art, it cannot be that nature is simply Good and art simply Bad; rather, MacLure argues, the art creates by pretending to be what it is not (129).

Lewis never directly answered the telling criticisms made by Nevo, MacLure and others, but he did modify his theory in his Cambridge Spenser lectures, posthumously published as *Spenser's Images of Life.* There he drew a diagram and said: "The House of Busirane is to the temple of Venus, as the Bower of Bliss is to the Garden of Adonis, in each case the bad compared to the good."[19] The House of Busirane is art (artificial); the Temple of Venus is art in symbiosis with Nature (civilization). The Bower of Bliss is nature and art, whereas the Garden of Adonis is simple nature. Obviously, in his later years he did give nature some part in the Bower. The Bower is "not putting itself forward as art but art trying to deceive, substitute for nature. *Trompe l'oeil.* The Garden is purely and simply natural" (23). When all is art, as in the House of Busirane, the product is bad; when all is nature, as in the Garden of Adonis, the result is good. But the combination of art and nature may be either good, as in the Temple of Venus, or bad, as in the Bower of Bliss; only art attempting to deceive is evil. Here Lewis is directly contradicting his earlier pronouncement that art in Spenser is always bad; however, these more mature and careful pronouncements have, in their very reasonableness, not attracted the attention of the earlier brash generalizations.

Since his death in 1963, it is his original Bower/Garden contrast which has continued to prompt significant readings of the text. Until recently, close readings predominated. Giamatti (1966), for example, agrees that in the Bower it seems impossible to make the correct distinctions:

> ...the artificial...infects all around it with its artificiality. The real grapes, compared to gems, suddenly acquire an artificial quality which is increased when they are juxtaposed with the truly artificial gold grapes. Art and nature are beginning to blur; the false and the real commence to merge as we go deeper into Pleasure's realm.[20]

John Bender (1972) devotes a section to "Illusion in the Bower of Bliss," adding substantive detail to Lewis's theory of art as artifice or deceit in the Bower. For instance, the gates of the Bower are illusory, demonstrating "transformations of natural substances by art" and representing "through images the eerie uncertainties and illusions of the Bower of Bliss."[21] Similarly the gem-like grapes are "the most artificial of natural things.... Perhaps all the grapes are 'made by art' and are in fact jewels shaped to look like clustered fruit" (184). Agreeing with Lewis that the ivy is one of the most significant examples of illusion, he argues that "because the eye is deceived, the intellect still will not believe what it knows to be true" (188). Spenser is showing not only art versus nature but illusion versus reality. Demonstrating "how wrongly motivated art inspires vice," Spenser "shows the dangers of Acrasia's amoral aesthetic" (196). What Lewis sketched out in five pages of generalization has been expanded by Bender into some twenty pages of careful documentation.

Antoinette Dauber (1980) has found in Lewis the impetus toward a reader-response approach to the Bower and its "compelling" beauty. "The reader, morally aware, knows that he should not allow himself to be seduced. But the powerful impression is not effaced when he repeats to himself, [as Lewis warned] 'this art is false, the nature unnatural, the sexuality corrupt.' "[22] Guyon's experience teaches the reader that there is no genuine vision lying behind Acrasia's veils of allegory. Everything in the Garden—Genius, the fountain, the girls in the fountain, even Acrasia herself—appears veiled, enticing Guyon who is "unschooled in such effects," does not "discern the hand of the artist, and remains unaware that the landscape itself conspires to beguil him" (164). Spenser shows "the shoddiness of Acrasia's product," thereby demonstrating "the difference between his art and hers" (169). In the Proem to Book III which immediately follows Guyon's destruction of the Bower, Spenser discusses his own allegory, "the proper use of the veil" (173). As Dauber's study illustrates, Lewis's art/nature distinction has contributed to the current emphasis on the self-reflexive nature of Spenser's statements about the poet's role within *The Faerie Queene.*

### *Art in* The Faerie Queen

Into the discussion of his thesis that Bower and Garden are distinguished by art and nature, Lewis slipped a digression, arguing that Spenser usually puts pictures and tapestries into places which he thinks evil—with the one exception of the House of Alma—because showing pictures is probably the only way "of allegorizing the fact that the external world enters as image into the human mind" (327). The Temple of Venus and the Garden of Adonis are natural, but the house of Malecasta and the House of Busirane include pictures. Lewis believed himself to have stumbled on another of the great antitheses which run through the poem, like Life versus Death or Light versus Darkness—the opposition of "natural and artificial, naive and sophisticated, genuine and spurious." The artifice of court life, the externals of the tournament, the pomps and vanities of the world are disparagingly compared with that Nature which is represented by the Noble Savage, by shepherds, by Una. In this second provocative generalization, Lewis is more sweeping and less accurate than in the Bower/Garden contrast.

Once again he has been answered by closer readings of the text. For example, Brooke accuses Lewis of faulty logic in excusing the paintings in the House of Alma: better to admit that Spenser used pictures "wherever it suited his allegory to do so."[23] Nevo points out that the Temple of Isis and Mercillae's palace—which cannot be termed evil—are adorned with gold and artifice, as are Britomart's shield and the glories of Cleopolis.[24] As the counter-examples accumulate, it becomes clear that to maintain Lewis's distinction would mean entering a long list of exceptions, rather like the desperate attempts to save Ptolemaic astronomy. Refining the theory is more economical.

MacLure's work on "Nature and Art in *The Faerie Queene*" is an outstanding close reading written to disprove one of Lewis's generalizations: he had argued "provocatively and incorrectly," McClure concludes, that art is used in a bad sense in Spenser.[25] Using one of Lewis's own favorite techniques—focusing on definitions—MacLure notes that the initial problem in Spenser's use of the terms nature and art is two-fold; the words themselves were "pretty well worn down" by the time Spenser used them, and in addition there is a variation of intensity in his use of the terms.[26] Sometimes they have their common meaning of nature as given, art as made, but nature can also mean the art of God and art itself can be viewed as evidence of man's nature, created in the image of God (171-172). Thus both terms, "art" and "nature," are ambivalent in Spenser. There is the natural which is good contrasted with the unnatural as evil, but there is also a bad nature, almost equivalent to the libido exemplified by Hellenore and the satyrs. (This distinction Lewis did recognize in *The Allegory of Love*, 329-330). However, there is also an ambivalence in the term "art." Art can indeed be sinister in its power to counterfeit nature and deceive, MacLure agrees: "As no reader of *The Faerie Queene* (or of C.S. Lewis) can fail to notice, Spenser chooses to present this capacity of art chiefly in its demonic aspect" of tempting and deceiving (174). In addition to the House of Busirane and the Bower of Bliss, which Lewis had mentioned, MacLure points to the false Florimell and the goldsmith at the house of Lucifera. MacLure demonstrates, however, that art can also be good in the Aristotelian sense of the "voices of reason and framers of civility," such as Bladud and the Orphic music which reduced discord to harmony, Prince Arthur's panoply, the illuminated New Testament which Redcrosse gives Arthur, and the garments of Belphoebe (175).

Intrinsically vulnerable to the counter example, hasty generalizations such as Lewis made about art in *The Faerie Queene* are easily disproven. The work of Brooks, Nevo and MacLure is sufficient to demonstrate that although Lewis was correct in his recognition of evil art in the Bower, he was blinded by his own theory to Spenser's delight in artificial beauty, in ornament and design for their own sake. The impromptu quality of this generalization is evident in his chatty introduction of it:

> I had intended only a short digression to show the deliberate contrast between nature and art (or reality and imitation) in all Spenser's good and bad places, but I find I have stumbled on another of those great antitheses which run through his whole poem (327-328).

Had he instead seized upon the real versus the imitation, with all its Platonic implications, as the great antithesis (as he actually does in the pages devoted to art versus nature) he would have initiated another useful distinction. As we have seen, Lewis himself later came to realize the falsity of that generalization he had seized on with such rash delight in *The Allegory of Love*. Not surprisingly, this section of his argument has now virtually disappeared from critical discourse.

### *Eroticism in the Bower and the Garden*

Most readers, Lewis says, approach Spenser with "the vulgar expectation" that the virtuous and vicious loves will be distinguished quantitatively; "that the vicious loves are going to be warmly painted and the virtuous tepidly—the sacred draped and the profane nude" (330). But Spenser's distinction in the Bower and Garden tend to work the other way—the essential contrast is between sterility and fertility. To support this theory, Lewis first points to the girls in the fountain and the ivy associated with them. He then compares the real Venus and Adonis in the Garden with a series of profane loves—the tapestry Venus and Adonis in the House of Malecasta, Cymochles and the nymphs, Acrasia and Verdant.

Spenser's girls in the fountain are memorably described by Lewis: "Acrasia's two young women (their names are obviously Cissie and Flossie) are ducking and giggling in a bathing-pool for the benefit of a passer-by: a man does not need to go to fairie land to meet them" (331). To avoid misunderstandings which might arise from a simplistic reaction to their nakedness, Lewis contrasts them with the Graces. Equally naked, the Graces are "engaged in doing something worth doing,—namely, dancing in a ring 'in order excellent' " (331). When they notice Calidore, they immediately vanish; their dance is not for his eyes and they have no sexual connotations at all.

This contrast of the girls in the fountain and the Graces was picked up by Frye and then by Alpers. Alpers objects that "the Naked Graces are not the healthy equivalent of the long erotic description of Acrasia's damsels as C.S. Lewis and Frye state." Only a single line describes them "and we are not meant to see a naked human body." Spenser is giving visual suggestion rather than pictorial description.[27] Lewis, however, never argued that the Graces are the good equivalent of "Cissie and Flossie" as the Garden is the good equivalent of the Bower; instead, he mentioned the Graces to disprove the facile assumption that nakedness *per se* is erotic in *The Faerie Queene*. Alpers is, in fact, agreeing with Lewis, though he vigorously objects to the "vulgar renaming" of the girls in the fountain. Curiously, that renaming has persisted so that the names Cissie and Flossie are used by critics such as Berger and Dauber without quotation marks and without attribution, as common terminology.[28]

On the whole, the sterility/fertility contrast has proven more valid than the art/nature distinction. As Graham Hough observes, the Bower is evil not because it is artificial but because it is sterile.[29] Yet the sterility/fertility contrast raises a real problem in connection with Acrasia's girls. If they, like the rest of the Bower, are supposed to suggest sterility, then why are they compared to Venus rising from "th' Oceans fruitful froth"? (xii. 65)[30]

Harry Berger suggests a solution which would maintain the generalization: the simile of the "faire star" represents not Spenser's evaluation but Guyon's. Although they are comically vulgar, the girls awaken Guyon to desire, apparently for the first time. They enact a ritual eternal in occurrence (hence the reference to Venus) but new to Guyon, who invests them with the glory of the true Venus.[31] Dauber recently amplified that idea, suggesting that it is the veiling of the girls in fountain and water which arouses Guyon's belief that they must be goddesses; he has not yet learned that the veils of the Bower hide no divine meaning.[32] Another possibility is that the girls merely seemed like Venus arising from the sea (xii.65), just as the "seeming beasts" were actually men, and the grapes and ivy were gold. The Bower is deceptive.

Lewis's use of the girls to prove his sterility/fertility contrast is dependent on the assumptions that they are "cheap" (this is probable, but not universally accepted) and that they appeal to the eyes only. But we do not know that they would have been loath to satisfy Guyon's "kindled lust" if the Palmer had not dragged him away. Lewis argues that there is no real action in the Bower, "only male prurience and female provocation" (332). However, this lack of action in the Bower may suggest more about Spenser's technique than it does about his morality. The Bower is presented as a tableau series; the particular scene shows Guyon looking at bathing girls as another will show Acrasia bending over Verdant "with greedily depasturing delight" while "through his humid eyes [she] did sucke his spright" (xii.73).

The girls in the fountain are closely associated with the ivy which trails in the water, suggesting both artifice and sterility. Lewis comments:

> Whether those who think that Spenser is secretly on Acrasia's side, themselves approve of metal vegetation as a garden ornament, or whether they regard this passage as a proof of Spenser's abominable bad taste, I do not know.... Is it possible now to resist the conviction that Spenser's hostile critics are precisely such wights who have viewed the Bower 'not well avis'd' and therefore erroneously deemed [the ivy] to be true? (325).

This petulance weakens his argument, for the ivy has no defenders. He would have done better to appeal to iconography by mentioning the traditional association of the ivy with lust, as a plant of Bacchus, an inconographical detail which had been emphasized by Lemmi in the *Variorum*.[33] The ivy would effectively support the sterility/fertility contrast—even the symbol of lust is not real.

After discussing the fountain and its occupants, he emphasizes the contrast in fruition between the real Venus and Adonis in the Garden and the pictured Venus and Adonis in the house of Malecasta. The tapestry Venus is not in the arms of Adonis but is secretly looking at him "with her two crafty spies." In the Garden, however, "Venus, in defiance of the forces of death... 'Possesseth him and of his sweetness takes her fill.' Nothing could be franker"; the fastidious reader might even object that the phrase "takes her fill" is too close to other appetites (331).

His second example of skeptophilia is Cymochles. Though he is surrounded by a "flock of wanton nymphs," the "wretched creature does not approach one of them," but lies in the grass "like an Adder lurking in the weedes" and peeps at them (332). Cymochles certainly does fit the thesis of inactivity. Although each girl attempts to outdo the others in showing him delights (one "all for tryall strips"), Cymochles's "fraile eye with spoyle of beauty feeds" (II.v.34) and that is all that happens.

His third example of suspended lust is Acrasia, discovered "posed on a sofa beside a sleeping young man, in suitably semi-transparent raiment" (332). Her breast, of course, is exposed to "hungry eyes," for those greedy eyes are the tyrants of the Bower. From these examples Lewis concludes that the Bower "is a picture, one of the most powerful ever painted, of the whole sexual nature in disease. There is not a kiss or an embrace in the island" (322). Once again, the sweeping generalization leaves Lewis vulnerable to the counter-example. His first illustration, the tapestry Venus and Adonis, can be countered by the scene which portrays

...with what sleights and sweet allurements she
Entyst the Boy, as well that art she knew,
And wooed him her Paramoure to be (III.i.35).

Lest we fear that she did not succeed in wooing, the narrator assures us that she "joyd his loue in secret unessspyde" (III.i.37), thereby filling in the lacuna in the tapestry series. The central scene is thus emphatically present in its stated absence from our view.

Since Lewis proposed the tapestries in the House of Malecasta as an example, it would be appropriate to counter with the tapestries in the House of Busirane. Depicting the evil of Cupid's "warres," they are full of action. Stanza 32 is far more explicit than anything in the Garden of Adonis:

Then was he turnd into a snowy Swan,
To win faire Leda to his louely trade:

O wondrous skill, and sweet wit of the man,
That her in daffadillies sleeping made,
From scorching heat her daintie limbes to shade:
Whiles the proud Bird ruffing his fethers wyde,
And brushing his faire brest, did her inuade;
She slept, yet twist her eyelids closely spyde
How towards her he rusht, and smiled at his pryde.
(III.xi.32)

This erotic action in the "bad" tapestries effectively invalidates Lewis's action/inaction distinction because this passage is so similar to the Bower. The Golden grapes are "lurking from the vew of couetous guest" as the gold and silver threads in the tapestries "lurked priuily/As faining to be hid from enuious eye" (III.xi.28). The gold hides "like a discolourd Snake, whose hidden snares/Through the greene gras his long bright burnisht backe declares" (III.xi.28), recalling the description of Cymochles lying in the grass like an adder.

Venus in the tapestries has been diligent about her traditional work, and Acrasia certainly has not been idle either. On her breast "through languour of her late sweet toyle/Few drops, more cleare than Nectar, forth distild" (xii.78). As Hough wryly observes, "I do not suppose the toil referred to is watering the garden."[34]

Two recent critics have observed that Lewis's misprision here reveals something about his own view of sexuality. Guillroy notes that this passage, like some others in *The Faerie Queene*, is

> not very far from pornographic.... The problem here, as with pornography, is precisely the nature of the visual image as a stimulus to desire. C.S. Lewis seized upon what seems to be the exclusively visual nature of the erotic stimulus to conclude that there are in fact no sexual relations at all in the Bower of Bliss, an interesting misreading since we are not told that the lover sleeping in Acrasia's lap has always been so immobile.[35]

Similarly, Greenblatt observes that in Lewis's picture of "male prurience and female provocation...the reader familiar with Lewis's work will recognize links to his criticism of erotic passages in *Hero and Leander* and *Venus and Adonis*, links to his conception of maturity and mental health."[36] Although his "brilliant account describes disturbing qualities that any attentive reader may recognize in the Bower," his insistence—against the textual evidence—that there is no activity in the Bower reveals his own prejudices, Greenblatt charges:

> What for Spenser is the place "Where Pleasure dwells in sensual delights" is for Lewis the realm only of frustration; all sexual activity is in this way reserved for the Garden of Adonis and hence tied securely to reproduction (171).

Although the action/inaction contrast has been largely disproven, this in no way invalidates the sterility/infertility contrast. There are no children in the Bower and no harvest but a counterfeit wine. Acrasia is as voluptuous as Venus, and has recently been as active, but she destroys whereas Venus creates, symbolically producing the fertility of mankind, beasts and plants.

*Destruction of the Bower*

When Lewis attempted to answer the charge of "actual sensuality and theoretical austerity," he assumed that by proving the Bower was a portrait of "vicious pleasure," a picture that "did justice both to the pleasantness and the vice," the necessity for the destruction of the Bower would be obvious. Filling the Bower with "sweetness upon sweetness and yet contriving that there should be something subtly wrong throughout," Spenser has demonstrated both the "skill [and] sincerity" of his allegory (333). Douglas Bush believed that Lewis had succeeded in his defense of Guyon's action: although the Romantics thought that Spenser was letting a "really voluptuous imagination have free reign in [in the Bower]...this wholly mistaken notion was happily killed by C.S. Lewis.[37] Guyon is "no rigorous puritan" for destroying that "beautiful nursery of sterile corruption." Its very subtlety is its danger, as Murphy agrees:

> The Bower is more dangerous than the Cave because it is so close to being right.... The relationship between art and nature in the Bower may be only one small step away from Spenser's concept of an ideal relationship, but the effect of that small step is enormous.[38]

The subtle perversions of the Bower have not reconciled all critics to its destruction; rather, they suggest that Guyon (or perhaps Spenser himself) is being intemperate, over-reacting to the allure of the Bower because of his own imperfections. Berger, for example, contends that Spenser "vacillates between the ethical conflict and the esthetic admiration." So lifelike and convincing are the images that they affect the poet even as he writes with full knowledge of their evil. Guyon lays waste the Bower in a "Puritan frenzy," destroying that which he is not mature enough to resist.[39] In this position Berger is close to Watkins's assertion, written some twenty-five years earlier, that Spenser creates "a beauty sensuous and sensual, at first without shame, then shadowed by a growing moral uneasiness which finally, intensified by self-distrust, smashed beauty like a looking-glass."[40] More recently, Madelon Gohlke has amplified this conception of Guyon as faulty: "By placing an inadequate hero in a situation which severely tests his resources, Spenser inexorably undermines the superficial fabric of his allegory."[41] Although on the surface it appears that Guyon must find the Aristotelian mean between extremes, the underlying conflicts, as exemplified in Guyon, remain unresolved. Not willing to recognize the presence of evil in Nature or in himself, "he clings to a pre-Christian outlook which robs him of his capacity to deal with a fallen world." A wiser man, she implies, could tolerate ambiguity and still resist temptation.

Many recent critics accuse Lewis of denying the ambiguity inherent in the conflict between the allure of the Bower and the need for its destruction. Hough agrees with Lewis that it is absurd to contend that Spenser is secretly on Acrasia's side, but he believes that Spenser's conscious moral position is not in perfect accord with his sensibility: "the image has assumed an independent life that works against the theme."[42] Although he is correct in demonstrating the differences between the Bower and the Garden, "in the course of making this argument good" Lewis "has involved himself in a denigration of the Bower of Bliss that leaves me unpersuaded," Hough concludes (164), accusing him of attempting to banish the moral tension between "a rational and world-denying morality" and "the blaze of earthly glory and erotic ecstasy" which is inherent in the romantic epic. Hughes had gone farther, siding with Gryll:

> For one defence of the allegory of Acrasia like that by Mr. Lewis...there are a dozen condemnations of the "Puritanism" which revelled in Guyon's destruction of the Bower.... When it comes to Guyon's famous curse on Gryll...most of us applaud the hog's stubborn individuality.[43]

Perhaps in reply to such criticism, Lewis re-emphasized, in a subsequent essay on Tasso, that early distinction between good and evil beauty. Both Spenser and Tasso describe the rescue of a young man from an enchanted garden full of erotic appeal; both poets are open to the charge of making the evil too beautiful, "so beautiful that the reader's sympathies go out to it, and it may be supposed that the poet's sympathies did the same."[44] If this were true, it would be a serious artistic flaw, "a fatal discrepancy between the profound and the superficial meaning of the poetry." In our industrial society, perhaps, "beauty has become so rare that we can no longer believe ill of beauty." But the old poets, like Tasso and Spenser, believed that a thing might be beautiful, "might be of a beauty to break the heart, and yet be evil" (116). We must look at the context. Spenser

> emphasizes the art of the evil garden in order that, six cantos later, he may contrast it with the naturalness of the good one.... The answer to depraved and artful sensuality [is] given by innocent and natural sensuousness.... Acrasia is...beaten...on her home ground (117).

In pointing to the larger structures of *The Faerie Queene,* Lewis anticipates some recent trends in Spenser criticism. Because Book II as a whole demonstrates the necessity for destroying the Bower, he could have strengthened his argument by emphasizing that Guyon's quest is to avenge Acrasia's destruction of Mordant. Her other victims litter the ground about the Bower. Cymochles, lying like an adder in the grass, has forfeited his full humanity, a precursor of the wild beasts which surround the Bower—those earlier victims of Acrasia—and of Verdant, who lies with her now and presumably will shortly join the beasts. Spenser knew what he was about in making the Bower so alluring, and he has told us exactly what to expect. Stanza 1 of canto xii warns us that we are coming to the point "of that same perilous sted,/Where Pleasure dwelles in sensuall delights,/Mongst thousand dangers, and ten thousand magick mights." On the way, Guyon and the Palmer must avoid the "Rocke of Vile Reproch," which is the end of "lustfull luxurie and thriftless waste." The Palmer asks, "What now is left of miserable wights,/ Which spent their looser daies in lewd delights,/But shame and sad reproach?" (xii.9) The floating islands are a preliminary encounter with that which seems "faire and fruitful," but once a man has put his foot there his error is irrevocable; he "wandereth euer more uncertain and unsure." Phaedria, the sea monsters, the false weeping damsel, and the sirens all prepare Guyon—and the reader—to be wary of false beauty. Inside the bower, Verdant is presented as another example of manhood forgotten in lust and laziness. Lest we overlook the moral, we are shown Verdant's arms in the tree and told: "His dayes, his goods, his botie he did spend:/ O horrible enchantment, that him so did blend" (xii. 80).

Nevertheless, there remains something in Spenser's description of "pleasant bowres," broken with "rigour pittiless" that "of the fairest late, now made the fowlest place," which cannot but tug at the heart. Reader-response critics have responded to Lewis by focusing on this problem of the reader's reluctance to see the Bower destroyed, a reluctance which is unchanged by the knowledge that it is evil. For example, Arlene Okerlund charges that

> C.S. Lewis and his followers have obscured this issue somewhat by pointing to the Bower's artificiality as the clue which will cause us to reject its false, contaminated beauty [and so reconcile us to its destruction; however, knowing that the Bower is evil] does not solve the problem that this evil possesses inherent attractiveness.[45]

She suggests that Book II provides "an education in temperance for both Guyon and the reader," for it is not until we have been seduced by the Bower that we will recognize and admit "our own intemperate desires."

Joan Klein approaches this problem of reader response by looking at parallels not in Book III, like Lewis, nor in Book II, like Okerlund and Hume (120-121), but in Book I. By making detailed comparisons between Archimago, that more obvious villain, and Acrasia, she demonstrates that Book I has prepared the reader to undergo the temptation of the Bower. We have already encountered a knight stripped of his armour by a fountain, a golden cup, alluring promises of rest from the struggle against temptation, a magician, and a beautiful temptress. Lest we miss the parallel, Archimago is introduced at the beginning of Guyon's quest to show that his aims are the same as Acrasia's: "For all he did, was to deceiue good knights./And draw them from pursuit of praise and fame,/To slug in slouth and sensuall delights" (II.i.23). Duessa reappears, beautiful once more, and pleads for Guyon's help in a scene full of dramatic irony. We have seen Duessa stripped, but Guyon has not; when we meet another beautiful woman, one who combines the wiles of Duessa with the magical powers of Archimago, we should remember and be prepared for a more subtle temptation. Acrasia is neither killed not exposed:

> Like the temptation she embodies, Acrasia remains forever beautiful.... Not until our wills approve Guyon's act, Spenser insists, can we hope to achieve the fruits of chastity and the issue of charity which are love, friendship, justice, and courtesy.[46]

De Neef believes that Spenser puts the reader in an awkward position in Book II in order to teach us about the limitations inherent in the golden world of poesy. In Book I it was easy to identify with Redcrosse; in Book II, "in habiting neither Alma's castle nor the Bower of Bliss, we are quite literally dis-placed from the narrative...forbidden to be Guyon."[47] The Bower itself is "the quintessential garden of the imagination...and an obvious analogue to the poet's own faerieland." Guyon acts for us in the Bower, "encountering the poetic fiction from within the narrative and teaching us that even here it has and is no privileged place." The Bower is perfect beauty, of the kind that can exist only in the imagination: "The Bower, like all poems, must be destroyed if life is to be lived" (108).

The politics of reading provides another influential response to the *Allegory*. Greenblatt believes that to acquiesce in the destruction of the Bower is not to achieve the fruits of charity or free the reader from the imagination, but rather to acquiesce in Spenser's imperialism, drawing into the discussion of the Bower a sinister element which Lewis had found only in Book V. An Irishman, Lewis admitted that in Artegall and his iron page Talus

> there is something I shall not attempt to excuse. Spenser was the instrument of a detestable policy in Ireland, and in his fifth book the wickedness he had shared begins to corrupt his imagination (*Allegory*, 349).

Although he does not acknowledge Lewis's rejection of this imperialism, Greenblatt asserts that Spenser's imagination was corrupted as early as Book II. "Spenser worships power," Greenblatt declares, and the destruction is his defense against "the threat of...absorption...self-abandonment, erotic aestheticism, the melting of the will, the end of all quests."[48] The Bower must be destroyed—as the alien cultures in Ireland and in the New World were destroyed—because they threatened English civilization by their appeal. Acrasia is treated with the same violence that Spenser himself exercised in Ireland—massacres, planned famine, military "executions." Pitiless destruction was seen not as "a stain but as a virtue" (186). A direct linkage with Book V would have made the argument stronger, but Greenblatt's interpretation must be disturbing for any defender of Guyon—or Spenser. It is far more pleasant to accept that Spenser's heart is on the side of Acrasia than that it is on the side of Talus.

Maureen Quilligan agrees with much of Greenblatt, finding in Virginia the model for the Bower, but adds sexual politics to her reading.[49] In Book II she sees Spenser presenting a difference between male and female perspectives: in the Bower, Guyon's experience "is a distinctly male version of the pornographic lure of the labyrinth's leisure" (188), while the Garden is presented from a female perspective. The Garden thus becomes an inversion of the Bower, as it was for Lewis, but in a gender-specific way: the boar which threatens Adonis is "a metonymy for fallen [male] bestiality" connected to "the threatened dismemberment of Actaeon, passed over in the erasure of that myth's presence from the text." Spenser specifically attributes Adonis's safety "eterne in mutabilitie" to Venus's power over the boar:

> Ne feareth he hencforth that foe of his,
> Which with his cruell tuske him deadly cloyd:
> For that wilde Bore, the which him once annoyed,
> She firmely hath emprisoned for ay (III.vi.48).

The "most comfortable and unthreatened viewpoint for reading the events in the garden is female," Quilligan argues. From this perspective, the garden's eroticism should be seen as "a vision of male sexuality brought safely and creatively under the control of an awesome female power." It is primarily the presentation, not the situation, which differs in Bower and Garden:

In a sense, Adonis's position is merely Verdant's passivity seen from a different perspective—one that insists on the cosmic legitimacy of the female Eros's triumph over a male Thanatos (196).

This is probably the reading which would have made Lewis the most uncomfortable, since he was not quite certain that Venus's divinity could compensate for the inferiority of her sex.[50]

The Bower retains its allure no matter what context is used to justify or to deplore its destruction. Thirty years ago, Robert Durling observed:

One of the obstacles to a correct understanding of Spenser's methods had been the wide acceptance of the notion that he was at heart of Acrasia's party; one wishes that Mr. C.S. Lewis's admirable discussion of the Bower in *The Allegory of Love* had laid that ghost.[51]

Obviously, it did not, as this survey of recent criticism demonstrates; nevertheless, Lewis did something more important—he redefined the terms of the discussion. One can still argue that Spenser sided with Acrasia, but, after Lewis, no one can assume that Spenser was a poet dominated by the senses who mistakenly believed himself to be an austere moralist.

Fifty years after *The Allegory of Love* was published, critics are still answering Lewis; even in this era of post-structuralism, his work remains the starting point for critical discourse on the Bower and Garden. Although he made a faulty generalization about art in *The Faerie Queene* and overstated the art/nature contrast in Bower and Garden, he was the first to distinguish between the two places. He also established the sterility/fecundity contrast which—so long as we allow action (present or implied) in evil places—is quite valid. But the correctness of Lewis's reading is the least important question we could ask about the enduring influence of his work; his boldest generalizations have incited some of the best subsequent readings of Spenser.

During the ebb tide of critical interest in epic grandeur, theological content, and allegorical form, Lewis began to rehabilitate the reputation of *The Faerie Queene*, restoring to us the teacher whom Milton had found to be as "sage and serious" as Aquinas. In the Spenser Society meetings, as well as in the pages of *Spenser Studies* or the *Spenser Newsletter*, C.S. Lewis is still frequently cited—not to settle critical arguments, but to start them. Nothing would have delighted him more.

## Notes

This article first appeared in *Seven* VII (1986), 41-60.

[1]Helen Gardner, Review of C.S. Lewis, *The Discarded Image*, in *The Listener*, 16 July 1964, p. 97. Because *The Discarded Image* appeared posthumously, Gardner took this opportunity to evaluate Lewis's contribution to medieval and Renaissance studies.

[2]See, for example, Kathleen Tillotson's review, which claimed that "no one could read it without seeing all literature a little differently for ever after," *Review of English Studies* 13 (1937), p. 477. The volume earned extravagant praise from such contemporary critics as Woodhouse, Gombrich, Tillyard and Chambers when it first appeared. Roche, although he disagrees with Lewis's definition of allegory, declared almost thirty years later: "His chapter on Spenser...is still the best introduction to the poem and by far the most sensitive reading," *The Kindly Flame: A Study of the Third and Fourth Books of Spenser's Faerie Queene* (Princeton: Princeton Univ. Press, 1964), p. 210. Graham Hough, beginning his own study of Spenser, declares, "By far my greatest debt in general criticism of *The Faerie Queene* is to the writings of Professor C.S. Lewis. Like so many others I found my first real guide to the reading of the poem many years ago in his *Allegory of Love*, and his work both here and in the history of sixteenth-century literature has been present to my mind throughout," *A Preface to the Faerie Queene* (New York: W.W. Norton and Company, 1962), p. 6.

[3]Nevill Coghill, "To the Martlets," in *Light on C.S. Lewis*, ed. Jocelyn Gibb (London: Geoffrey Bles, 1965), pp. 51-52. Compare this account with that in the Minutes of the Martlets Society, Number 238 (Bodleian library, MS. Top Oxon. d 95/4, fo. 17) which records a technical paper by Lewis, on language and metrics. (The Martlets was an Oxford literary society, primarily for undergraduates at University College.) Lewis's first references to *The Faerie Queene* are in letters to his childhood friend Arthur Greeves; he finished reading the poem in early 1916, concluding with adolescent condescension, "Of course there are dull and childish passages, but on the whole I am charmed." The holograph letters to Greeves are available in the Marion E. Wade Collection at Wheaton College. On Spenser see 049, 053, 147, 158 and 207. The letters have been published as *They Stand Together: The Letters of C. S. Lewis to Arthur Greeves (1914-1963)*, ed. Walter Hooper (London: Collins, 1979).

[4]C.S. Lewis, *The Allegory of Love: A Study in Medieval Tradition* (Oxford: Oxford University Press, 1936), pp. 321-22. Subsequent references will appear as *Allegory*.

[5]For a post-structuralist approach to Spenser's language, see particularly A. Leigh De Neef, *Spenser and the Motives of Metaphor* (Durham, N.C.: Duke University Press, 1982) and Jonathan Goldberg, *Endlesse Worke: Spenser and the Structures of Discourse* (Baltimore: The Johns Hopkins Press, 1981).

For various types of political readings, see such works as Stephen Greenblatt, *Renaissance Self-Fashioning: From More to Shakespeare* (Chicago: University of Chicago Press, 1980); Richard Helgerson, *Self-Crowned Laureates: Spenser, Jonson, Milton, and the Literary System* (Los Angeles: University of Los Angeles Press, 1983); and Maureen Quilligan, *Milton's Spenser: The Politics of Reading* (Ithaca: Cornell University Press, 1983); Robin Headlam Wells, *Spenser's Faerie Queene and the Cult of Elizabeth* (London: Croom Helm, 1983).

[6]For an overview of Lewis's critical work and methodology, see my *C.S. Lewis* (New York: Ungar, 1981), chapter 4; and Francis Morris, "Metaphor and Myth: Shaping Forces in C.S. Lewis' Critical Assessment of Medieval and Renaissance Literature" (Unpublished Ph.D. dissertation, University of Pennsylvania, 1977).

[7]See, for example, Antoinette B. Dauber, "The Art of Veiling in the Bower of Bliss," *Spenser Studies* I (1980), p. 163; Quilligan, 64n; Greenblatt, 170. For an almost paradigmatic reaction to Lewis's work—accepting the broad outlines but rejecting the detail—see Anthea Hume, who acknowledges her debt to Lewis's concept of allegorical cores but develops a substantially different list of where they occur. *Edmund Spenser: Protestant Poet.* (Cambridge: Cambridge University Press, 1984), p. 109.

[8]John Milton, "Aeropagitica," in Frank Allen Patterson, ed. *The Student's Milton* (New York: Appleton-Century-Crofts, 1961), p. 731. Recent studies focusing on intertextuality have given much attention to "Spenser's Milton." See, for example, A.K. Hieatt, *Chaucer, Spenser, Milton: Mythopoeic Continuities and Transformations* (1975); Quilligan; John Guillroy, *Poetic Authority: Spenser, Milton and Literary History* (New York: Columbia Univiversity Press, 1983); and the annual Spenser/Milton session at MLA, sponsored jointly by the Spenser Society and the Milton Society. See particularly John King, "Milton's Bower of Bliss," paper read at the Spenser/Milton session, MLA 1985.

[9]On Lewis's part in the Satanist controversy, beginning with Blake and Shelley and involving such twentieth-century critics as Mario Praz, E.M.W. Tillyard, Denis Saurat, Walter Raleigh, Douglas Bush, Edgar Stoll, and William Empson, see my dissertation, "Rehabilitations: C.S. Lewis's Contribution to the Understanding of Spenser and Milton" (State University of New York at Albany, 1976), chapter 8. Lewis's position—that the result of Satan's choice is progressive degradation—became generally accepted as World War II changed the critical reaction to Satan. His self-important posturings began to sound too much like Hitler's.

[10]William Butler Yeats, *Poems of Spenser* (1902), reprinted in John R. Elliott, ed, *The Prince of Poets: Essays on Edmund Spenser* (New York: New York University Press, 1968), pp. 17-18.

[11]*Times Literary Supplement*, 27 February 1930. Cited in *The Works of Edmund Spenser: A Variorum Edition* (Baltimore: The Johns Hopkins Press, 1933), II, p. 16.

[12]See, for example, Mammon's promise in Jonson's "The Alchemist," IV, 1, 11. 166-169; and Polixenes in "The Winter's Tale," IV, iv, 11. 94-95. Spenser's passage "All that which all fare works doth most aggrace,/ The art, which all that wrought, appeared in no place" is a rather literal translation of Tasso "E quel, che il bello e il caro accresce all'opre,/L'arte che tutto fa, nulla si scopre." Cited by Lewis in "Tasso," *Studies in Medieval and Renaissance Literature*, ed. Walter Hooper (Cambridge: Cambridge University Press, 1966), p. 117.

[13]Janet Spens, *Spenser's Faerie Queen: An Interpretation* (New York: Russell and Russell, 1934), p. 122. Lewis praises her work on symbolism in *Allegory*, p. 333.

[14]Edmund Spenser, *The Faerie Queene*, II.xii.50 in *Spenser: Poetical Works*, ed. J.C. Smith and E. De Selincourt (London: Oxford University Press, 1912). All subsequent references will be to this edition.

[15]G. Wilson Knight, "The Spenserian Fluidity" from *The Burning Oracle* (1939) reprinted in *Elizabethan Poetry*, ed. Paul J. Alpers (London: Oxford University Press, 1967), p. 337; A.S.P. Woodhouse, "Nature and Grace in *The Faerie Queene," ELH* 16 (1949) reprinted in *Elizabethan Poetry*, pp. 350-360.

[16]N.S. Brooke, "C.S. Lewis and Spenser: Nature, Art and the Bower of Bliss," *Cambridge Journal 2* (1949), reprinted in A.C. Hamilton, *Essential Articles for the Study of Edmund Spenser* (Hampden, Connecticut: Archon Books, 1972), pp. 13-28.

[17]Brooke's own comparison between the Bower and the House of Alma is rather forced, but his work serves as a valuable corrective to Lewis's generalization.

[18]Millar MacLure, "Nature and Art in *The Faerie Queene*," *ELH* 28 (1961), reprinted in *Essential Articles,* p. 177.

[19]C.S. Lewis, *Spenser Lectures* (Bodleian library MS fac. d. 135), p. 10. Alastair Fowler expanded these cryptic notes into *Spenser's Images of Life* by explaining elliptical phrases and providing transitions between ideas; I have cited Lewis's own words here.

[20]A. Bartlett Giamatti, *The Earthly Paradise and the Renaissance Epic* (Princeton: Princeton University Press, 1966), p. 272.

[21]John B. Bender, *Spenser and Literary Pictorialism* (Princeton: Princeton University Press, 1972), pp. 179-180.

[22]Dauber, p. 163.

[23]Brooke, p. 22.

[24]R. Nevo, "Spenser's Bower of Bliss and a Key Metaphor from the Renaissance Poetic," in *Essential Articles,* p. 34.

[25]MacLure, p. 170.

[26]Lewis's best scholarship in this area is *Studies in Words* (Cambridge: Cambridge University Press, 1960). He invents an Ur-language, which is essentially a myth of origins, in his own fantasy, *Out of the Silent Planet.* The concern for language pervades the other volumes in the interplanetary series, culminating with the destruction of the N.I.C.E. by Merlin's words of power in *That Hideous Strength.*

[27]Paul J. Alpers, *The Poetry of The Faerie Queene* (Princeton: Princeton University Press, 1967), p. 13.

[28]Harry Berger, *The Allegorical Temper: Vision and Reality in Book II of Spenser's Faeire Queene* (New Haven: Yale University Press, 1957), p. 218; Dauber, p. 164.

[29]Graham Hough, *A Preface to The Faerie Queene* (New York: W.W. Norton and Company, 1962), p. 163.

[30]Alpers, p. 315.

[31]Berger, p. 218.

[32]Dauber, p. 167.

[33]*Variorum* II, 383. In Lewis's novel, *That Hideous Strength,* the sinister aspect of the N.I.C.E. is symbolized by the laurel in the formal garden which looks "as if it were made of cleverly painted and varnished metal." This artificial garden is, as one would anticipate, contrasted to the good, natural garden at St. Anne's, the bastion of Logres. In a further reference to Spenser's Garden of Adonis, the ending of the novel is highly erotic, with all the beasts and people under the benign influence of Venus; the mating rituals of the animals take place in the Garden.

[34]Hough, p. 164. Mark Rose, surveying the controversy, concludes that "Lewis is quite right to emphasize the general absence of activity in the tapestry," *Heroic Love: Studies in Sidney and Spenser* (Cambridge: Harvard University Press, 1968), p. 87.

[35]Guillroy, p. 39.

[36]Greenblatt, p. 170.

[37]Douglas Bush, *Mythology and the Renaissance Tradition in English Poetry* (1932; rpt. New York: W.W. Norton, 1963), p. 93.

[38]S. Murphy, "Love and War in *The Faerie Queene,*" in *Eterne in Mutabilitie,* ed. Kenneth Archity (Hampden, Conn: Archon Books, 1972), p. 137. See also M. Pauline Parker, *The Allegory of The Faerie Queene* (Oxford: Clarendon Press, 1960), p. 150.

[39]Berger, p. 237.

[40]W.B.C. Watkins, *Shakespeare and Spenser* (Princeton: Princeton University Press, 1950), p. 178.

[41]Madelon S. Gohlke, "Embattled Allegory: Book II of *The Faerie Queene*," *ELR* 8 (1978), p. 138.

[42]Hough, p. 164.

[43]Merritt Y. Hughes, "Spenser's Acrasia and the Circe of the Renaissance," *JHI* 4 (October 1943), p. 381.

[44]C.S. Lewis, "Tasso," p. 116. Compare Lewis's own treatment of the beautiful but evil sorceress in his Narnia books, particularly *The Lion, the Witch, and the Wardrobe, The Magician's Nephew,* and *The Silver Chair.* For other connections between Lewis's criticism and his fiction, see John Ulreich, "Prophets, Priests, and Poets: Towards a Definition of Religious Fiction," *Cithara* 22 (1983), pp. 3-31.

[45]Arlene N. Okerlund, "Spenser's Wanton Maidens: Reader Psychology and the Bower of Bliss," *PMLA* 88 (1973), p. 64. For an interpretation of reader psychology based on Aquinas, see Zailig Pollock, who argues that readers react with anger to Guyon's destruction of the Bower because of the connection of the irascible and concupiscible impulses. "Concupiscence and Intemperance in The Bower of Bliss," *SEL* 20 (1980), pp. 43-58.

[46]Joan Larson Klein, "From Error to Acrasia," *HLQ* 41 (1978), p. 199.

[47]De Neef, p. 108. See also pp. 109-110 on Phaedria and Acrasia as false poets.

[48]Greenblatt, pp. 171-173. For a political interpretation more flattering to Spenser, see Robin Wells, who argues that as a direct inversion of the *hortus conclusus* topos associated with the Virgin Mary and then with the Virgin Queen, the Bower makes Acrasia the antithesis of Elizabeth and of her avatar Belphoebe. According to Robin Wells, Spenser is thereby praising the Queen for her temperate reign and instructing her on the necessity for correct use of artifice: "if that art is abused, it will destroy all that temperance has achieved," pp. 68-69.

[49]Quilligan, p. 67n.

[50]C.S. Lewis, "Neoplatonism in Spenser's Poetry," in *Medieval and Renaissance Literature,* p. 155. Lewis found Spenser's equation of Venus as Form and Adonis as Matter profoundly disturbing. In a comic alphabet poem, written during the same period as *The Allegory of Love,* he had written, "M is the Many, the Mortal, the Body, the Formless, the Female, The Thoroughly Shoddy./ N is not-Being which sinks even deeper./ More formless, more female, more footling—and cheaper." "Abecedarium," *The Oxford Magazine,* 30 November 1933, p. 298. Fortunately, his attitude toward women changed, particularly after his marriage to Joy Davidman. See the references cited in my article, " 'Surprised by Joy': C.S. Lewis's Changing Attitude Toward Women," *Mythlore* 4 (1976): pp. 15-20.

[51]Robert M. Durling, "The Bower of Bliss and Armida's Palace," *Comparative Literature* 6 (1954), p. 113.

# Visions and Revisions: C.S. Lewis's Contributions to the Theory of Allegory

*Paul Piehler*

C.S. Lewis's *The Allegory of Love* may fairly be reckoned the greatest of his scholarly works, and indeed one of the most influential literary histories of the century. My first encounter with it takes me back to undergraduate days, when I recollect being instructed by a kindly tutor, himself a very considerable medievalist, not to bother reading the original *Romance of the Rose,* since Lewis's version in *The Allegory of Love* made so much more satisfactory reading. (Admittedly this incident did take place within the hallowed walls of Lewis's Magdalen itself.) Even today, some fifty years after its initial appearance, the work seems quite as popular with undergraduates as it was in my time as a coherent and compulsively readable introduction to courtly love and to allegory.

Allegory, it must be admitted, does seem to be even more difficult to define than other literary genres, as this essay should demonstrate. Nonetheless it is a little startling to find that Lewis's admired and authoritative work embodies a striking and somewhat overlooked inconsistency in the definition of allegory which forms the theoretical basis of its literary interpretations. I refer to the complex and thought-provoking discussion of allegory in relation to symbolism (44-48), from which I shall for the sake of clarity extract only one major point.[1] Explicitly, for Lewis, the scenes and personages of allegory appear to be no more than rather trivial fancies. "The allegorist leaves the given—his own passions—to talk of that which is confessedly less real, which is a fiction." This contrasts with the symbolist who "leaves the given to find that which is more real." Thus, for Lewis, allegory is by no means to be considered a serious "mode of thought, but merely a "mode of expression"( *Allegory* 45, 48). This theoretical judgment, which, as we shall see, is based on definitions of allegory and symbolism sufficiently current and orthodox at the time, is, however, strikingly contradicted by the tone and implications of his actual interpretation of allegorical texts. At times, indeed, he recognizes quite explicitly that allegory is capable of exploring reality directly, as when he warns us not to think that in turning to *The Romance of the Rose* "we are retreating from the real world into the shadowy world of abstractions" (115). Concerning a Roman Christian in mental struggle against the assaults of vice Lewis wrote "For such a man allegory will be no frigid form. It is idle to tell him that something with which he has been at death-grips for the last twenty-four hours is an 'abstraction' " (61). Talking of the decline of allegory in the late fifteenth century, as manifested in the work of the poetaster William Neville, Lewis implicitly reverses his theoretical position once more: "The earlier poets used allegory to explore worlds of new, subtle, and noble feeling, under the guidance of clear and masculine thought: profound realities are always visible while we read them" (255).

My contention here is that this inconsistency is no trivial oversight, no banal case of a man forgetting his theoretical position when he comes to his practical interpretations. To investigate the causes of this palpable discrepancy in Lewis's interpretation of allegory we shall need to make some scrutiny of the evolution of the genre. Through this we can reach some working definitions of allegory, before we look at the particular significance of Lewis's position in the history of allegorical criticism.

Our procedures should be ruthlessly empirical. By this I mean that one should start by identifying and using as a basis for interpretation only those works of literature, iconography, or exegesis which have been most frequently and confidently described as allegorical by the generality of readers and scholars. Thus we should have in our minds the common characteristics of such works as *The Divine Comedy, Piers Plowman, Everyman, The Faerie Queene,* and *Pilgrim's Progress* as we pursue the discussion. My assumption here is that the consensus of readers in identifying such works as allegorical implies an intuitive sense of the nature of allegory that, mysteriously enough, goes much deeper than explicit critical definitions and discussions. To start, on the other hand, from the etymologically based dictionary definition of allegory as 'otherspeaking' and apply that principle to any literary work in which an intelligent and ingenious critic can find meaning (or 'subtext') beyond the strictly literal may lead to every kind of stimulating insight but is liable to make the definition of allegory practically co-terminous with that of literature itself.[2]

Nonetheless, when we interpret allegory etymologically with the great traditional allegories in mind it is not difficult to see that to define it as 'other speaking' can in fact make a lot of sense provided that one interprets 'other' as referring to precisely what all such allegories do in fact speak of, that is an 'other,' non-material or super-natural, reality. Viewed in this light, one perceives the primary allegorical procedure to be the transposition of elements and events from non-material reality into material images and events comprehensible in terms of everyday experience and yet betraying some hint of their other-worldly origin.

Thus whatever one's personal feelings about the reality of the 'other' worlds of medieval allegory, it seems hardly likely the allegorists themselves would agree with Lewis's formulation that they were leaving a 'given' to talk of a 'less real' world. They would surely believe the exact opposite, holding such an opinion to be more characteristic of "The mooste partie of this peple that passeth on this erthe," who, in the words of Langland's Lady Holychurch

Have thei worship in this world, thei wilne no bettre,
Of oother hevene than heere holde thei no tale!
(*Piers Plowman* B. Passus I 7-10)

It could nonetheless be objected that the above interpretation of 'other speaking' as referring to other and superior realities still accounts for too much,—if not for literary behaviour in general, at least for the behaviour of, say, myth and parable, as well as allegory. How may we modify our definition in order to clarify the necessary distinction between allegory and myth? Lewis himself wrote in the preface to *The Pilgrim's Regress* that "when allegory is at its best, it approaches myth, which must be grasped with the imagination, not with the intellect" (13). The point is an important one, but the polarity implied between allegory and myth, while characteristic of the "romantic" notion of allegory that Lewis inherited, is too sharp to represent the complexities of the medieval allegorization of myth. For the fundamental experiences represented in such allegory resemble and are developed from those of myth inasmuch as they consist almost exclusively of encounters with that 'other' reality, as it manifests itself in the form of spiritual powers and places.[3]

But there are also significant differences. Such experiences tend to be more sharply distinguished from the everyday realities of what was interpreted as normal life in the mythic period, a life in which mythic and empirical realities seem to be ever more inextricably blended or confused as one ascends back along the stream of man's psychic evolution, so that finally everyday and 'other' realities appear indistinguishable.[4] But as myth transmutes into allegory, to enter the other reality demands special circumstances. The supernatural beings who appear so frequently and freely, if alarmingly, in the haunts of men are now only to be met with in visionary experience, most usually in remote paradises or other sacred places of the after or inner life.

But Lewis's dictum, just quoted, suggests that as allegory approaches myth it becomes less intellectual as it becomes more imaginative. (This is, admittedly a somewhat confusing way of putting the case, so far as historical development is concerned, since allegory as a genre gradually developed out of and separated itself from myth in the first centuries of this era.) Nonetheless, one may find much of value in the observation if we merely reverse the movement and look for a process of allegory becoming more intellectual and (in a special sense) less imaginative as it evolves out of myth. The increased rationality is manifested in a number of different forms. The supernatural powers that portray the active forces of the otherworlds are either given reassuring identifications as personified abstractions or, if still appearing under the identity of the ancient 'mythic' gods, yet demonstrate greater rational consistency of behavior than their pre-allegorical counterparts. The same holds for otherworld places. (One has only to compare the mysterious and terrifying menace of Aeschylus's Erinyes in the *Oresteia* with the predictable onslaughts of the personified vices in Prudentius's *Psychomachia* or the grim shadowy Hades of *Odyssey XI* with the awesome but well-organized underworld of Dante's Inferno.)

The allegorical hero similarly manifests a higher rationality in a more intellectual response to his encounters with otherworld powers, and a greater concern for the implications of such experiences in his personal and moral life. Such increased rationality is most in evidence in the great series of dialogues between hero and spiritual power which distinguished the allegorical tradition as it develops from the *Shepherd of Hermas* (c.150 A.D.) to the *Commedia* and beyond. These dialogues typically incorporate extensive and profound analysis of the ethical, spiritual, and psychological aspects of the hero's predicament, with the aim of achieving a harmony or integration of the disparate intellectual and imaginative elements.

Medieval allegory thus functioned in part as a mode of establishing rational control over the intimidating, excessively powerful psychic forces dominating man's inner life during the mythic era. Personification, so scorned by Lewis as representing the greater in terms of the lesser reality, is thus rather to be seen as a mode of identifying and coping with dangerous if not uncontrollable mental phenomena (*Allegory,* 45-48). But medieval allegory also treated very extensively of a world universally acknowledged to be more real, the world of the pneuma, or transcendence. Where some allegories, such as the *Psychomachia,* remained limited to the psychological level, most of the greater allegories treated extensively of theophany, of numinous encounters with such beings as Boethius's Lady Philosophy, of Dante's Beatrice, often in paradisal or infernal regions equally numinous. In medieval terms this is clearly the realm of the greater reality that Lewis's symbolist aims at, but of course in medieval literature it seems most difficult (for reasons we shall see later) to find symbolic imagery existing independently of an embracing allegorical structure. In fact while psychic allegory is clearly distinguishable from the allegory of the numinous, and most allegories show a tendency one way or the other, the two types are frequently found closely intermingled, since, for the medieval at least, the two areas if not overlapping are evidently continguous.

These confusions in the text of *The Allegory of Love* are, however, chiefly significant in illustrating a crucial turning point in the understanding of allegory, and it is to the history of allegory we must now turn. It must be frankly admitted that the origins of allegory as a critical term are quite undistinguished and uninteresting, except to the most dedicated student of classical rhetoric. It is simply one of a long and hardly exciting list of figures of speech that Greek and Roman rhetoricians managed to discover, or perhaps more accurately "invent" in the texts of their poets. As such it could be described as a somewhat elaborate form of metaphor whose significance or reference tended towards the elusive.

Its appearance in a typical classical rhetoric, the *Ad Herennium*, (1st cent. BC) makes the point. Identified as *permutatio*, ('substitution') it is classified as a figure of speech rather than thought (*verborum* rather than *sententiarum exornatio*) and described as made up of a number of metaphors, denoting one thing by its words but something else in its meaning. The most elaborate example runs: "When the dogs take over the functions of wolves, who on earth can we trust with the cattle?" (Ad *Herennium* 4:34.46). In another rhetorical handbook of the period, Cicero's *De Oratore*, III xli 166, we find the warning that allegory should not be excessively allusive, or it will degenerate into a riddle. These extremely limited descriptions remained popular in rhetorics and other handbooks not only during the classical period but even through the Middle Ages and Renaissance, in fact right up to modern times, inspite of the astonishing things that were shortly going to happen to the humble little figure of speech.[5]

It should be noted that while these books of rhetoric had the ostensible purpose of teaching oratorical and poetic composition, the figures they found there are fundamentally byproducts of natural human expression, and by no means necessarily occur in speech or text as a result of any conscious intent to employ figures of rhetoric. Thus creation of these mini-allegorical figures is quite secondary to interpretation. The point is all the more worth making in that the next phase of this history also involves allegory in the eye of the reader rather than in the pen of the writer. In the second century AD Plutarch commented concerning the attempts of literary critics of the day to reconcile the Homeric epics with contemporary morality that this practice of *hyponoia* or discovering hidden or underlying meanings in a story or myth was now generally being termed *allegoriai*, allegorising.[6]

One may surmise that practitioners of this highly controversial activity were happy to associate their methods with the humbler but less tendentious skills of the teachers of rhetoric. If the street corner rhetoricians 'ornamented' their political attacks by 'allegorically' referring to the rascals in power as dogs turned wolfish, then might not the ancient, sacred, but frequently embarrassing legends of the gods be explained as similar, if somewhat more philosophical instances of allegory. Thus, as the Stoic disputant Balbus explains in Cicero's dialogue *On the Nature of the Gods,* the seemingly unedifying legend that Saturn had the habit of eating his children is simply to be interpreted as Time gorging himself insatiably (*insaturabiliter*) on past ages (*De Natura Deorum* II 64). As one might imagine, Balbus's arguments are not too enthusiastically received by the other contributors to the dialogue, and it is easy to see that people who had to defend traditional pieties on such a desperate basis needed all the help they could get. Thus the concept of allegory has from the beginning suffered from its curious double origins, innocent if unexciting figure of speech and daringly controversial method of saving the moral integrity of the established religion. We already begin to see the sources of the confusion about the nature of allegory that manifests itself in *The Allegory of Love.*

This form of exegesis, necessary, as we have noted, in order to rationalize the menacing psychic forces of an earlier era, was nonetheless something of a minority taste in the pre-Christian period. By and large it was only the Stoics, and by no means all of them, who felt any personal or philosophical need to save so much as even the appearance of such ancient pieties. But with the advent of Christianity the allegorical method quite swiftly took on a new and urgent relevance. The pious intellectual Christian reading conscientiously through his Old Testament, found much to cause him anxiety. Was he merely exchanging one outmoded superstition for another? Augustine explained the problem—and its solution:

> I joyed also that old Scriptures of the Law and the Prophets were laid before me, not now to be perused with the eye to which before they seemed absurd...and with joy I heard Ambrose, in his sermons to the people, oftentimes most diligently recommend this text for a rule unto them, The letter killeth, but the spirit giveth life, whilst those things which taken according to the letter seemed to teach perverse doctrines, he spiritually laid open to us, having taken off the veil of the mystery. (*Confessions VI 4*).

By the time Ambrose and, more especially, Augustine himself had completed its development, the new Christian allegorical method had become an intellectual system that was to dominate biblical and indeed all literary interpretation for the next ten centuries. What was the magic Augustinian formula that transformed the sickly seedling of Stoic *hyponoia* into Christian allegoresis, a robust monarch of the forest, unpeturbed by time or enemies through the turbulent centuries that followed? First, he severed any links with the discredited pagan allegorising, criticizing it in much the same terms as its earlier pagan opponents as being implausible, arbitrary and after the fact.[7] Then he proceeded to seal off Christian allegoresis from the kind of criticism that had so damaged its pagan predecessor. Even if the Old Testament did contain incidents disturbing to contemporary morality, yet satisfactory interpretation could always be found. Did Jacob lie to his father Isaac in order to steal the blessing from his brother Esau? Yes, the incident really did occur—Augustine will have nothing to do with the pagan practice of denying the historical actuality in favor of the allegorical interpretation alone—but it occurred for a special reason. Moses recorded the incident so that the enlightened Christian could perceive the interpretation: as Jacob deceived Isaac by putting on the goat skins so Christ bore the sins of others for man's salvation.[8] For it is the Holy Ghost that writes these meanings into history and inspires the prophets who record them. Does it matter that many different interpretations could be and indeed were made of the same incident? Not in the slightest, for the truth of the interpretation lies in its correspondence to the intention of the great director-writer of the whole scenario—and the intention is the furtherance of charity. Thus any interpretation that furthers that end is true, so that between alternate true readings no conflict can exist.[9] In the later medieval exegetical tradition pagan literature was once more admitted into respectability, when treated with appropriate allegorical techniques, but this was less a reversal of Augustine's position than a tribute to the completeness of the Christian conquest of paganism and the all-conquering effectiveness of the allegorical method.

Does anything in Augustine's achievement of perfecting this long-maturing system of allegorical interpretation prepare us for the coming of the great allegories of the Middle Ages? The direct connections are quite weak. Interpreting myth is really quite a different occupation than writing one's own allegories. And yet, given the irrelevance and triviality of the material to be found in the rhetorical texts, it is hardly surprising that medieval poets would be tempted to find some theory of their allegorical activities in the exegetical procedures. Dante attempted this in the *Convivio* and the results are quite interesting. When he gives us his own version of the famous fourfold scheme of biblical exegesis into which Cassian and others had systematized the Augustinian methods, Dante's adaptation seems ingenious enough, but one cannot quite see a poet actually composing along those lines, especially as the two highest senses, moral and anagogic, have to be illustrated, it turns out, from sacred rather than secular texts. However, when his own *Commedia* comes into question in the famous letter to Can Grande, his attempt at exegesis runs:

> In the literal sense the topic of the whole work is the state of souls after death, and that alone, for the whole purpose of the work is directed towards that. But in the allegorical sense the topic is man, who, through his merits or his failings, and exercizing his freedom of choice, receives his just reward or punishment. (para 8).

Such allegorical interpretation is certainly accurate, on what medieval scholars would have termed the moral or tropological level of interpretation, though it is hardly profound or revealing. One's feeling for the *Commedia* is scarcely enhanced. Modern attempts to continue the task of performing a proper scriptural fourfold exegesis on the *Commedia* have gone very far beyond the embryonic point where Dante wisely left it, but have hardly achieved any deeper enlightenment.[10] The problem, once more, arises from a confusion of allegorical traditions. The fourfold method was a system of allegorizing pre-allegorical texts. Creative allegory, of which the *Commedia* is the ultimate example, has its allegorical significances built into it, and can hardly be allegorized once more without some absurdity.

Thus in the Middle Ages we already find allegorical theory inadequate to account for what actually happens in allegorical texts. What follows in succeeding centuries, however, will add further to complication and confusion, and I must ask my reader to bear some further attempts at unravellment before returning to Lewis's text. The sixteenth and seventeenth centuries saw of course the great outbreaks of iconoclasm where distrust of any attribution of spirituality to a physical object produced large scale physical destruction of sacred art everywhere the protestors could succeed in what they regarded as purifying the churches. With the new emphasis on the literal and objective it is not surprising to find Calvin condemning the allegoresis of the Bible as not merely mistaken and useless but no doubt inspired by the devil. Luther more mildly allowed allegory to the poets but considered it unworthy of the attention of theologians.[11] After Spenser allegory becomes rare in polite English literature for more than a century, and when it does revive again it reappears in a form that would surely have given much surprise (and doubtless little gratification) to any of the great allegorists whose names we have taken as touchstones.

The classical period produced a couple of rather slight allegories that we have refrained from mentioning to this point since their effect on either allegorical theory or the literary tradition was up to the Renaissance in fact rather marginal. They were *The Choice of Hercules* (attributed to Prodicus) and *The Table of Cebes*. Early in the eighteenth century, however, they suddenly achieved, in a period of neo-classical enthusiasm, a quite remarkable vogue. In the first Hercules makes a choice between two ladies who offer him respectively a life of pleasure or a life devoted to the pursuit of virtue. In the second a young man is instructed by a sage, with the visual aid of a temple painting, how to conduct life's journey in such a way as to reach the Palace of True felicity and avoid the byways leading to false pleasures and destructive passions. The success of Addison in reviving this allegorical form in his "The Vision of Mirzah" (in *The Spectator* 159) was universally celebrated, the elegantly written but rather slight work being hailed by one critic as having "a grandeur and solemnity of imagery, with an elegance and melody of language that stand unrivalled in English literature"[12]

The eighteenth century is the first period in this history where we can see a close and accurate relationship between the theory and the practice of allegory. Unfortunately this exact relationship was achieved only as the result of a quite drastic simplification, some would say attenuation, of both the critical theory and the creative output. With a remarkable degree of agreement, critics called for and admired allegories that were brief, clear and straightforward. They should "blend the agreeable with the useful" (Heinle 7). Medieval allegory equivalently was condemned for the obscurity attendant upon its length and complexity. So popular was this revived genre that Addison complained that if he printed all the allegories that were sent to him as editor of *The spectator*, "my book of speculations would have been little else but a book of visions" (*Spectator*, no. 524).

Nonetheless periodical editors found plenty of room for this popular art form right through the neo-classic period. The basic structure of these allegories does, however, owe somewhat more to the medieval tradition and less to classical example than the critics usually acknowledged. The incorporation of the allegory within a dream, and the presence of a helpful spiritual personification to elucidate and guide one through the allegorical landscape, though by no means incompatible with the spirit of the classical allegories, are thematically closer to the medieval example. But scope and tone are entirely classical. For what as been left out of the medieval tradition (which in this sense extends as late as Bunyan) is the high seriousness and intense intellectual and spiritual commitment of the earlier heroes. There is none of the spiritual anguish that so frequently forms the prelude to the allegory nor the ecstasy that accompanies the final vision of salvation. Nor does one find intense and long drawn out intellectual dialogue with the spiritual guide. Nor, most important of all, is there any dimension of the numinous, the transcendent, in the neo-classic productions. All is confined, elegantly and prettily, to the moral and psychological levels of allegorization. Anagogy, the high spiritual level, is simply lost. The Vision of Mirzah itself offers its readers a last glimpse, as it were, of transcendence, the further shores beyond death, but they are too remote or too fog-shrouded from Mirzah's vantage point to constitute more than a bare though wistful acknowledgement of their existence in the scheme of things. After Mirzah, the allegorists content themselves almost exclusively with the conditions of the moral life in their present existence.

Such limitations on the expression of human experience did not, of course, outlast the neo-classical period. Indeed, as soon as the bounds of man's aspirations were so rapidly and dramatically extended by the 'Romantic Rebellion' allegory became deeply suspect as an art form as a result of its patronage by the discredited cultural "ancien regime". Reacting, perhaps sometimes overreacting, to the neoclassic insistence on taking over the structural forms and abandoning the deeper and more sustained spiritual explorations of medieval allegory, the romantics once more took up the spiritual journey, while abandoning the now discredited structures which in the allegorical tradition had sustained such explorations.

Thus, we come finally to the point where Lewis's descriptions of allegory begin to make historical sense. The great exemplar of romantic attitudes towards allegory is of course Coleridge who, in *The Statesman's Manual,* describes it in the well known and influential definition as essentially a translation, usually of abstract ideas, into poetic imagery. Such a negative description was by no means unjustified in terms of the allegorical essays of the time, though of course quite inadequate to describe the profounder emotional range and wider metaphysical reach of medieval visionary allegory.

It is interesting to see that both Wordsworth and Coleridge intuited the weakness of contemporary allegorizing with some precision. Wordsworth, in the 1802 Preface to the *Lyrical Ballads* would accept the personification of abstract ideas as "prompted by passion," but claims he has "endeavoured utterly to reject them as a mechanical device of style" (232). For Coleridge, "the personification of an abstract being" is appropriate as used "only by a person under the highest emotion,..."[13] Symbolism, on the other hand, is described by Coleridge in far more interesting terms as "characterized...by above all the translucence of the eternal through and in the temporal."[14] This description of course fits medieval allegory quite admirably, but the break in tradition cut off the romantics both from its theory and its practice. (It is not surprising, therefore to find the best symbolic poetry of this period to exist in lyric and in fragment, where a tradition of structure to sustain a venture into transcendence is less of a necessity.)

Our long foray into the history of allegorical theory and practice is almost complete. The Coleridgean polarity of allegory and symbolism clearly underlines Lewis's theoretical position in *The Allegory of Love.* What then precisely is the achievement of Lewis's work that so transcends its theoretical inconsistencies? To describe this in detail would be to describe most of the book, apart from its opening remarks on Courtly Love and on Allegory and Symbolism. For Lewis grasped instantly and intuitively that the poetry he was reading at its best far transcended the limitations that the neo-Coleridgean definitions would place upon it. Thus, not only in the few direct acknowledgements we have quoted at the beginning but also in his wise and deep-probing appreciation and interpretation of such allegories as *The Romance of the Rose*, interpretation that one of my tutors once was so rash to prefer to the original poem itself. For, inspite of all his theoretical misgivings concerning the value of allegory, evidently he came to love and appreciate the form as no scholar had before him. And it is after all on true enjoyment of the text, living the world of the allegorist, that any valid interpretation must be based. In the recovery of allegory, Lewis's role was a heroic one, the re-discoverer of forgotten texts, the restorer of forgotten splendours and subtleties to the "common reader" of medieval literature.

Here he is, for example, on *The Court of Sapience:*

> For I must confess that more than once as I progressed slowly through these brightly coloured and indistinctly shaped landscapes, half pleased and half tired with the names of Asteryte, Charbuncle, Crisopras, and Auripigment...more than once I found myself reminded of Milton. It is very unlikely that the explanation lies in any real similarity of poetic art: it is of Milton's theme, not of his style, that we are reminded. He wrote of paradise; but the old poet seems rather to have written *in* Paradise, to be himself paradisal in his piety, his cheerful gravity, his childlike love of matter. (*Allegory* 263-64)

Not only does such literary appreciation lure one into reading and enjoying this forgotten work, to share the experience that Lewis has so personally offered to us, as to a friend, but also, offers, as it were, a sharing of a world larger than the formal bounds of literature itself. In a climate of thought which was turning increasingly colder and more restricted, where philosophy was being restricted to analysis of the devices by which philosophy is expressed, where literature refers only to other literature and criticism is only about other criticism, to read Lewis on allegory or any other subject is to accept an invitation to walk out of the claustrophobia of the operating theatre into a landscape as fresh, open and inexhaustible as the universe itself.

Nor is his critique of *The Court of Sapience* merely "fine-writing." The shift in perception between and fifteenth century allegorical visionary and the iconoclastic non-participated worldview that underlies *Paradise Lost* is distinguished here in a manner that anticipates Owen Barfield's studies in the history of consciousness.[15]

One could continue the tale indefinitely with appreciations of Lewis insights and subtleties, all communicated in so unportentous, so good humoured and relaxed a fashion that it is easy to overlook their depth and resonance. His casually phrased remarks, for instance, on Spenser's allegorizing of popular mythology as "translations into the visible of feelings else blind and inarticulate" gets very close to the heart of what is perhaps the most significant function of allegory in the evolution of the cultural process; his distinction between Catholic and Protestant attitudes to allegory his observation that Catholics allegorize into "bricks and mortar" reality what Protestants are content to leave on the level of literature surely says something penetrating and equally seminal about differing religious modes of representing the ineffable. But I would prefer to leave this most inexhaustable topic with a simple instance of Lewis's ability to see many sides to a question, to allow the opposition to have its say. Here he is taking for a moment a most Ariostan and UnEnglish view of Spenser's Britomart:

> As for Bradamant [heroine of the *Orlando Furioso*] inimitable Bradamant, by her side Britomart is little better than a big-boned country girl. Her speech is dull and pretentious, her love-sorrows without dignity; she carries her nurse about with her, and often suggests the *anglaise* of continental tradition. (*Allegory* 312; 323; 306)

Well, to such an observer the link between Britomart and the continental view of British girls was obvious enough, but for the rest of us the lightning flash of Lewis's wit illuminates what seems the most impossible incongruities in a manner that simultaneously startles, convinces, and delights, as indeed the best kind of wit is bound to do.

If I have demonstrated anything here it is perhaps that the flaws in the writing of a great man are likely to have more significance, and to be more fruitful to study, than the truisms that the rest of us get by with. In *The Allegory of Love*, leaky vessel as it may have been in respect of its theoretical underpinnings, Lewis opened up the routes for the recovery of what is arguably, from certain points of view, the greatest of western cultural achievements and indisputably its most undervalued.[16]

## Notes

[1]Oxford, 1936. Other useful discussion of allegory by Lewis may be found in the *Letters of C.S. Lewis,* 271, 273-4, 283, as well as in the preface to *The Pilgrim's Regress.*

[2]As pre-eminently explored in Angus Fletcher, *Allegory, The Theory of a Symbolic Mode.*

[3]See my *The Visionary Landscape*, 1-8 and passim.

[4]See, e.g., Owen Barfield, *Saving the Appearances.*

[5]Similar definitions occur, for example, in Cicero, *de Oratore* XXVII 94; Quintilian, *Institutio Oratoria,* VIII vi 44; Isidore, *Etymologiarum,* I xxxvii, 22, 26; Matthew of Vendome, *Ars Versificatoria* III 43.

[6]*Moralia* 19 E-F. I owe this reference and much other assistance here to Philip Rollinson's learned and stimulating study, *Classical Theories of Allegory and Christian Culture.*

[7]*City of God* VII 5, 19-26; *On Christian Doctrine* III vii.

[8]*Against Lying,* X 24, as referred to by Rollinson, 61-63.

[9]*On Christian Doctrine* III x, xv, xxvii, and passim.

[10]Cf. Johan Chydenius, *The Typological Problem in Dante,* (Helsingfors: Societas Scientiarum Fennica, 1958).

[11]See e.g., J. Calvin, *Les Commentaires de Jean Calvin sur L'Ancien Testament,* ed. A. Malet (Geneva: Labor et Fides, 1961), I 47; M. Luther, *Works,* ed. J. Pelikan, St. Louis, Mo., 1958, I 90-1.

[12]Contributor to *The Looker On,* no. 22, as cited by Edwin Heinle, 11-12.

[13]*Shakespeare Criticism,* II 103. See M.H. Abrams, *The Mirror and the Lamp* 291.

[14]*The Statesman's Manual,* 437-8.

[15]See especially Barfield's *Saving the Appearances,* and for a more specific study of Milton's non-participated account of Paradise, see my "Milton's Iconoclasm," 121-35.

[16]I am hoping to show, in a forthcoming article, how Lewis's fiction has also, in a different dimension, played a very considerable part in the movement to recover this lost tradition.

# Works Cited

Abrams, M.H. *The Mirror and the Lamp.* Oxford: Oxford UP, 1953.

Barfield, Owen. *Saving the Appearances.* New York: Harcourt, 1957.

Coleridge, Samuel Taylor. *The Statesman's Manual.* W. Shedd, ed. New York: Harper, 1856.

Fletcher, Angus. *Allegory, The Theory of a Symbolic Mode.* Ithaca: Cornell UP, 1964.

Heinle, Edwin. "The Eighteenth Century Allegorical Essay." Diss. Columbia University, 1957.

Lewis, C.S. *The Allegory of Love.* Oxford: Oxford UP, 1936.

——. *Letters of C.S. Lewis.* Ed. W.H. Lewis. New York: Harcourt, 1966.

——. *The Pilgrim's Regress* Grand Rapids: Eerdmans, 1958.

——. *The Letters of C.S. Lewis* Lewis, W.H. ed. New York: Harcourt, 1966.

Piehler, Paul. "Milton's Iconoclasm." *Evolution of Consciousness.* Shirley Sugerman, ed. Middletown, CT: Wesleyan UP, 1976. 121-35.

——. *The Visionary Landscape.* Montreal: McGill-Queen's UP, 1971.

Rollinson, Philip. *Classical Theories of Allegory and Christian Culture.* Pittsburgh: Duquense UP, 1981.

Wordsworth, William. *Lyrical Ballads.* H. Littledale, ed. Oxford: Oxford UP, 1911.

# Style and Substance in the Prose of C.S. Lewis

*David H. Stewart*

We recognize the voice of C.S. Lewis whether he writes a scholarly essay, a sermon, or a children's story. In the latter, sentence length will be shortened and diction simplified; but the cadence and imagery are unmistakable, and the sense of total concentration on subject matter (the sense of the writer's and reader's being, as it were, immersed in the story or argument) is everywhere the same. Only his poems might have been written by someone else, but this can be explained by his acceptance of traditional stanzaic forms and meters that conventionalize any utterance. His prose is so uniform and lucid that it resists analysis, partly because it seems to violate the premise that style and substance are inseparable. Of course, a critic who accepts that premise may claim that, whatever the genre, Lewis's substance does not vary (he is always a Christian apologist) hence his style never changes. *The Silver Chair* and *The Allegory of Love* are parts of a single book.

How may we describe Lewis's style without repeating "euphonious vacuities" that a recent critic detected in virtually all stylistic criticism?[1] We might follow the older models provided by George Saintsbury or Bonamy Dobree,[2] but these have come to seem inadequate. Or we might follow recent linguistic models through "deep structure" and the transformation of strings and kernels, but this would be so repugnant to Lewis personally and so at variance with his own philological understanding of language (not to mention its questionable validity quite apart from Lewis)[3] that the attempt seems pointless.[4] Perhaps the best approach of all, though it may seem amateurish to linguists, is W.K. Wimsatt's introduction to *The Prose Style of Samuel Johnson* which is a miniature encyclopedia of the subject and deserves its status as a classic statement. "The question what the author ought to have said is the true difficulty in judging style.... It is the only difficulty, for it is the only question, and it is one we implicitly answer every time we judge style. We do it by our sense, more or less definite, of what the author intends to say as a whole, of his central and presiding purpose."[5]

My thesis is that Lewis's language expresses traditional ideas about a writer's "possession" by the *logos,* but let me first note what other critics have said and also what Lewis believed about the process.

*I*

Commentary on Lewis focuses almost exclusively on the content and structure of his work. This is natural because his scholarly and religious books must be judged mainly in terms of their substance, that is the quality and cogency of their evidence. His fiction and poetry draw heavily from the content of his referential discourse, hence they too attract attention mainly in terms of their substance. Lewis, being a literary theorist in addition to his other callings, invites commentators to examine the "art" of his literary performances mainly insofar as they become the forms or vehicles for his ideas.[6]

Underneath his forms and structures, however, is a foundation, namely language and style. The Lewis canon rests on a medium of words and sentences. Can anything of substance be said about them to help explain the power and appeal of his work? The fact that they draw little attention to themselves and that critics bypass them with courteous but cursory remarks suggests that there is not much to say.

What is one to make of Peter Bayley's quip that Lewis is "a sort of Drydenesque Chesterton?"[7] This double metaphor sounds apt because Enlightenment prose rhythms do echo in Lewis's writing and because both Dryden and Chesterton were conservatives alive to many facets of their times. In like manner John Wain's observation that Lewis "had a naturally rhetorical streak in him"[8] is convincing. But the question remains, how does Lewis manage his words so that we hear a Dyrdenesque, Chestertonian rhetorician?

The closest we come to insights about Lewis's style turn up almost casually in commentators who are interested in bigger things. For example, Walter Hooper, in his introduction to the poems, finds that Lewis's "wonderful imagination is the guiding thread" to his "clear and sparkling prose."[9] For James Como, Lewis's "pellucid style" was "simple, precise, conversationally rhythmic (Lewis always wrote for the ear)....,and strikingly vivid."[10] Chad Walsh believes that Lewis's style is a combination of his early attempts at the realism of "Boxen" and the romance of "Bleheris." It is a "modest style...,straight to the point, lean, free of inflated language and the technical jargon of the professions. At the same time, thanks particularly to the use of exact metaphors, it is capable of modulating into highly poetic effects...."[11] True enough. But what constitutes an "exact" metaphor or a "poetic" effect?

Such casual references become crucial when they are linked with the very texture of Lewis's mind, as in Raymond P. Tripp's assertion that Christianity disclaims "all knowledge that comes from history while claiming that God entered history to make it meaningful. . . . Christianity has it both ways, and so does Lewis; and this is precisely the contradiction informing his consistently inconsistent style." Thus readers look for truth in Lewis but find only devotion "embedded or, rather, incarnated in the style of chiliastic agnosticism."[12] (We shall return to the problem of truth and language.)

Perhaps the most thoughtful remarks on Lewis's style are Nevil Cogill's:

> There is a magistral quality in the English in his finest work. . . . The marks of this style are weight and clarity of argument, sudden turns of generalization and genial paradox, the telling short sentence to sum a complex paragraph, and unexpected touches of personal approach to the reader, whom he always assumes to be as logical, as learned, as romantic, and as open to conviction as himself. Not that in fact he was easily open to conviction; perhaps "open to argument" would be a truer description. . . . His sentences are in homely English, and yet there is something Roman in the easy handling of clauses, and something Greek in their ascent from analogy to idea.[13]

Coghill's key word is "magistral," which he applies to Lewis's scholarly books, not his fiction or poems; but Coghill's description of the style applies generally. Perhaps "magistral" is a little heavy, especially when one recalls Lewis's miraculous facility, his practice of correcting a rough draft only once before making the fair copy.[14] Knowing this, we may be tempted to discount his language on the ground that he could not have thought carefully about it if he wrote with such ease. Or we may dismiss his language because it is merely facile rhetoric, however magistral.

But before either praising or blaming Lewis's style on the basis of subjective impressions of it, we may profitably assemble some of his own statements about the matter and decide what light they shed on his practice.

## *II*

Lewis claims flatly that "language is an instrument of communication. The language which can with the greatest ease make the finest and most numerous distinctions of meaning is the best."[15] The *meaning* of a book Lewis defines as "the series of system of emotions, reflections, and attitudes produced by reading it."[16] Of course, the communication of meaning is not confined to print, and Lewis acknowledges that love-talk or hate-talk are not language at all but a sort of verbal gesturing.[17] Moreover, there are communicable concepts and feelings that transcend language. For example, Lewis characterizes the feeling of grief that he experienced after his wife died as an emotion that was beyond "mere verbal thinking."[18] The idea of God is similar.

Approaches to God can occur only obliquely. Thus in the chapter of *Miracles* called "Horrid Red Things," he notes that the word " 'sonship' is not used of Christ in exactly the same sense in which it is used of men." On the other hand, "the assertion that Jesus turned water into wine was meant perfectly literally."[19] His point is that "all speech about supersensible [which includes psychology, economics, and poetry as well as God] is, and must be, metaphorical in the highest degree."[20]

Myth, as Lewis uses the word, is closely associated with God: "giants, dragons, paradises, gods and the like are themselves the expressions of certain basic elements in man's spiritual experience [i.e. myths]. In that sense, they are more like words—the words of a language that speaks the else unspeakable—than they are like the people and places in a novel."[21] For Lewis, the connection between myth and God is explicit. In a letter to Arthur Greeves (October 18, 1931), he called Christ a "true myth."

> Pagan stories are God expressing Himself through the minds of poets, using such images as He found there, while Christianity is God expressing Himself through what we call 'real things.' Therefore it is *true,* not in the sense of being a 'description' of God (that no finite mind could take in) but in the sense of being the way in which God chose to (or can) appear to our faculties. The 'doctrines' we get *out* of the true myth are of course *less* true: they are translations into our *concepts* and *ideas* of that wh. God has already expressed in a language more adequate, namely the actual incarnation, crucifixion, and resurrection.[22]

Now if "the man who does not consciously use metaphors talks without meaning,"[23] how does Lewis bridge the space between meaning and truth? By mathematics and poetry. Lewis believes that social scientists write nonsense one hundred percent of the time while writers of children's stories do so only forty percent of the time and mathematicians as little as ten percent. Poets rank even higher. Lewis's preference for them does not imply that imagination alone is the organ of truth. Quite the contrary: with poets, "we are not talking of truth, but of meaning: meaning which is the antecedent condition both of truth and falsehood, whose antithesis is not error but nonsense. I am a rationalist. For me, reason is the natural organ of truth; but imagination is the organ of meaning. Imagination, producing new metaphors or revivifying old, is not the cause of truth, but its condition."[24]

There are two reasons why, in the presence of a poem, we may not reach a "condition of truth." First, one may be a poor reader who thinks of style "not as a linguistic means by which the writer produces whatever results he desires but as a sort of extra—an uncovenanted pedantry tacked on to the book proper, to gratify some specifically 'literary' or 'critical' taste which has nothing to do with the ordinary pleasures of the imagination."[25]

It is equally possible for the writer to fail. As much as Lewis liked George MacDonald, he conceded that his writing was undistinguished and fumbling except when the wisdom and "holiness that are in him triumph over and even burn away the baser elements of his style."[26] The same applies to Rider Haggard whose *She* Lewis admired. The book suffers from a "continuous poverty of style, by which, of course, I do not mean any failure to conform to certain *a priori* rules, but rather a sloth or incompetence of writing whereby the author is content always with a vague approximation to the emotion, the reflection, or the image he intends, so that a certain smudging and banality is spread over all."[27]

To reach a "condition of truth" requires a style that is like a lens, which we are expected not to look *at* but to look *through*. The lens must be "clean" so that it does not "smudge" the image of the world that we inspect. Lewis uses an analogous image to show why writers are not original in any important sense. We must be, he claims, "as little as possible ourselves..., clean mirrors filled with the image of a face that is not ours."[28]

The second requirement for a "condition of truth" resides in myth-making which Lewis thinks may not be a species of literary art because myth "does not essentially exist in *words* at all." Form and content are separate because a myth comes to us not in a single form but in many versions. By contrast, in a lyric poem, "the words are the body and the 'theme' or 'content' is the soul." In myth, on the other hand, "the imagined events are the body and something inexpressible is the soul: the words, or mime, or film, or pictorial series are not even the clothes—they are not much more than a telephone."[29]

In the poem "The Birth of Language," Lewis postulates a diachronic debility in words. They begin as nameless "intelligible virtues." Then they take on names and become "facts," whence they deteriorate into "truth" and finally into everyday meaning. A true poet can "lift the curse" so that words may "feel in dreams" their celestial origin. This is a fanciful vision of language, but it registers Lewis's conviction that words have lives of their own. They are god-given, which is to say they come to us from outside.[30]

What are we to make of this assembly of Lewis's statements about language? We might simply conclude that the most perfect communication is a myth embodied in a poem. And we might suggest that Lewis borrowed this notion from Barfield.[31] But first we should turn to Lewis's texts to see if we can find some keys in them that will unlock the secret of his effectiveness. We can approach them in three ways: by examining his revisions, his images, and the oral quality of much of his work.

*III*

Because he moved from first draft to fair copy in one jump, we cannot watch the evolution of a text. Nor would we gain much by comparing his juvenilia or the poor writing in his early poems or in *The Pilgrim's Regress* with later work. There is, of course, the published abridgement of *That Hideous Strength*[32] in which he practiced his own advice to authors, namely that their "first duty...is to entertain" and that they are "to avoid ornament, [and] to set down as simply and clearly as possible what it was they had to say, then to go through it and remove all purple passages or anything that seemed to be particularly fine writing."[33]

Evidently, Lewis's task was to reduce the length of *That Hideous Strength* by thirty percent. The simplest way for him to have done this was to remove entire sub-sections of chapters. (There are eighty-four sub-sections distributed unequally within the seventeen chapters.) Or he might have removed entire characters or plot lines that readers found to be redundant or superfluous, for example Miss Ironwood, Hingest, or even Merlin. Instead, he went through the entire novel line by line, altering single words, omitting phrases, sentences, and (rarely) full paragraphs; so that the overall "architecture" remains exactly the same. The amount of rewriting is minimal. It occurs only when continuity demands a summary or transition.

It is difficult to answer the question, "which version is better?" because readers who come to the abridgement after enjoying the original will feel somehow cheated. Readers unimpressed by the book will no doubt say, "The briefer, the better." In neither case, I think, would one wish to claim the alteration of form substantially changed the substance. Stories that transmit myths can take many forms. You can throw away the "means of communication" once you have the myth in your head. Thus when someone told Lewis the story of Kafka's *Castle,* his actual reading of the novel added nothing.[34] Once we know that*That Hideous Strength* involves an averted "second fall" of man, this time in the twentieth century, we recognize its affinity with *Perelandra, Paradise Lost, Genesis,* and countless other versions. Lewis' own rendering in this particular novel is equally intelligible and effective in both versions.

Examining the revision of a large novel is cumbersome, so let us take a briefer example of Lewis's practice. In *The Pilgrim's Regress* (1933), there is a poem which John "sang" at the moment when he discovered God and therefore found his own voice:

He whom I bow to only knows to whom I bow
When I attempt the ineffable name, murmuring *Thou;*
And dream of Pheidian fancies and embrace in heart
Meanings, I know, that cannot be the thing thou art.
All prayers always, taken at their word, blaspheme,
Invoking with frail imageries a folk-lore dream;

And all men are idolaters, crying unheard
To senseless idols, if thou take them at their word,
And all men in their praying, self-deceived, address
One that is not (so saith that old rebuke) unless
Thou, of mere grace, appropriate, and to thee divert
Men's arrows, all at hazard aimed, beyond desert.
Take not, oh Lord, our literal sense, but in thy great,
Unbroken speech our halting metaphor translate.[35]

In 1964 Lewis's revision was printed under the title "Footnote to All Prayers."

He whom I bow to only knows to whom I bow
When I attempt the ineffable Name, murmuring *Thou,*
And dream of Pheidian fancies and embrace in heart
Symbols (I know) which cannot be the thing Thou art.
Thus always, taken at their word, all prayers blaspheme
Worshipping with frail images a folk-lore dream,
And all men in their praying, self-deceived, address
The coinage of their own unquiet thoughts, unless
Thou in magnetic mercy to Thyself divert
Our arrows, aimed unskillfully, beyond desert;
And all men are idolators, crying unheard
To a deaf idol, if Thou take them at their word.

Take not, oh Lord, our literal sense. Lord, in Thy great,
Unbroken speech our limping metaphor translate.[36]

Four things stand out in the revision. By moving lines 5-6 and 11-12, Lewis strengthens the logical sequence of his reiterated depiction of man's verbal inadequacies in God's presence. The picture of idolators crying to an idol is a fitting conclusion to the previous lines. Second, Lewis enhances the consistency of his imagery by foregrounding the idea of counterfeit offerings. Graven idols in stone or metal are bad substitutes for words. Third, Lewis replaces vague or abstract terms with more specific terms. Perhaps "symbol" is only a slight improvement over "meaning" (line 4); but "worshipping" for "invoking," "images," for "imageries," "deaf" for "senseless," "magnetic mercy" for "mere grace" are dramatic steps toward specificity. The best example is the shift from "address/One that is not (so saith that old rebuke)" to "address/The coinage of their own unquiet thoughts," which relocates our attention from God to man. Fourth, Lewis adjusts the rhythm. Adding and removing parentheses in each case appropriately decelerates and accelerates tempo. In the thirteenth line, replacing "but" with "Lord" creates a caesura, doubles the word's force by repetition, and adds stateliness at the same time that it provides oral force. This is how we would *say* it.

We may call Lewis's revisions a logical-lexical-aural process, with each element clarifying meaning and enhancing the poem. Lewis says better what he ought to say (in Wimsatt's sense) by this tripartite process.

## *IV*

The key to Lewis's imagery may be found, I think, in a passage from *English Literature in the Sixteenth Century* where he describes the rhetorical component in the education of that century.

> We must picture them growing up from boyhood in a world of 'prettie epanorthosis', paranomasia, *isocolon*, and *similiter cadentia.* Nor were these, like many subjects in a modern school, things dear to the masters but mocked or languidly regarded by the parents. Your father, your grown-up brother, your admired elder schoolfellow all loved rhetoric. Therefore you loved it too. You adored sweet Tully and were as concerned about asyndeton and chiasmus as a modern schoolboy is about country cricketers or types of aeroplane. But against what seems to us this fantastic artificiality in their education we must set the fact that every boy, out of school, without noticing it, then acquired a range of knowledge such as no boy has today; farriery, forestry, archery, hawking, sowing, ditching, thatching, brewing, baking, weaving, and practical astronomy. This concrete knowledge, mixed with their law, rhetoric, theology, and mythology, bred an outlook very different from our own. High abstractions and rarified artifices jostled the earthiest particulars. They would have found it very hard to understand the modern educated man, who, though 'interested in astronomy', knows neither who the Pleiades were nor where to look for them in the sky. They talked more readily than we about large universals such as death, change, fortune, friendship, or salvation; but also about pigs, loaves, boots, and boats. The mind darted more easily to and fro between that mental heaven and earth: the cloud of middle generalizations, hanging between the two, was then much smaller. Hence, as it seems to us, both the naivety and the energy of their writing. Much of their literary strength (when at the end of the century they became strong) is bound up with this. They talk something like angels and something like sailors and stable-boys; never like civil servants or writers of leading articles.[37]

Lewis's attitude toward rhetoric was on the whole negative.[38] The important thing here, however, is his empathy for young sixteenth century scholars. I think he understood them by "reading himself" back into their time, by projecting his own deliberate boyishness into the boyhood of Spenser's and Shakespeare's contemporaries. Whether this is legitimate or not as a way to understand history is, for my purpose, beside the point. What is crucial is Lewis's assumption about how great writing gets done: by yoking the exalted with the homely. —That Lewis speaks personally and candidly here is confirmed in his poem "A Confession," in which he portrays himself as

> one whose doom
> Keeps him forever in the list of dunces,
> Compelled to live on stock responses,

Making the poor best that I can
Of dull things....[39]

To have written so much and so well about Highest Things through the medium of stock response and homely or mundane things is a challenge to which all great writers rise. It is Lewis's way. The wider the gap between high abstraction and low metaphor, the more delight we take, so long as the surprising congruity illuminates. This is why every reader's list of favorite passages from Lewis's work includes homely images or analogs for grand objects.

For all Adam knew, God might have had other cards in His hand.[40]
Of each of us some great poet has made a rape when we still wore Eton collars.[41]
(Donne's) love poetry is *Hamlet* without the prince.[42]
This world is a great sculptor's shop. We are the statues and there is a rumour going around the shop that some of us are some day going to come to life.[43]
We laugh at honour and are shocked to find traitors in our midst. We castrate and bid the geldings be fruitful.[44]
God is a 'host' who deliberately creates His own parasites.[45]
No seed ever fell from so fair a tree into so dark and cold a soil as would furnish more than a faint analogy to this huge descent and re-ascension in which God dredged the salt and oozy bottom of creation.[46]
Amiable agnostics will talk cheerfully about 'man's search for God.' To me, as I then was, they might as well have talked about the mouse's search for the cat.[47]

As commentators always say, these are "genial" or "vigorous" figures. Why so? Because the distance between object and image is the distance between angel and stable-boy; because homeliness and familiarity are so surely yoked with abstraction. Lewis found the verbal donkey to carry the weight of glory that was his message.

To be sure, the homeliness of Lewis's images, the clarity and simplicity of his style, may be faulted by some readers. C.E. Montague observes that, "if you are going to stand out for clearness at any price, then you are going to shut yourself out from a good many things. For a good many things cannot be put quite clearly except by being put falsely."[48] Cyril Connolly warns that "a writer who thinks himself cleverer than his readers writes simply (often too simply), while one who fears they may be cleverer than he will make use of mystification...."[49] I have heard readers complain that Lewis's imagery is too "pat" and that his "facile" clarity makes them uncomfortable because "real truth" cannot be as simple as Lewis makes it seem.

One answer to such complaints is the old adage that if you can't explain something clearly to someone else, you don't understand it yourself. Good writers always make the rough places plain. But this will not help the sceptics of our time who, as Bonamy Dobree claims, "instinctively mistrust any one who pontificates" because "in our present confusion our only hope is to be scrupulously honest with ourselves, so honest as to doubt our own minds and the conclusions they arrive at." The pontificator "is not being faithful to the movement of his mind; he is taking things for granted, and he fills us of to-day with uneasiness."[50]—If you think confusion or ambiguity are virtues, Lewis is not your man. The indubitable consonance of his images will vex you, send you down to Schoenberg.

*V*

As important as imagery is in defining the character of Lewis's language, the oral quality of his writing is even more so. Most of his published words were either designed for oral presentation as lectures, sermons, and radio talks or were read aloud to the Inklings. Moreover, the fact of orality, as we have come to recognize in recent years, means a good deal more than the incoporation of "conversational" or informal turns of phrase in an otherwise bookish discourse. Whether or not we have actually heard Lewis's recording of *The Four Loves* or read Carolyn Keefe's analysis of his voice,[51] we often have the illusion that Lewis sounds like Augustine or Socrates. He works close to his subject and close to his listener so that you can sometimes almost feel a tug at your sleeve. How does this happen?

This royalty is less apparent in Eve, partly because she is in fact Adam's inferior, in her double capacity of wife and subject, but partly, I believe, because her humility is often misunderstood. She thinks herself more fortunate than he, because she has *him* for her companion while he 'like consort to himself can nowhere find' (IV, 448) and obeys his commands 'unargued' (IV, 635). This is humility, and, in Milton's view, becoming humility. But do not forget that it is to Adam she speaks; a lover to a lover, a wife to a husband, the Queen of earth to the King. Many women in love, many wives, perhaps many queens, have at some time said or thought as much. Portia wished that for Bassanio's sake, she might be trebled 'twenty times herself. A thousand times more fair, ten thousand times More rich', and protests that, as things are, 'the full sum of her is sum of nothing', 'an unlesson'd girl'. It is prettily said and sincerely said. But I should feel sorry for the common man, such as myself, who was led by this speech into the egregious mistake of walking into Belmont and behaving as though Portia really *were* an unlessoned girl. A man's forehead reddens to think of it. She may speak thus to Bassanio: but *we* had better remember that we are dealing with a great lady. I am inclined to think that critics sometimes make the same mistake about Eve. We see her prostrate herself in spirit before Adam—as an Emperor might kneel to a Pope or as a Queen curtsies to a King. You must not think but that if you and I could enter Milton's Eden and meet her we should very quickly be taught what it is to speak to the 'universal Dame'. Even Satan, when he has said that she is 'not terrible', is constrained to add 'though terrour be in Love And beautie, not approacht by stronger hate' (IX, 490). Even for Adam, though she is 'made so adorn for his delight', she is also made 'so *awful* that with honour he may love' (VIII, 576; italics mine). There is no question, you see, of a boy and a girl tumbling on a bank; even for him there is that in Eve which compels deference, the possibility of *Daungier*.[52]

Five things about this passage (from a "dry," scholarly book on Milton's *Paradise Lost*) make Lewis's presence seem tangible. (1) The imperatives ("but do not forget. . .;" "*we* had better remember;" "you must not think") increase the urgency, the "volume," of his message, making it importunate but not presumptuous. (2) The "I" is intimate and personal without the faintest ingratiation. (3) His *ethos* as a speaker combines two kinds of authority: he knows his subject, as the constant citations of Milton's text and Shakespeare's analogous texts show; he also knows the world outside his literary subject, the world of common men and women, and reveals ways in which both this knowledge and the knowledge within a great text illuminate each other reciprocally. (4) He has an uncanny knack of anticipating the flow of his listener's mind, so that he is always ready with an answer just when you are ready with a question. This is why we seem to be actually conversing with him. (5) The plurality of pronouns (I, we, you, he-she) hastens us into various angles of vision. We must for an instant *become* Eve, Adam, Milton, many women, a common man, Portia, some critics, a Pope, a Queen, Lewis, Satan, a courting boy and girl, and (breathlessly) ourselves. Lewis holds all these viewpoints together for us as if they were fish in a small bowl—a dazzle of color and movement.

When Lewis finishes with you—or when you finish with him—you emerge as you do from a Platonic dialogue or Augustine's Confession, acutely aware that you were engaged in working rhetoric, not showpiece rhetoric. This is true of everything he wrote, fiction and non-fiction alike. He "works" his audience.

His perfection of a style that approximates a kind of dialog with his listener (sometimes with himself or God) places him among those writers of the twentieth century who have rediscovered the miracle of language and freed themselves from cant. (God "never talked vague, idealistic gas.") One thinks of recent Soviet writing by Voinovich, Zinoviev, or Solzhenitsyn in which the Russian language, sterilized for fifty years by Marxian verbicide, returns to its roots in the soil and in the church and thus begins to sound human again. One also thinks of the growing concern about the origins and consequences of literacy. Eric A. Havelock,[53] Samuel Ijesseling,[54] Rudolf Pfeifer,[55] J. Goody and I. Watt[56] have all moved beyond McLuhan's more popular work. This renewed concern for orality (and therefore rhetoric) is relevant to an understanding of Lewis's language in two ways: it suggests revisions in our attitude toward his *ethos* as speaker and his relationship with the *logos*.

Despite his professed rationalism, Lewis was no disciple of Descartes and Kant who imagined that language was a neutral medium that rational men could control, thereby becoming lords and masters of their own thought. Such an assumption has collapsed in our time, and I think it collapsed for Lewis at the time of his conversion. Like Socrates and Nietsche, Lewis knows that far from speaking in his own person, he is spoken through by the Word. This, I take it, is what he means when he likens himself to a clean mirror "filled with the image of a face not our own," or when he compares a mythic story to a telephone that cannot speak itself but can transmit otherwise inexpressible messages.

Knowing that language is saturated with dead metaphors and that all communication about supersensibles, is metaphoric, Lewis perhaps conceded more to Scientific language than he should have when he compared it with Ordinary and Poetic language in his essay "The Language of Religion."[57] In any case, his insistence on imagination as necessarily ancillary to the "condition of truth" places him on the side of those who know that you cannot possess the *logos* but only be possessed by it.

This happens because of the way imagination works. When we express it, we use the strange locution, "It occurs to me to say" rather than "I think." Properly so, because imagination comes from memory, mother of the Muses. To speak from memory, we must listen to words planted inside our heads, words that are not our own. To utter truth at all in the Greek sense of *alethia* (rather than *episteme*) is literally to *un*-forget.

It is both natural and inevitable that a Christian writer (except certain dogmatists) will exalt imagination, as Lewis does when he says it may create the "condition of truth." His authority for this is not merely Romanticism nor yet Platonism. It is more ancient than either. It is at once pre-Socratic and Hebraic.[58] It is Homer's invocations of the Muse, Hesiod's confession that his philosophy was suggested to him by Mnemosyne, Isocrates' eulogy to the *logos* in "Nicocles," and it is continuously Biblical. No prophet of the Lord or disciple of Christ presumed to speak in his own voice. Always it is the *logos,* the God, who speaks *through* them. "For it is not you who speak, but the spirit of your father speaking through you." (Matthew, 10:19-20)

Educated as a twentieth century rationalist, Lewis does not dwell on this ancient side of the communication process, in part because it came so naturally to him (as it did for sixteenth century scholars). The tutorial system at Oxford, the penchant he had for debate, the duty imposed upon him as a Christian to propagate the faith: all of these made him an evangelist—or a sophist (in the original sense of the word). Reference to this ancient tradition recurs frequently in his work.

Who but Lewis would begin an attack on Evolutionism with the sentence: "I come to bury the great Myth of the nineteenth and early twentieth Century; but also to praise it?"[59] In *That Hideous Strength* he postulates a Great Tongue, a divine language of which human language is a faint imitation, but one we must use as a distant echo of the primal Voice. In *The Weight of Glory,* he explains *glossolalia* by means of some sort of transposition: "the incredible flooding of those very sensations we now have with meaning, a transvaluation, of which we have no faintest guess." This sense of a mind "flooded" with meanings from outside is an exact rendering of the ancient "possession." His comment on Homer's poet Phemius illustrates this. Phemius claimed to be both "self-taught" and "god-inspired." It sounds contradictory, but Lewis explains that "god's instruction is given internally, not through the senses, and is therefore regarded as part of the Self, to be contrasted with such external aids as, say, the example of other poets."[60]

Usually, however, Lewis follows Augustine for whom truth was incommunicable except by an inner teacher. For Augustine, one can communicate and *recollect* through words but not *learn.* Truth is not a word but an inner event prepared for by Grace. Like Lewis's "myth," truth is the "inexpressible soul" contained within a "body" of language and imagined events. Thus Lewis claims that God "is inside you as well as outside: even if we could understand who did what, I do not think human language could properly express it."[61] Thus also, the only way you can understand either religious dicta or poetry is to "meet them with a certain good will." You must "trust" them.[62] You will understand not when you are ready but when God is ready. Only then will you be *en logoi,* that is "taken into account" by the Word.

This limitation, far from inhibiting speech, makes efforts to communicate all the more imperative. The stakes are high indeed both for the pagan who wanted Power and for the Christian who wants to hear the Good News and share it with others. It is here that Lewis and Augustine sound alike. Augustine: "...it is a mark of good and distinguished minds to love the truth within words and not the words. Of what use is a gold key if it will not open what we wish? Or what objection to a wooden one which will, when we seek nothing except to open what is closed?"[63] Lewis: "My task as a writer about Christianity was...simply that of a *translator*—one turning Christian doctrine, or what he believed to be such, into the vernacular, into language that unscholarly people would attend to and could understand. For this purpose a style more guarded, more *nuance,* finelier shaded, more rich in fruitful ambiguities...would have been worse than useless."[64]

We might be tempted to commit the same error here that Paul Goodman did when he claimed that Milton's sonnets lacked style because "a powerful diction is artificially neutralized in the interest of thought and feeling."[65] Better, I think, to acknowledge that Lewis's Christianity gave him what the *logos,* the Muses, always give: a measureless accession of meaning that floods and fertilizes language. Always it is some revealed truth that exalts mere sophistry and transforms Isocrates or Demosthenes or Augustine from rhetoricians into prophets. By "occupying" them, the *logos* magnified their personal *ethos.* The same applies to mere versifiers who embrace a great truth and become poets, though of course truth alone is no guarantee of excellent poetry.

Primarily, then, Lewis's susceptibility to the Western oral tradition forbade his talking "like civil servants or writers of leading articles." This cost him the allegiance of many twentieth century intellectuals who typically say, "How *dare* you speak to me like that! Who do you think you are?" Far from blocking the view with his own ego, he tried to remove himself, to become a "clean" lens or mirror. His engaging us in the Great Conversation, his homely images, his revisions of texts are parts of one aim: to let the past live in us. In Tolkien's words, he was among those who "preserve the ancient *pietas* towards the past."[66]

If this seems too exalted, we may recall his advice in 1954 to an American schoolgirl: "Always write (and read) with the ear, not the eye. You shd. hear every sentence you write as if it was being read aloud or spoken. If it doesn't sound nice, try again."[67]

### *VI*

In *The Voyage of the "Dawn Treader,"* there is an episode that may serve as a parable for Lewis's work. Lucy discovers a "Magician's Book" filled mainly with spells. Then she comes upon an illustrated story and says, "That is the loveliest story I've ever read or ever shall read in my whole life." She wants to re-read it, but the pages of the book will not turn back. Henceforth for her, a good story is one that reminds her of the story in the Magician's Book.

As you remember the Narnia books, they may seem to be like Lucy's story, models of what good stories should be long after the story-line and characters have faded. Writers of another, perhaps greater, kind leave characters indelibly impressed on your mind (Oedipus, Aeneas, Lear, Sorel, Karenina, the Karamazov brothers), but you would not say of any of their stories, "this is the loveliest story I've ever read." Is it possible that every story Lewis told (and he told only old stories, from the ones about literary history to the ones about God) is the best telling we can find in this century? "The books or the music in which we thought the beauty was located will betray us if we trust them; it was not *in* them, it only came *through* them, and what came through was longing."[68]

## Notes

[1]Louis Milic, "Metaphysical Criticism of Style," in *Modern Essays on Writing*

*and Style,* ed. P.C. Wermuth (New York: Holt, Rinehart and Winston, 1969), 57.

[2]George Saintsbury, *A History of English Prose Rhythm* (1912; rpt. Bloomington: Indiana University Press, 1965). Saintsbury's "table of feet" is still suggestive despite H.W. Fowler's harsh words about all mechanical approaches to style in his entry on "Rhythm" in *A Dictionary of Modern English Usage.* Dobree's *Modern Prose Style* (Oxford: Clarendon, 1934) is always insightful, but his approaches are so eclectic that they provide no pattern.

[3]Let one extreme example suffice: Gunther Kress and Robert Hodge, *Language and Ideology* (London: Routledge & Kegan Paul, 1979). This book, like many "post-Chomskian" commentaries on language and literature, could have been written by Mark Studdock during his Belbury phase.

[4]After all, Lewis shared Owen Barfield's dislike for one of the patron saints of structural linguistics, I.A. Richards. In *Poetic Diction* (1928; rpt. New York: McGraw-Hill, 1964), Barfield denounced Richards and Ogden's *The Meaning of Meaning* as a "ghastly tissue of empty abstractions" 135.

[5](New Haven: Yale University Press, 1941), 10-11.

[6]*The Longing for a Form,* ed. P.J. Schakel (Kent, Ohio: Kent State University Press, 1977) is a typical example.

[7]"From Master to Colleague," *C.S. Lewis at the Breakfast Table and Other Reminiscences* (New York: Macmillan, 1979), 82.

[8]"A Great Clerke," *Ibid.*, 69.

[9]C.S. Lewis, *Poems,* ed. W. Hooper (New York: Harcourt 1964), vi.

[10]"Introduction," *C.S. Lewis at the Breakfast Table,* xxix.

[11]*The Literary Legacy of C.S. Lewis* (New York: Harcourt, Brace, Jovanovich, 1979), 128; 245.

[12]"Chiliastic Agonisticism and the Style of C.S. Lewis," in *Man's "Natural Powers:" Essays for and about C.S. Lewis* (Denver: Society for New Language Study, 1975), 30; 33.

[13]"The Approach to English," *Light on C.S. Lewis* (New York: Harcourt, Brace & World, 1965) 590-60; 65.

[14]*Ibid.*, 64. Luke Rigby reports that he wrote "mostly in the evenings, when he was too tired (as he once said to me) for serious work." "A Solid Man," *C.S. Lewis at the Breakfast Table,* 43.

[15]*Studies in Words,* 2nd ed. (Cambridge: Cambridge University Press, 1967), 6.

[16]"On Criticism," *Of Other Worlds: Essays and Stories,* ed. W. Hooper (New York: Harcourt 1975), 56.

[17]*Studies in Words,* 325.

[18]*A Grief Observed* (New York: Bantam, 1976), 43.

[19]*Miracles* (New York: Macmillan, 1947), 81.

[20]*Ibid.*, p. 74. Relying heavily on Barfield's *Poetic Diction,* Lewis worked out the implications of this position in "Bluspels and Flalansferes: A Semantic Nightmare," *Selected Literary Essays,* ed. W. Hooper (Cambridge: Cambridge U P, 1969), 251-65.

[21]*A Preface to Paradise Lost* (London: Oxford U P, 1942), 57.

[22]*They Stand Together: The Letters of C.S. Lewis to Arthur Greeves,* ed. W. Hooper (London: Collins, 1979), 427-28. Cf. *Miracles,* chapter 15.

[23]"Bluspels and Flalansferes," 263.

[24]*Ibid.*, 265.

[25]"High and Low Brow," *Selected Literary Essays,* 271.

[26]"Preface," *George MacDonald, An Anthology* (New York: Macmillan, 1947), xxvi.

[27]"High and Low Brow," p. 269. Lewis would likely have agreed with Rudyard Kipling who told Haggard: "You didn't write *She* you know,...something wrote it *through* you." *Rudyard Kipling to Rider Haggard: A Record of Friendship*, ed. M.N. Cohen (Rutherford, N.J.: Fairleigh Dickinson University Press, 1965), 100.

[28]"Christianity and Literature," *Christian Reflections* (Grand Rapids: Eerdmans, 1967), 7.

[29]"Preface," *George MacDonald, An Anthology*, xxvi-xxviii. "What flows in you from the myth is not truth but reality (truth is always *about* something, but reality is that *about* which truth is), and, therefore, every myth becomes the father of innumerable truths on the abstract level.... Myth is the isthmus which connects the peninsular world of thought with the vast continent we really belong to." "Myth Became Fact," *God in the Dock* (Grand Rapids: Eerdmans, 1970), 66.

[30]*Poems*, 10-11.

[31]*Poetic Diction*, chapter 5. On the nature of metaphor, see Barfield's "poetic Diction and Legal Fiction," in *Essays Presented to Charles Williams*, ed. D. Sayers, et. al. (London: Oxford U P 1947), 125.

[32]*The Tortured Planet* (New York: Avon, n.d. [1958]). The abridgement contains 254 pages by contrast with 382 pages in a comparable full edition.

[33]Robert F. Havard, "Philia: Jack at Ease," *C.S. Lewis at the Breakfast Table*, 220-21.

[34]"Preface," *George MacDonald, An Anthology*, p. xxviii. Modern critical orthodoxy demands the organic unity of form and content, but this article in the Creed causes problems. Louis Milic says that most stylistic critics know little about the facts of language and are prone to romantic exaggeration and a Rhetoric of Metaphysics. "It is my impression that some of this disorder may derive from the debilitating belief that style and content are inseparable and the resulting unwillingness to attempt anything that might seem to show trust in their disjunction." *Op. cit.*, 56. Lewis approaches this matter cautiously: a literary work "both *means* and *is*. It is both *Logos* (something said) and *Poiema* (something made)." Thus you cannot claim "the whole goodness of a literary work is in its character as Poiema, for it is out of our various interests in the Logos that the Poiema is made." *An Experiment in Criticism* (Cambridge: Cambridge U P, 1961), 132 and 137.

[35](Grand Rapids: Eerdmans, 1933), 144-45.

[36]*Poems*, p. 129.

[37](New York: Oxford University Press, 1954), 61-2.

[38]James Como, "Introduction," *C.S. Lewis at the Breakfast Table*, xxvii-xxviii.

[39]*Poems*, 1.

[40]*A Preface to Paradise Lost*, 127.

[41]"High and Low Brow," 277.

[42]"Donee and Love Poetry," *Selected Literary Essays*, 123.

[43]*Mere Christianity* (New York: Macmillan, 1952), 140.

[44]*The Abolition of Man* (New York: Macmillan, 19477), 35.

[45]*The Four Loves* (New York: Harcourt, Brace, Jovanovich, 1960), 176.

[46]*Miracles*, 117.

[47]*Surprised by Joy* (New York: Harcourt, 1955), p. 227. All of the examples of Lewis's images are what the Renaissance called ornaments (or "praises" or "lights") of speech. As Walter Ong has noted, we moderns have lost the feeling for such

ornaments—and been impoverished. "Ramist Rhetoric," in *The Province of Rhetoric*, ed. J. Schwartz and J.A. Rycenga (New York: Ronald, 1965), 236-39.

[48]"Only Too Clear," in *Modern Essays on Writing and Style*, 267.

[49]*Enemies of Promise* (New York: Macmillan, 1948), 17.

[50]*Modern Prose Style*, 220-21.

[51]"Notes on Lewis's Voice," in *C.S. Lewis Speaker and Teacher*, ed. C. Keefe (Grand Rapids: Zondervan, 1971), 169-78.

[52]*A Preface to Paradise Lost*, 120.

[53]Eric A. Havelock, *Origins of Western Literacy* (Toronto: The Ontario Institute for Studies in Education: Monograph Series/14, 1976).

[54]Samuel Ijsseling, *Rhetoric and Philosophy in Conflict: A Historical Survey*, tr. P. Dunphy (The Hague: M. Nijhoff, 1976).

[55]Rudolf Pfeifer, *History of Classical Scholarship* (New York: Oxford U P, 1968).

[56]J. Goody and I. Watt, "The Consequences of Literacy," *Comparative Studies in Society and History*, V (1962-63), 304-26, 332-45.

[57]*Christian Reflections*, 130.

[58]George Kennedy explains in detail the differences and similarities between Judeo-Christian and Greek rhetoric in the seventh chapter of *Classical Rhetoric and Its Christian and Secular Tradition from Ancient to Modern Times* (Chapel Hill: U of North Carolina P, 1980). Lewis seems to have been wary of mysticism, but I think he might have approved Evelyn Underhill's description of the psychological state and the language of mystical expression in *Mysticism* (Cleveland: World, 1955), 252-53:

"In Dante, the transcendent and impersonal aspect of illumination is seen in its most exalted form. It seems at first sight almost impossible to find room within the same system for this expansive vision of the Undifferentiated Light and such intimate and personal apprehensions of Deity as Lady Julian's conversations with her 'courteous and dearworthy Lord,' or St. Catherine's companionship with Love Divine. Yet all these are really reports of the same psychological state. . . .

"It must never be forgotten that all apparently one-sided descriptions of illumination—more, all experiences of it—are governed by temperament. 'That Light whose smile kindles the Universe' is ever the same; but the self through whom it passes, and by whom we must receive its report, has already submitted to the moulding influences of environment and heredity, Church and State. The very language of which that self avails itself in its struggle for expression, links it with half a hundred philosophies and creeds. The response which it makes to Divine Love will be the same in type as the response which its nature would make to earthly love: but raised to the nth degree. We, receiving the revelation, receive with it all those elements which the subject has contributed in spite of itself. Hence the soul's apprehension of Divine Reality may take almost any form, from the metaphysical ecstasies which we find in Dionysius, and to a less degree in St. Augustine, to the simple, almost 'common-sense' statements of Brother Lawrence, the emotional ardours of St. Gertrude, or the lovely intimacies of Julian or Mechthild."

[59]"The Funeral of a Great Myth," *Christian Reflections*, 82.

[60]"Christianity and Literature," 8. Lewis adds: "To the Christian [unlike the unbeliever] his own temperament and experience, as mere fact, and as merely his, are of no value or importance whatsoever: he will deal with them, if at all, only because they are the medium through which, or the position from which, something universally profitable appeared to him."

[61]*Mere Christianity*, 130.

[62]"The Language of Religion," 141.

[63]*On Christian Doctrine,* tr. D. W. Robertson, Jr. (Indianapolis: Bobbs-Merrill, 1958), 136.

[64]"Rejoinder to Dr. Pittenger," *God in the Dock,* 183.

[65]Quoted in Nils Enkvist, "On Defining Style," *Modern Essays on Writing and Style,* 24.

[66]"Beowulf: The Monsters and the Critics," in *Beowulf,* ed. J. F. Tuso (New York: Norton, 1975), 112-13.

[67]*Letters of C. S. Lewis* (New York: Harcourt Brace Jovanovich, 1966), p. 291.

[68]*The Weight of Glory and Other Addresses* (New York: Macmillan, 1949), 4-5.

# Fighting "Verbicide" and Sounding Old-fashioned: Some Notes on Lewis's Use of Words

*Paul Leopold*

I don't think I shall provoke any violent disagreement if I say that the four most prominent features of C.S. Lewis's style are: lucidity of argument; vividness of illustration; an immoderate use of quotation (like Lamb's); and a defiant old-fashionedness—a set purpose not to move with the times. I am concerned in this essay only with the lucidity and the old-fashionedness, though I hope what I have to say will throw light on the whole texture of Lewis's style. My focus will be on the evidence furnished by one of the smallest, but most telling, elements of style, the choice of vocabulary.

Of course what I call "lucidity," and ascribe to Lewis's intelligence, some would call "simplism" and ascribe to his "complacency." For the present such critics and I need not quarrel; for my purpose is purely descriptive. I am not going to insist on the intelligence; I am only going to describe, and try to analyze, what I think no reader of Lewis can fail to see. And one cannot read much of him without noticing how—for better or worse—he is always lighting the subject up, always giving the impression, at least, of dealing with it thoroughly, of searching its very corner and tracing its very implication. His characteristic approach to anything is the formal argument: he is always defining his terms, listing his points, setting up his elenchus, and concluding with Euclidian—not to say Kirkpatrician—finality. His prose makes heavy use of the colon and of sentences beginning with *But*.

Nor is it only in argument that Lewis writes thus. He narrates, describes, and speculates in the same "hard-edged" manner. All is flood-lit: there are no long shadows, no *sfumato* twilight evanescence. In style Lewis is far closer to Chesterton than to Morris; yet the clarity of his manner can also, paradoxically, deepen the dimness of his matter. Lewis often leads us *per mirabilia,* but in the midst of the thickest mystery his reason and imagination seem still to be trying their best to comprehend the object; so that it is largely by the measure of their failure that we come to apprehend something of the super-rational and the unimaginable. Even if you think the apprehension illusory, you must admit that on the imaginative level the technique works. Reading Lewis, we sometimes seem to be looking down a well under the midsummer sun at noon, and still we cannot see to the bottom.

Those who find Lewis's lucidity specious are apt also to find his old-fashionedness offensive. And I am not sure the offense is always altogether accidental. There is something pugnacious about his refusal to be modern, even on the level of the choice of a particular word or phrase. That this was a conscious refusal, and not (in the French sense) a *naiveté,* is clear from the extent and depth of Lewis's philology. For not only *Studies in Words* and essays like "Bluspels and Flalansferes," but notes and comments scattered throughout his critical works and elsewhere, show Lewis to have been a writer who thought (and knew) unusually much about language, and who was particularly conscious of the import of its minutiae (e.g. the difference between "don't have" and "haven't got" or the appropriateness of the term *Scotch,* as opposed to *Scottish*). John Wain has pointed out that the attitude Lewis assumed of an "Old Western Man" surviving like a bemused dinosaur in a cultural Ice Age was, like every don's public figure, something of a construction—a persona (68-69). The mask may have fitted the man unusually well, but Lewis was, after all, chronologically a Modern; younger, indeed, than Eliot or Pound or Picasso. On the other hand, to call his old-fashionedness a "pose" would be utterly misleading. No attitude was ever more sincere. If it was a disguise, it was the kind of disguise that reveals rather then conceals. The motive to it surely came from deep within—from regions where affection and affectation are still joined in Barfieldian "primal unity." Nothing could be more natural than the way Lewis's language continually reminds us that we are in the company of a man who holds the sort of solid and sensible—or smug and stodgy—views our great-grandfathers took for granted. Yet when clarity demands modern diction and vocabulary Lewis never hesitates to use them.

But of course clarity with Lewis, as with every writer, depends chiefly on his understanding of his own arguments and his ability to see them from the reader's point of view. Beyond this, Lewis is a master of technique, remarkable particularly for his cogent marshalling of paragraphs and his almost eighteenth-century deftness at projecting parallels and turning antitheses. But I should add that his clarity also owes much to the accuracy of his vocabulary—which, for much of what he has to say, means the archaism of his vocabulary. From even the most colloquial of his prose there jut forth, like fragments of ancient sculpture in a Dark Ages wall, certain verbal antiquities—words, phrases, or sense of words and phrases, no longer in current use. His art makes their meaning inevitably clear and their oddity, often, unnoticeable. And they give his style an extended range and a suggestion of timelessness (itself an old-fashioned ideal). Beside them, and more numerous, are words and phrases not yet totally corrupted or extinct, but in danger of becoming so: and of these, of course, every use is a blow struck against "verbicide." And finally there are certain words and phrases, not specially needful for precision, which Lewis draws from the recent rather than the remote past, and which contribute to his "dinosaur" persona. Though they were not all current in the age of that monarch, I shall refer to them for convenience as "Edwardianisms."

I am not suggesting that Lewis was necessarily conscious of any of the peculiarities of usage I am going to point out. Probably he was conscious of some, unconscious of others, and half-conscious of perhaps the majority. But the question of self-consciousness is unimportant. His style is, in any case, no accident. Like all good styles, it fits its content the way a man's skin fits his body. *Stilus virum arguit.*

Archaism skillfully employed can help prevent the erosion of meaning and repair damage already done. It is a lamentable fact that, as Rose Macaulay noted, dictionaries "are always telling us of words 'now used only in a bad sense' " (*qtd. in On Stories* 105). But Lewis invariably uses words like *pompous, condescending, pious* and *righteous* in a good, or at least, neutral, one. And when he revives an old word for its precision he is careful to shore it up with a precise definition and explanation, as with the Greek names of the Four Loves, the Latin *Venus,* and the English *begotten* describing the Son's relation to the Father (*The Four Loves* 85; *Mere Christianity* 138).

But there is another vein of old-fashionedness in Lewis's style, of which even those who like it will recognize George Orwell's acerbic description in a review of *Beyond Personality*:

> One must make some allowance for the fact that these essays are reprinted broadcasts, but even on the air it is not really necessary to insult your hearersforth (*Collected Essays* 264).

" 'Specially' for 'especially.' " That detail perfectly reflects the whole stodgy, avuncular manner that disaffects so many readers of Lewis (and how like Orwell to spot the telling trait in a single omitted letter!). Americans may sometimes mistake Lewis's Edwardianisms for mere Britishisms, but usually the defiant out-of-dateness is hard for anyone to miss—all the "capital's" and "corking's" and "toppings"; all the "golly's" and "by gum's"; all that constant suggestion that the author is talking to a male audience about a "man's world." For it was certainly old-fashioned by the forties and fifties to represent callow youth so often under the figure of a "schoolboy," or to use as one's impersonal subject so rarely "one" or "they" or "people," but rather "men" or "a man." Open Lewis anywhere and you find things like, "when a man makes a moral choice," "I never met a man who," "Hypocrisy can do a man good," "Nothing...is more astonishing in any man's life," "Men have differed whether you should have one wife or four." Few writers since Dr. Johnson, I suspect, have leaned so heavily on this idiom.

At the same time Lewis cared seriously about the erosion of meaning, and opposed it by precept as well as example. Often he appeals to our sense of linguistic responsibility. "The greatest cause of verbicide," he warns in the Introduction to *Studies in Words,* "is the fact that most people are obviously far more anxious to express their approval and disapproval of things than to describe them" (7). Indeed, on this fact hang all the lesser causes—"inflation" (e.g., *enormous* for "great"), appropriation of a word "as a party banner" (e.g., *liberal* and *conservative),* and "verbiage," which he defines as the use of a word "as a promise to pay which is never going to be kept," (e.g., calling a thing "significant" "with no intention of ever telling us what it is significant of" (*Studies in Words* 7)—a pedant might add that even to call a thing "important" begs the question of what it imports!).

But even allowing such looseness as *significant* in an absolute sense, one has reason to be shocked at the crippling and killing of words that continues apace. It seems almost miraculous that language remains as capable of fineness and subtlety as it is. All the knives and chisels have been used as screwdrivers and crowbars so often that we are amazed to see them still able to carve lifelike figures with precision. Part of the explanation may be that languages, like other living things, renew themselves as they die; men continually mar old meanings, but they continually make new ones. Another part may be in a principle Ruskin somewhere noted: Bad taste, though there is always more of it around than good taste, is essentially random, and its manifestations therefore cancel each other out; but the manifestations of good taste, various as they are, reinforce each other with a consistency drawn from their common root in Truth. The same may be said of good and bad language. There too order builds an order, quickly and conspicuously, as a brick wall rises above masses of rubble. It is not really a losing struggle, but we must wage it all the time. Lewis has some suggestions:

> Our conversation will have little effect; but if we get into print—perhaps especially if we are leader-writers, reviewers, or reporters—we can help to strengthen or weaken some disastrous vogue word; can encourage a good, and resist a bad, gallicism or Americanism. (*Studies in Words* 7)

The following examples of how Lewis fights this good fight come from a rather narrow range of works, and from those places in the larger range where the hooks and crotchets of memory happen to have taken hold. If my examples recall any better ones to the reader they will have done as much as I hoped of them. The only books I have thoroughly perused for this purpose are *The Problem of Pain, Mere Christianity, Miracles, Surprised by Joy, Reflections on the Psalms,* and *Letters to*

*Malcolm*, these constituting most of the non-fiction in which Lewis speaks in his own voice to a large, popular audience. As such, they are the books in which he is most likely to have seen an opportunity to nudge the mass of speakers an inch or two in the direction of what he considered the ideal language, towards that language (as he defines it) which makes "with the greatest ease...the finest and most numerous distinctions of meaning" (*Studies in Words* 6).

My first example comes from the title of the first book mentioned above, and it raises an issue which deserves discussion at some length. Lewis always uses *problem* to mean something like "a perplexing question proposed for solution"; he never uses it as a synonym for *trouble* or *affliction*. This latter sense was, however, already common in his time, and has by now become probably the prevalent sense in both England and America. We hear the word used that way everywhere. People on television talk about their "family problems," their "drug problems," their "sexual problems," etc.; instead of "the trouble with," people now say, "the problem with." Now it is my contention that behind this new habit of speech there lurks the old heresy of what may be called secular Pelagianism, by which I mean the faith—falsely supposed to have been wiped out by two world wars, etc.—that all felicity not forbidden by the material nature of things is reachable by man's intelligence and will. To professors of this faith there is something vaguely defeatist about talking of person's "griefs" or "troubles" or "afflictions." These are all things to be endured: they require of the sufferer patience and resignation. But a "problem" is something to be solved: it is no occasion for the passive virtues; it requires pluck and imagination and a spirit of optimism.

All this sounds very well. And to be fair, a humane impulse is usually the mainspring of this heresy (as Lewis acknowledged). It is certainly kinder to speak to a drunkard's family of the "problem," than of the "curse" of his alcoholism. And the same can be said with regard to all curable, or potentially curable, ills. Hope must not be made a sacrifice to patience. But what of the ills that cannot—or at least cannot right now—be cured? To define these as "problems" is to remove them from the arena in which the virtue of patience can be exercised, and therefore to discourage the very virtue that most needs to be encouraged. The substitution of *problems* for *afflictions* is thus a minor symptom of the same cruel tenderness which has replaced the manly concept of punishment in prison with the chilling and disheartening one of "rehabilitation in a correctional institution." It is the old paradox: "Damn braces. Bless relaxes." I don't know that anyone yet speaks to the dying or the bereaved about their "problem"; but such a development is conceivable. It is no good to say that "semantic ramification" has already turned *problem* into two distinct words. It hasn't. Everyone is conscious of the connection, and the new branch continues to draw meaning from the common root. Nor is it possible to excuse most users of the new word on the ground that their usage is casual and they have never reflected on its implications. The force of a word never depends entirely on the speaker's, or the hearer's, consciousness of it. The present widespread currency of the word *problem* to describe those things that used to come under the old concepts of "affliction," "trouble," etc. tends to deny patience the name of virtue and strip suffering of its dignity. It is a symptom of that terrible optimism whose final product is despair.

To the lure of such optimism Lewis was, of course, totally immune. His own nature was too deeply pessimistic. He was not inclined to make a virtue of impatience, and far from flattering hope with palliatives like *problem,* the tendency of his style was to temper it with plain talk; for he knew that in the end plain talk stays hope more firmly than the most "supportive" flattery.

The subject of homosexuality offers a good example. Lewis never speaks of the thing with reproach, and once even suggests that in certain circumstances it promoted virtue (*Surprised by Joy* 90); but he always refers to it as a "perversion." Conditions may produce different relative values, but nature is nature and facts are facts. Similarly, those who are not theists, however virtuous, he calls "atheists"; and the uncivilized, however noble, "savages." I recall a critic (I've forgotten who) giggling in print over Lewis's matter-of-fact characterization of Shelley as a "heathen"—though the critic, I believe, admired Shelley far less than Lewis did. And (to return to *problem*) I recall a discussion with a friend being mired in cross-purposes until I discovered that he thought *The Problem of Pain* referred to the trouble caused by the presence of pain rather than to the riddle posed by its existence. But I think few readers who stick with Lewis for long continue to make stuck mistakes.

Lewis naturally avoids euphemisms; not entirely; it would take a Diogenes to go through life eschewing them all, but pretty nearly so. The subject is somewhat complicated, and is worth introducing with some general observations.

Euphemisms may be divided into three groups: what we may call euphemisms of deprecation like "*vixit,*" "the dickens," "if something should happen to me," and "fourteen" (applied to the thirteenth floor of a building); euphemisms of obfuscation like population resettlement," "pacification," "affirmative action," "*Endlösung*"; and euphemisms of delicacy like "rest room," "gift" (for a bribe), "sexual intercourse," and "slow achiever." The first kind, which are superstitious in motive and relatively stable in meaning, do no evident harm to language. Lewis never uses them. He is not superstitious, and he always calls death, the devil, and damnation by their proper names. The second, which are political in motive and decidedly verbicidal, scarcely concern us. Lewis described himself as a "political skeptic" and wrote almost nothing in support or opposition to a political position[1]; if he ever used a euphemism of obfuscation he did so ironically (as when he conjectured that future persecution of Christians might be called "reeducation of the ideologically unfit")[2]. The third kind, euphemisms of delicacy, may be anything from charitable to quasi-hysterical in their motivation, are extremely volatile in their meaning, and do a great deal of harm to language. We may describe them as nice words for nasty things—or for things inconveniently or untowardly sensational. Decency often demands, but convention almost always exaggerates, their use (our age does so as much as the Victorian, though our areas of delicacy are different). Their volatility presents an interesting paradox.

The trouble with giving nasty things nice names is that, as everyone has observed, the nastiness of things has more power to affect words than the niceness of words has to affect things. A euphemism of delicacy is like a "respectable front" that does not even hide what is behind it; it is like tissue paper used to wrap coal. Refer to dung as "roses" and you only make the word *roses* malodorous.

The result, of course, is that such euphemisms need continually to be replaced. Our century has seen the once genteel gallicisms *saloon* and *toilet* (the latter a word whose literal reference, to a small cloth, is almost absurdly wide of its euphemistic application) become in certain contexts coarse. *Freak*, for "freak of nature" (representing *lusus naturae*), was apparently once regarded as a humane euphemism. The older term, *monster* (Latin *monstrum*, a "showing" or "omen"), implied the disgrace of divine displeasure; *freak* made monstrosity into a mere accident, a caprice of nature. But the new word in its turn became offensive, and now some want to call the deformed "special people." If their usage prevails, *special* will become, in that application, a nasty word, and a new euphemism will have to be found. We see the process repeating itself again and again. But mankind's faith in the power of names over objects apparently has very deep roots, for no amount of contrary evidence seems able to overthrow it.

The oddest thing about the shift from *monster* to *freak* is that, according to their literal meanings, it is the former which is really the more dignified term. This was not so among the pagans, for whom the birth of a misshapen man or beast could be regarded as pointing only to some evil. But the coming of Christianity must have changed that. For not only does its whole tenor recommend compassion rather than revulsion, but its Founder has left a specific teaching relevant to the point. When his disciples demanded of him why a certain man had been born blind Jesus answered, "that the works of God should be made manifest in him" (John 9:2). What to pagans had been a re*monstr*ance thus became for Christians a de*monstr*ation. Horace and Cicero use *monstra* mainly for hideous things like sea serpents: Saint Jerome uses it, translating *tépata*, for the wonders of the prophet Elijah (Ecclus. 48:15) and of God (Sap. 19:8).

Lewis employs the usual euphemisms for the acts and organs of generation and evacuation. The only alternatives, as he points out, are "gutter words, scientific words, or nursery words."[3] He does not seem to care whence he fetches his expressions: archaisms like "the act of kind" do equal work with quasi-scientific latinisms like "sexual intercourse" (though he does not hesitate to use *intercourse,* and even *ejaculation,* in a non-sexual sense).[4] On the other hand, Lewis seldom uses *sex* to mean "country matters." Almost always in his writings it refers to what some people nowadays (usually very solemnly) call "gender"; when Lewis wants to speak of the emotions and behavior associated with the generative act he is more likely to use *lust* or *amorousness* or *lasciviousness* or—on a level of more precise abstraction—*Venus* and *Eros* (although once in *The Four Loves* he commits the error of confusing these—"Without Eros none of us would have been begotten"—meaning of course "without Venus").

But where he has a decent alternative I think it is safe to say Lewis never uses a euphemism. What the cant of our time calls "erotica" he calls "pornography," not to denigrate but to describe it. And he is not shy of applying the word *pornographic* to writers like Ovid (*An Experiment* 126); nor shy of defining it, as it can only be defined, in terms of intention: the pornographic representation of "Venus" is that which appeals to the nerves rather than the imagination. With the same matter-of-factness Lewis regularly calls practical malice "wickedness" (a rare word in this age of psychological explaining), and "pre-marital sex" "fornication." Orual, the narrator of *Till We Have Faces,* is always described—and describes herself—as "ugly," even "extremely ugly." She is neither indifferent to her looks nor disposed to self-laceration. Her ugliness hurts her, but (like Lewis) she is a person who calls things by their right names. It would never occur to her to describe herself as "homely" or "plain." And so beautiful is her frankness that the word *ugly,* applied to her, loses some of its ugliness. And thus in the reader's imagination the tyranny of appearance suffers a small defeat.

Such a process, however, takes time; the reader who only dips into Lewis may find the frankness shocking. A friend of mine was put off by the first sentence of *The Discarded Image,* "Medieval man shared many ignorances with the savage, . . ." "How can anyone in 1962 talk about 'savages'!" I explained that Lewis undoubtedly meant the word only in its anthropological sense and intended no slur on anyone. But to my friend this defense made no difference; he felt the word as a slur and, as Johnson said to Boswell, "Sensation is sensation." To twentieth-century people who feel about human inequality the way nineteenth-century people felt about human reproduction, the word *savage* is indecent, and those who use it either insensitive or malicious. But Lewis in 1962 was only speaking plain, as he always did.

Lewis was deeply moved by the lines in the nineteenth Psalm likening the Law to the desert sun's "blinding, tyrannous rays hammering the hills, searching every cranny (*Reflections* 56). It is a good image, too, of Lewis's rigor and his ruthlessness. His prose "pierces everywhere"; unfortunately, it is not always "disinfectant."

But Lewis's refusal to emphasize, like his use of archaisms, concerns us mainly as a means to resist "verbicide." He is always fighting on several fronts with several kinds of weapons. In his popular works we find not only revived archaisms like *salt* in the sense of "lustful" (from *assault*), *infest* (as an adjective), *knave, wolf's head, forsooth, to overcrow, profane* (for "secular"), but also neologisms like *event* (in approximately the physicists' sense), *behaviors,* Rudolf Ottos's *numinous* (before it became commonplace), and even Kahlil Gibran's notorious *togetherness* (though that was no true neologism: the *O.E.D.* cites it from 1656!).[5] Most of all, we find everyday words used with their old, straightforward—and now often forgotten—meanings.

In *The Problem of Pain* we find *published* in the sense of "made public" (58); *primitive* used (without comment on the fact) eulogistically (72); *movement* in the sense of "motion of the mind, will, or desires" (75); *beast* simply for "non-human animal" (78, 129); *enormous* in the archaic sense of "exceedingly wicked" (89); *enthralled* with the notion of actual enslavement (92); *plausible* meaning (as always in Lewis) "specious" (96, 129); *toys* in the sense of "trifles" (106); *motions,* like *movement* above, for *motus animi* (120); *pious* as a eulogistic term (141); *big* in the sense of "pregnant" (149); *symphony* as an abstract noun (150); and *generation* for the *res agens,* the action, not the result, of "begetting" (153).

The radio talks edited as *Mere Christianity* show Lewis using a "broad, rough, and highly colored style, like scene-painting" (as Aristotle recommended for "popular eloquence"). Their almost total lack of cultural allusion is made up for by an abundance of vivid illustration; no other work of Lewis's is so dense with metaphors and similes. Since listeners cannot stop to think about words, he makes in this book his largest concessions to the inaccuracies of the vernacular—it is here, for example, that he talks the most about "sex." Yet he departs from the "dangerous sense" of *crazy,* using it for "physically broken down" (72); he uses *Christian* in a merely descriptive sense (101), *chastity* for "abstention from *unlawful* sexual intercourse" (88ff.), and *heathen* to refer to the far-from-brutish-or-benighted Aristotle. Here too he makes a careful rehabilitation of *Nature* in the sense that embraces moral law. And, let it be observed, that merely to have spoken or written without irony, words like *chastity* and *heathen* was to fling a defiance at the decay of meaning.

In *Miracles* we have *fat* for "fertile or fruitful" (155); *imbecility* for "feebleness" (not necessarily mental) (149); *aphrodisiac* as an adjective with no specific reference to things ingestible (119); *atheist* applied, with no suggestion of opprobrium, to W.T. Kirkpatrick, the "man who taught me to think" (73); *scenery,* as always since his first conversation with Kirkpatrick, with an implicit reference to the theater (68); and "what some modern people call 'ambivalent' " (129)—though he elsewhere uses this neologism without apology. We also have *enjoy* in the technical sense (so important to Lewis) of Sir Samuel Alexander, which Lewis glosses by the old Humanist trick of combining it with a near synonym—

> The item which we. . .label "Reason" always turns out to be somehow different from the reason we ourselves are enjoying and exercising. (27)

*Surprised by Joy* contains *free of* in the old legal sense—"We were thus free of two very different social worlds" (11); *idea* in an almost Platonic sense—"It troubled me with what I can only describe as the Idea of Autumn" (19); *fantastic* for what could exist only in fantasy (ibid.); *stuff* for "cloth" (24); and *assumption* for the *res agens* of "putting on" clothing (25). Here too (as always) Lewis uses *sadism* in the proper—i.e. the psychopathological—sense, spring it rather cunningly on the reader by first describing such a man as all who use words loosely would call a "sadist" and then observing: "Everyone talks of sadism nowadays but I question whether his cruelty had any erotic element in it" (27). (It would have risked considerable misunderstanding to say, following the terminology he adopted in *The Four Loves,* "any venereal element"!) *Sophisticated* and *sophistication* occur five times in *Surprised by Joy* (37, 58, 58, 70, 85), only once without the root connotation of sophistry and corruption. Non-sexual *intercourse* occurs twice (45; 148); *condescension,* which Lewis somewhere else calls "a beautiful word which we have spoiled," appears in a good sense (75); *patient* is used in the general sense of "one who undergoes something" (77); and he describes as "formal" an activity (California-style surfing) which, because its formalities are of recent origin, careless speakers would call "informal." He uses E.B. Pusey's *antitheist* for "atheist" in the dyslogistic sense (95), and he uses the recent journalese (I think originally military) term *V.I.P.* (87).

In *Reflections on the Psalms* we find frequently *temptation* and *wickedness* in their straightforward senses without irony; we find *irresistible,* which is used vulgarly only to describe temptations, applied to the way textual evidence can create conviction in the mind of a judicious reader (34). We find *pious* and *piety* in their plain sense, without sneers or irony (44, 45, 47); *patronize* meaning not just "to look down on," but "to look down on from the arrogance of conscious benefaction—i.e. like a patron" (60); *the good life* in Aristotle's (and Bishop Gore's) sense of "the life of virtue," and not (of course) in the current debased sense of "the life of pleasure" (63); *congenial* with its etymological force conspicuously operative (87); and *compulsion* applied to force coming from without, and not (as always in these psychologizing times) to force coming from within (93, 98).

The *Letters to Malcolm* yield non-sexual *intercourse* (12, 38, 107); *personal* in the philosophic sense, and not, of course, in what Lewis claimed he was surprised to discover in the "usual uneducated" one—viz., "corporeal" (21, 22); *depreciate* for what some people mean by "deprecate" (Lewis always made the correct distinction between these even to the unusual degree of writing "self-depreciatory," though he admitted it was a rear-guard action) (26); *event* in the literal, but increasingly rare, sense of "outcome" (31, 61, 64) and in something like Whitehead's philosophic sense (39, 90); *afflictions* (41, 43) unconfounded with *problems* (48, 59); *to utter* without reference to speech but in the general sense of "to cause to go out" (49, 70, 72, 73); *profanely* meaning "without the light of revelation" (49); *patient* in the general Latin sense (52 & *passim*); *creatures* for "created things," not necessarily animate (73); *motive* for "motif" (85); *sensible* for "perceptible by the senses" (114); and *scandal* with the notion of the "stumbling-block" always implicitly present (119 passim).

Everything Lewis wrote shows his awareness of the history of meaning stored up in words (as Owen Barfield said), like "the energy of sunlight in coal" (*History* 13). Barfield taught Lewis many things, but nowhere, I suspect, was his influence greater than in this. Lewis's philological writings—and much in the style of all his writings—would have been very different without books like *History in English Words* and *Poetic Diction* and the ideas in them tossed between their author and his friend in conversation. I don't think one ever meets any form of the word *ruin* in Lewis without hearing some faint rumbling echo from the pages Barfield devoted to that word in *Poetic Diction* (116-126).

One will hardly ever find Lewis using a word contrary to the tenor of its semantic history. *Nice* has a very peculiar history; apparently it comes originally from *nescio* ("I know not"), and it still sometimes has the sense of "neat" or "fastidious," which was its usual sense before it acquired the modern one of vaguely "agreeable, pleasant, etc." Since nicety, or "fastidiousness," is a vice to which Lewis was somewhat addicted it is also a vice which he was always ready to rebuke—as was Spenser, who seems to have suffered from it too (*Allegory* 316). Is it altogether fanciful, I wonder, to see traces of the word's etymology, all the way back to its primary sense of "ignorant," in that most memorable of Lewis's satiric inventions, the acronym of the National Institute for Coordinated Experiments?

The propensity to pun seems to prevail in many of the writers we should particularly distinguish as "verbal geniuses"—I mean writers, like Shakespeare and Joyce, whose receptivity to words and quickness to associate them appears to be particularly keen. I think Lewis was this sort of writer; yet he rarely makes a pun. Most of the few examples of his punning come from the informal correspondence; the best I can recall (though it is perhaps not original) occurs in the postscript to a letter to Owen Barfield (*Letters* 162-63). The letter contains a series of pessimistic grumblings, tongue-in-cheek but clearly evincing a disgruntled frame of mind: "Nearly everybody has been ill here.... I hear the income-tax is going up again. The weather is bad and looks like getting worse," etc. Then comes the P.S.: "Even my braces are in a frightful condition. 'Damn braces,' said Blake." And yet even this, in a way, is something deeper than a pun.

For the essence of the true pun is that it keeps you on the surface, makes the medium of discourse itself turn suddenly and hilariously opaque. To be sure, there are semi-transparent puns, like Hamlet's "a little more than kind and less than kind," where a kinship of sense shows faintly beneath the similarity of sound. But when Hamlet answers Horatio's "this is wond'rous strange" with "And therefore as a stranger bid it welcome," he is engaging in a different kind of wordplay; one which, by throwing together what use and inattention had put asunder, displays not the opacity but the transparency of language. He is restoring a "primal unity": he is reminding his friend that strangers and strangeness have something essential in common, and that consequently he who receives a specter may be entertaining an angel unaware. If we must call this a "pun," we should at least distinguish it as a "transparent pun." Of course "transparency" is a matter of degree. But it has become so common to make no distinction that there is now hardly a blunter instrument in the critical vocabulary than the word *pun*. I once heard a man in a discussion of *Paradise Lost* describe the poet's calling upon the Holy Spirit to inspire him as "Milton's punning on 'spirit' and 'inspire.' " He might as well have said that Milton would be punning if he called on the Lord Protector to protect him. It is one thing to speak of a spirit inspiring, a form informing, or a pressure impressing; it is quite another to speak of creases increasing, tails entailing, clothes enclosing, or choirs inquiring.

"Damn braces" is in itself a pure—"opaque"—pun, yet in its literal, and biographical, context it points to something beneath the surface. For we feel sure that Blake's proverb must have bubbled up into Lewis's mind at that moment initially as a consolation, and can hardly read the footnote without a sense that it breaks the spell of grumpiness in the body of the letter, and that on more than one level.

Lewis could certainly relish a pun for its own sake. In more than one place he repeats with mirth the story of the bishop, addressing a girls' school after their performance of *A Midsummer Night's Dream*, saying, "This is the first time I have seen a female Bottom." But on the rare occasions when he himself employs paronomasia it is almost always of the decidedly "transparent" kind.

When, in *The Problem of Pain* (92), he speaks of the masochist's "enthralled," he is combining a literal and a figurative sense of the word to produce a sort of semantic stereoscopy which brings the nature of the perverted passion into relief. When, in *Reflections on the Psalms* (82), he suggests that present worship on earth may be to future glorification in heaven as the tuning up of an orchestra is to the playing of a symphony, he calls the present worship "promise not performance" and thus allows the word *performance* to resonate with both its general and its specifically musical or theatrical meaning. In *Letters to Malcolm* (91) he says that if he were preaching a certain doctrine in public, "I should have to pack it in ice, enclose it in barbed-wire reservations, and stick up warning notices in every direction," thus "punning" (if you like) on *reservations*; and further on (121) he speaks of the wish of liberal theologians for "the gilt-edged security of a religion so contrived that no possible fact could ever refute it," doing the same with *security*. There is a pregnancy, if not quite a "transparency" in these puns. They are allusive, and what they allude to is not merely whimsical: a fenced-off tract of public land is a good "objective correlative" to a mental reservation; a stock certificate does provide security in the sense of comfort as well as declare it in the sense of a guarantee.

Some languages, like Latin and German, require the feminine form for nearly all adjectives and nouns that refer to females. While English always distinguishes between *king* and *queen, father* and *mother, duke* and *duchess, host* and *hostess, waiter* and *waitress, actor* and *actress*, it allows the speaker to choose whether or not to make the sex distinction between *sculptor* and *sculptress, aviator* and *aviatrix, heir* and *heiress*, and many others; though if a single (i.e., epicene) form is preferred, it must be the masculine; and this time-honored sense of the masculine as the representative gender for both sexes is evidently shared even by radical feminists, who will sometimes call stage players of both sexes "actors" but never "actresses."

"Sensation is sensation." But it doesn't always follow reason. The title of Lewis's essay on the ordination of women, "Priestesses in the Church" (*God in the Dock* 234-39), has probably kept many an indignant person from ever finding out what his thoughts were on that subject. One can easily see—and I am sure Lewis saw—that some people would regard the employment of the optional feminine suffix in *priestess* as an insult. Yet if Lewis himself had thought it insulting to add—*ess*es adscititiously, he would hardly have described the woman he loved as both a "poetess" and a "Jewess."[6] And anyway, *is* the form *priestess* optional? It never seems to be in a pagan context. No one calls Vestals or Sibyls "priests," and even the wise women of modern Haiti are called "priestesses." It would seem that the offense lies less in the distinguishing of sex than in the suggestion of paganism. But that is exactly Lewis's point: the word *priestess* suggests paganism because priestesses are essentially a pagan thing. Those who believe the church's traditional denial of the sacerdotal office to women is only the result of accidental historical conditions, from which the world has now emerged, ought, one would think, to want to redeem the word *priestess* from its exclusively pagan connotations; ought, in fact, to insist on it. But "sensation" has its own reasons: and there surely enters into this case the paradoxical feeling of many modern feminists (though not of the older ones) that to define a woman as a woman is somehow to belittle her. (Curiously, the functions of receiving and feeding are still apparently felt by everyone to require a sex-distinguishing suffix if the agent is female; no hostess wants to be called a "host," or waitress a "waiter.")

But of course the real modern impulse, as Lewis observed in the essay on "priestesses," is to treat everyone as a neuter (if *hostess* and *waitress* are discarded, it will be in favor of terms like "reception person" and "meal attendant"). Orwell's prophecy of an Anti-sex league has, in a sense, come true. For sex is one of the awkward facts that get in the way of the general modern tendency to make people interchangeable. Lewis knew better than to condemn this tendency out of hand; for he saw that it was probably an inevitable concomitant of democracy. In his view it may be well, for the sake of justice, that a government treats its citizens as interchangeable neuters: it may "be a useful legal fiction. But in Church we turn our back on fiction" (*God in the Dock* 238).

It was also, as I have been arguing, a characteristic of Lewis's style to turn its back on fictions; to eschew the bland, the fashionable, the euphemistic—everything that confounds or shifts or glosses over the truth. And in turning away from such fictions he often turned towards the language of the past.

Perhaps the most often quoted phrase of Lewis, in academic discourse, is the description of the content of Books XI and XII of *Paradise Lost* as an "untransmuted lump of futurity (*A Preface* 129). The phrase of course owes much of its impact to the combination of a strong Anglo-Saxon monosyllable with two polysyllabic latinisms (change "lump" to "agglomeration" and the phrase falls to pieces); but it owes its precise meaning—as many who quote it may not realize—to an alchemical metaphor. Lewis also used it in *The Problem of Pain*, referring to "those untransmuted lumps of atheistical thought which often survive in the minds of modern believers" (138).

In his popular works such historical allusions are relatively rare—as are archaisms revived solely for their flavor. Of the latter we find in *Surprised by Joy*, for example, only the odd *nay* (176), *he who* (190), the *whereof* type of relative adverb (177 etc.), and a jocular *Papist* applied to J.R.R. Tolkien. *The Problem of Pain* gives us "for long centuries" (77), "all the days of our life" (ibid.), *brethren* (106), *uncovenanted* (80)—all scriptural-sounding and easy to understand.

But the old-fashionedness everyone really notices in Lewis's style is what I have called his "Edwardianism." This is the thing that alienates; this is what stuck in Orwell's throat; this is what John Wain finds barely tolerable—the headmasterly manner, the parenthetical "homey little asides," the obtuse clarity and thundering redundancy: of what Tolkien (privately) called Lewis's "ponderous silliness."[7] One may like or dislike, tolerate or execrate, this aspect of the style—and the man—but it is hard to pay no attention to it. To most readers of Lewis, I suspect, it is either attractive or repellent.

One of its most interesting manifestations on the lexical level is the word *nursery*. Not that the thing did not survive the Edwardian era; but the word's associations tend to be old-fashioned, and there is something almost obsessively nostalgic about Lewis's frequent use of it. You will hardly find a literal or figurative reference to childhood anywhere in his writing into which he has not contrived to work the word *nursery*, as either a noun or as an adjective. His wife had been a "nursery governess to a lion-cub" (*Smoke on the Mountain* 7); the Machiavellian formula, "not to be, but to seem, virtuous," is one "whose utility we all discovered in the nursery" (*English Literature* 51); the eating preferences of children are "nursery gastronomy" (*Reflections* 13); and so on. If a Freudian (*absit omen*) ever does a "close reading" of Lewis, he will find fruitful matter for inference in this word.

A Marxian critic might also have something to say about *nursery*, and even more about some of the other "Edwardianisms." For this part of Lewis's style is deeply soaked in connotations of class (which is, of course, what Orwell was especially sensitive to). And it is in this manner, as John Wain suggests, that Lewis's logic is most apt to be weak or his facts wrong. (75)

For instance, to illustrate the error by which misguided piety rejects the miraculous as "beneath God's dignity" Lewis offers this analogy: "When schoolboys begin to be taught to make Latin verses at school they are very properly forbidden to have what is technically called 'a spondee in the fifth foot'."[8] Now observe: on the one hand the illustration assumes that schoolboys learning to make Latin verses are a reasonably familiar part of the reader's experience (otherwise why not use some other example of the *quod licet Jovi* commonplace, as Lewis could easily have done?). On the other hand the manner of its presentation assumes that the reader won't know what a "spondee" and a "fifth foot" are and, rather than wish to be taught, will be content with a *de haut en bas* dismissal of the matter as a technicality. (Lewis has an annoying way of telling people, "Of course you wouldn't be interested in this.") By trying to have it both ways Lewis puts himself into a false position. Moreover, though he speaks of these schoolboys in the present tense, we know they belong more to the past. An odor of snobbery clings to the whole business. We feel that Lewis is reminding the majority of his readers that they lack the good fortune to have known the good things of the good old days.

Perhaps it is true that only fools believe—and knaves pretend to believe—that this sort of gesture is intended as a reactionary put-down. Still, it can have that effect. Perhaps the most scandalous example is the passage John Wain quotes (though he unfairly misrepresents its context) from *Reflections on the Psalms.* Lewis remarks of certain despicable but respected villains that the state of affairs might have been better in which such men were "blackballed at every club, dropped by every acquaintance, and liable to the print of riding-crop or fingers across the face if they were ever bold enough to speak to a respectable woman" (59). Surely Wain is right to describe the tone of this passage as "silly truculent." Even more interesting are the Miniver-Cheevyish implications of its content—rather like those of the passage in *Mere Christianity* where Lewis speaks as if the morality of duelling were still an urgent question (98)! The voice we hear is above all that of the *laudator temporis acti.*

And here I think Wain's assessment is right. What strikes one more than anything else about Lewis is that he was what the Italian Futurists (those paragons of silly truculence) called a *passatista.* He was, as he described himself, "a lover of the past," (*God in the Dock* 264). And this, I think, accounts for his widespread appeal on a superficial level to the "nostalgic" and the conservative, while a certain antipathy keeps many of those who are not particularly charmed by the past from being able to see him clearly. John Wain could; but he was Lewis's pupil and friend. Had he read him as a stranger, one wonders if he would have thought any more of him than Orwell did.

## Notes

[1]See note to John Roynton Priestley, Sept. 18, 1962, in the Humanities Research Center, The University of Texas at Austin. Referred to in a Checklist by Joe R. Christopher in *CSL: Bulletin of the New York C.S. Lewis Society*, Nov. 1980: 7.

[2]"And thus when the command is given, every prominent Christian in the land may vanish overnight into Institutions for the Treatment of the Ideologically Unsound." "The Humanitarian Theory of Punishment" in *Twentieth Century: An Australian Quarterly Review*, vol. III, No. 3 (1949): 5-12; reprinted in Walter Hooper, ed., *God in the Dock* (Grand Rapids: Eerdmans, 1970): 287-94.

[3]See the essay "On Four-letter Words" in Walter Hooper, ed., *Selected Literary Essays* (Cambridge: Cambridge UP, 1969): 169-74; and "Prudery and Philology" in *The Spectator*, CXCIV, 21 Jan. 1955: 63-4; rpt. in *Present Concerns* 87-91.

[4]E.g., *Surprised by Joy* 45; *Letters to Malcolm: Chiefly on Prayer* 115.

[5]*Salt: Surprised by Joy* 166; *infest: The Problem of Pain* 16; *knave: Surprised by Joy* 99; *wolf's head: Reflections on the Psalms* 59; *forsooth: Surprised by Joy* 161; *to overcrow: Miracles* 57; *profane: Problem of Pain* 95; *event: Letters to Malcolm* 39, 90; *behaviors:.Letters to Malcolm* 114; *numinous Surprised by Joy* 188; *togetherness: Problem of Pain* 35; and *The Four Loves* 57.

[6]*Poetess* in his foreword to Joy Davidman, *Smoke on the Mountain: The Ten Commandments in Terms of Today* (London: Hodder and Stoughton, 1963): 7; *Jewess* in a letter to Dom Bede Griffiths, O.S.B., dated 30 April 1959, in *Letters of C.S. Lewis* 285.

[7]From a letter to Christopher Tolkien, 12 Sept. 1970: "I have just received a copy of C.S.L.'s latest: *Studies in Words*. Alas! His ponderous silliness is becoming a fixed manner." Humphrey Carpenter, ed., Letters of *J.R.R. Tolkien: A Selection* (London: George Allen and Unwin, 1981): 302.

[8]*Miracles* 99; for another instance see, in the same book, 167: "These small and perishable bodies we now have were given to us as ponies are given to schoolboys."

# Works Cited

Barfield, Owen. *History in English Words*. London: Faber 1953.

——. *Poetic Diction*. London: Faber, 1952.

Carpenter, Humphrey, ed. *Letters of J.R.R. Tolkien: A Selection*. London: Allen and Unwin, 1981.

Lewis, C.S. *The Allegory of Love*. New York: Oxford UP, 1958.

——. "Cross-Examination." *Decision* Oct. 1963: 4. Rpt.in Walter Hooper, ed. *God in the Dock*. Grand Rapids: Eerdmans, 1970.

——. "The Death of Words." *The Spectator* 22 Sept. 1944. Rpt. in Walter Hooper, ed. *C.S. Lewis "On Stories" and Other Essays in Literature*. New York: Harcourt, 1982.

——. *English Literature in the Sixteenth Century Excluding Drama*. Oxford: Clarendon Press, 1954.

——. *An Experiment in Criticism*. Cambridge: Cambridge UP, 1961.

——. Foreword. *Smoke on the Mountain: The Ten Commandments in Terms of Today*. By Joy Davidman. London: Hodder and Stoughton, 1963.

——. *The Four Loves*. London: Collins, 1960.

——. "The Humanitarian Theory of Punishment." *Twentieth Century: An Australian Quarterly Review* 3 (1949): 5-12. Rpt. in Walter Hooper, ed. *God in the Dock*. Grand Rapids: Eerdmans, 1970.

——. *Letters to Malcolm: Chiefly on Prayer*. New York: Harcourt Brace Jovanovich, 1964.

——. *Mere Christianity*. New York: Macmillan, 1952.

______ *Miracles*. London: Collins, 1960.

______ *"Notes on the Way," Time and Tide* 14 Aug. 1948: 830-31. Rpt. in Walter Hooper, ed. *God in the Dock*. Grand Rapids: Eerdmans, 1970.

______ *"On Four-letter Words." Selected Literary Essays*. Ed. Walter Hooper. Cambridge: Cambridge UP 1969.

______ *A Preface to Paradise Lost*. Oxford: Oxford Paperbacks, 1960.

______ *Present Concerns*. Ed. Walter Hooper, New York: Harcount, 1987.

______ *"Priestesses in the Church?" God in the Dock*. Grand Rapids: Eerdmans, 1970.

______ *The Problem of Pain*. New York: Macmillan, 1962.

______ *Reflections on the Psalms*. London: Collins, 1961.

______ *Studies in Words*. Cambridge: Cambridge UP, 1960.

______ *Surprised by Joy*. London: Collins, 1959.

Lewis, W.H., ed. *Letters of C.S. Lewis*. New York: Harcourt, 1975.

Orwell, George. "As I Please." *The Tribune* 27 Oct. 1944. Rpt. in Sonia Orwell and Ian Angus, eds. *The Collected Essays, Journalism and Letters of George Orwell*. London: Secker and Warburg, 1960, p. 264.

Wain, John. "A Great Clerke." *Encounter* May 1964. Rpt. in James Como. *C.S. Lewis at the Breakfast Table and Other Reminiscences*. New York: Macmillan, 1979, 68-77.

# Part III:

# C.S. Lewis: The Critic as Imaginative Writer

# Sub-Creation and Lewis's Theory of Literature

*Margaret L. Carter*

In C.S. Lewis's *Perelandra,* Satan in the body of the scientist Weston tempts the Green Lady, the Eve of that world. The concept of art is brought up by the Adversary and appears to be regarded as perilous, at best. Particularly telling is the Lady's reaction to the notion of "creation" with a small "c": "When she had at last been made to understand what creative meant she forgot all about the Great Risk and the tragic loneliness and laughed for a whole minute on end" (132). And it is the Evil One who offers a justification for the existence of fiction: "Because the world is made up not only of what is but of what might be. Maleldil [God] knows both and wants us to know both" (104). Yet Lewis's career makes it clear that he does not consider art or fictoin diabolical. And a Christian poet, like any other, must be, in some sense, "creative." Is literature a legitimate vocation for a Christian? If so, what sort of literature is lawful for him to produce? To what extent must his art be purely mimetic, and mimetic of what?

We search largely in vain for the answers to these questions, even in the wide range of essays collected in Nathan Scott's anthology, *The New Orpheus,* published in 1964. Dorothy Sayers' introductory comment that most discussions of Christianity and literature juxtapose the two "only at the ethical circumference" (3) applies to many of the articles in this volume. Her own essay, covering the same concepts as her *Mind of the Maker* (i.e., the artistic trinity), comes to the conclusion that "creation" is the distinctive Christian contribution to aesthetic theory. David Jones' "Art and Sacrament" presents art as the uniquely human activity; animals, not being free, and angels, not being corporeal, cannot be "makers." When he tells us, "All art re-presents," we find ourselves approaching a fundamental principle that may validate the existence of the Christian poet (52). The same may be said for G. Ingli James' principle that personal experience is a "mystery" that can be conveyed only in the concrete form of art, not in conceptual statements (192). On the subject of the form and content of Christian fiction, we get little help toward a theoretical grasp of the achievement of a science-fantasy master like Lewis. Must a whole vast province of fiction be declared forbidden ground with a condemnation like Elizabeth Sewell's pronouncement, "The healthy imagination does not work with supermen and space ships and robots with electronic brains"? (390). (It is only fair to note that Sewell does defend the expansion of the imagination, despite what seems to be an unaccountable blind spot toward certain kinds of fiction.) Or can we find a way to keep Narnia, Middle Earth, and the science fiction of Madeleine L'Engle?

Lewis' own critical writings show us a way to this goal.... We find, as might be expected, a change in his attitude over the years. His earlier remarks on Christianity and literature assign art a permitted but limited place in the Christian life, while his later writings on the subject seem to allow art a function of greater importance. In the lecture "Learning in War-Time" (1939) Lewis raises the question of "how it is right, or even psychologically possible, for creatures who are every moment advancing either to heaven or to hell, to spend any fraction of the little time allowed them in this world on such comparative trivialities as literature or art, mathematics or biology" (44). (We notice in passing that he includes pure science on the same footing as liberal arts.) Whatever justifications may be advanced for the study of literature must apply *a fortiori* to the production of literature. Lewis clears the ground by reminding us that in the Christian view art and learning occupy no privileged position; like all our "merely natural activities," they acquire value only by being performed "to the glory of God" (48). This condition, of course, presupposes that the activity in question is useful or at least harmless. One use of Christian culture is as a defense against the anti-Christian use of culture. Since "a cultural life will exist outside the Church whether it exists inside or not" (50), it is the duty of some Christians to pursue the learned vocation in order to combat the enemy's misuse of art and learning. Besides this negative value of liberal studies, this lecture offers a positive value in "the pursuit of knowledge and beauty, in a sense, for their own sake, but in a sense which does not exclude their being for God's sake" (49). By attending to the object in itself, as end rather than means, we paradoxically find the object a road to "the vision of God" (49). The humble and somewhat tentative nature of this suggestion is shown by Lewis' haste to assert that the learned vocation is a path to the Glory for some people but by no means all or even the majority. He also points out the hazard of this way of life, the danger of allowing personal ambition to supplant the disinterested appetite for truth and beauty.

A similar awareness of the limits and dangers of the cultural life seems uppermost in the papers collected as the essay, "Christianity and Culture" (1940). In this series of columns from the journal *Theology* Lewis addresses the problem of reconciling the exaggerated claims sometimes made for culture with Christian values. In what sense is liberal knowledge a good, and how is it related to the Good in the spiritual sense? A brief survey of Christian sources reveals few authorities who attribute any worth to "culture." Lewis proceeds cautiously in attempting to rehabilitate this realm of human endeavor. Beginning at the lowest level, that of economic necessity, he defends the learned profession as a way of making one's living, since the New Testament clearly forbids Christians to be a burden on others. "Provided, then, that there was a demand for culture, and that culture was not actually deleterious, I concluded I was justified in making my living by supplying that demand" (20). "Innocent pleasure" (20) is certainly not an evil and may be a legitimate use of culture. The second valid reason for a Christian's cultivation of liberal knowledge is to combat its misuse. This point presents "culture as a weapon" (21) in much the same way "Learning in War-Time" does. Lewis' third point defends the use of the liberal arts for pleasure, as already mentioned. His fourth point confronts the hazard posed by the fact that "the values assumed in literature were seldom those of Christianity" (21). Some of the "sub-Christian" values he mentions may be designated with relative approval as belonging to "the highest level of merely natural value lying immediately below the lowest level of spiritual value"; honor, for instance, or romantic love, may be a "schoolmaster" to lead its devotees to Christ (22). Such ideals may lead some souls to conversion. The liberal arts may also prepare the way for conversion in a more general sense, by undermining the intellectual provincialism against which Lewis so often inveighs.

So far the possible good in the liberal arts seems to be merely contingent. Is there no justification for viewing culture as good in itself? Lewis struggles with the problem of non-moral goodness and its relation to the Good. A well-written book is "better" than a poor one, just as a healthy person is "better" than a maimed one. But does a Christian have a duty to strive for such non-moral excellence? Contrary to Cardinal Newman's position that "one of the moral duties of a rational creature was to attain to the highest non-moral perfection it could" (19), Lewis, though apparently he would like to accept this conclusion, finds little Scriptural or patristic support for it. (On this point Dorothy Sayers, especially in *The Mind of the Maker,* seems more helpful, with her insistence on the maker's serving the integrity of the work.) As in "Learning in War-Time," Lewis suggests as the chief positive value of art a kind of Platonic avenue to the Beatific Vision. The sub-Christian values found in art are "dim antepasts and ectypes of the truth," compared to moonlight, which can be recognized for its proper worth as reflected sunlight (24). Conceding that "culture has a distinct part to play in bringing certain souls to Christ," Lewis still stresses the existence of the "shorter, and safer, way" open to most of humanity (24). The limitations of liberal studies are still uppermost in his argument.

The nearly contemporaneous "Christianity and Literature" (1939), in contrast to the two essays just discussed, does not adress the quesion of whether literature should be produced at all. Rather, it inquires what attitude a Christian writer or critic should take toward his material. In the criticism prevalent in the thirties Lewis discovers a tone or atmosphere incompatible with the Christian picture of reality. The characteristic metaphors of this criticism use words like "creative," "spontaneity," and "freedom," producing an image of "bad work flowing from conformity and discipleship, and of good work bursting out from certain centers of explosive force. . . which we call men of genius" (2). Lewis' strategy, as in "Christianity and Culture," is to search the New Testament for light on the validity of this view of art. His argument focuses on certain Pauline passages dealing with hierarchy (for instance, the discussion of male-female relations in I Corinthians 11). Lewis notes that in orthodox theology the proper relationship of an inferior to a superior is one of imitation. By means of imitation an "original divine virtue" passes "downwards from rung to rung of a hierarchical ladder" (5). Again Lewis takes an almost Platonic position in his insistence that there is one original Good of which all inferior goods are but reflections. Indeed, he explicitly states that a Christian literary theory ought to "have affinities with the Platonic doctrine of a transcendent Form partly imitable on earth" (6).

Here Lewis goes to the extreme of declaring that New Testament theology "leaves no room for 'creativeness' even in a modified or metaphorical sense" (7). An artist cannot bring any new thing into existence, nor should he aim at self-expression, but should attempt to "embody in terms of his own art some reflection of eternal Beauty and Wisdom" (7). Taken in its full rigor, this position would seem to align us with Plato in *The Republic*. What use is art if it presents only a mimesis of something more real than itself? Given the opportunity, should we not turn from the imitation to the reality? Lewis points out that the Christian, recognizing literature as a secondary good, does not fall into the error of taking it too seriously. Unlike some pagans, he is not taken in by the "fussy and ridiculous claims of literature that tries to be important simply as literature" (10). Literature on frivolous subjects can be enjoyed for nothing more than what it is, while literature on solemn subjects borrows its importance from the theme. Here a simplistically mimetic theory seems unavoidable.

But what, exactly, is the Christian artist to imitate? Is he representing some external object perceived through the senses (the severely limiting Platonic position)? Is the producing, in Aristotle's terms, a mimesis of an action? Or of some aspect of "eternal Beauty and Wisdom" itself? Lewis suggests a broader answer to this question in his essay "On Stories," first presented in 1940, but published in its present form in 1947. This article investigates the appeal of "stories," defined as romances, fictions in which plot rather than characterization is paramount. Are such tales read mainly for suspense and excitement? Lewis' own experience tells him otherwise. In the kind of romance he enjoys, the plot is a vehicle for an atmosphere, an imagined world—a "something else" difficult to define. The Indian milieu of *Last of the Mohicans,* the subterranean imprisonment at the climax of *King Solomon's Mines,* the terror of outer space in *First Men in the Moon,* the giants in fairy tales are some examples of the kind of imaginative experience to which Lewis refers. One advantage of art is that it allows us to contemplate such "permanent aspect[s] of human experience" which "the narrow and desperately practical perspectives of real life exclude" (10). That most of the tales cited in this essay involve the marvelous shows that Lewis is not recommending "Realism" in the sense of photographic imitation of everyday life. The plot, the temporal sequence of events, is often trying to capture "something that has no sequence in it, something other than a process and much more like a state or quality" (17). This atemporal object of imitation suggests, to readers of Lewis' theological works, the eternal Now in which God dwells. In ordinary human life, as in art, we "grasp at a state and find only a succession of events in which the state is never quite embodied" (19). Lewis seems to be hinting that this "state," which we hope to enjoy in Heaven, may sometimes be attained, though imperfectly and transitorily, by art:

> In life and art both, as it seems to me, we are always trying to catch in our net of successive moments something that is not successive. Whether in real life there is any doctor who can teach us how to do it, so that at last either the meshes will become fine enough to hold the bird, or we be so changed that we can throw our nets away and follow the bird to its own country, is not a question for this essay. But I think it is sometimes done—or very, very nearly done—in stories. (19-20)

At this period in his career, then, Lewis takes a cautious attitude toward the potential hazards and benefits of literature. He classifies the liberal arts, including literature, as secondary, derivative goods, which may be enjoyed only if they are not assigned exaggerated importance. He declares that the Christian artist must be a mimetic artist. The rigor of this stand, however, is softened by a hint that mimesis may include an imaginative apprehension of some aspect of the Divine. As an artist in *The Great Divorce* informs his colleague, newly arrived at the foothills of Heaven, the legitimate motive for art "was because you caught glimpses of Heaven in the earthly landscape. The success of your painting was that it enabled others to see the glimpses too" (80). Lewis suggests, moreover, that fiction unrealistic in terms of ordinary life may nevertheless offer us "an image of what reality may well be like at some more central region" ("On Stories" 15).

These hints are developed to their fullest extent in *An Experiment in Criticism*. In this work we find fruitful discussions of myth, fantasy, and the kinds of realism. Lewis' argument in this book for the difference between using and receiving art reveals a concept of the autonomy of the work of art not made explicit in his earlier critical statements. In *Experiment in Criticism* he cautions us against using art as either solely a stimulus to our own emotions and reveries or solely a source of "ideas" in the abstract sense. In reading a great work of fiction we are not thinking about "any such generality as human life," but about things "concrete and individual," valued "not for any light they might throw hereafter on the life of man, but for their own sake" (65). The good reader "never mistakes art either for life or for philosophy" (68). Though literature is still mimetic—words, since they carry meaning, inevitably direct our attention to things beyond themselves—"mimesis" need not imply that literature receives all its value from its content.

Must the content be "realistic" in the sense generally understood? Lewis approaches this question by distinguishing between two kinds of realism, "realism of presentation" and "realism of content" (59). The first comprises the use of sensuous detail to make an imagined situation vividly concrete. "Realism of content," as the term implies, comprises fictional events that conform to the probabilities of everyday life. The two kinds of realism, as Lewis points out, may exist in combination or independently. The plays of Racine, for instance, though rich in psychological probability, contain no realism of presentation. A great many marvelous tales, on the other hand, clothe their impossible events in "realistic" images. Lewis draws attention, with clear disapproval, to the twentieth century's valorization of realism of content. The tacit principle that "a fiction cannot be fit for adult and civilised reading unless it represents life as we have all found it to be, or probably shall find it to be, in experience" runs counter to the taste of most of the human species in all times and places (60). Even within the realm of non-fantastic fiction, the reader must distinguish between two kinds of "truth to life," the kind exemplified by probable fiction such as *Middlemarch* and the kind embodied in possible but exceptional stories like *Great Expectations*, in which the characters' reactions may be credibly typical, but the initial situation is not.

What of fiction whose events are contrary to nature as we know it? Lewis' remarks on literary fantasy constitute a defense. He first distinguishes this kind of fiction from "fantasy" in the psychological sense. The egoistic reveries to which the word "fantasy" is often applied are, he shows, directly opposed to the literary phenomenon called by the same name. "Egoistic castle-building," as he calls the former, features the daydreamer as hero, with vicarious satisfaction as its aim (53). But there exists another kind of reverie, in which the daydreamer is not a character but a spectator, creating an imagined world for its own sake. This kind of psychological fantasy is akin to literary art and provides a clue to the nature of fantastic fiction. Fantasy (literary sense) is *less* likely than "realism" to pander to egoistic wish-fulfillment impulses. Stories that are mainly "guided or conducted egoistic castle-building" (53) must present a superficial resemblance to ordinary life in order to allow the reader to identify with the hero's success. Fantastic fiction, in contrast, demands disinterested appreciation; it says, "I am merely a work of art. You must take me as such—must enjoy me for my suggestions, my beauty, my irony, my construction" (56). We might conclude from this contrast (though Lewis does not explicitly say so) that the Christian reader ought to prefer fantastic over "realistic" fiction, since the former invites self-forgetful contemplation and offers little opportunity for the indulgence of depraved appetite. Yet this kind of fiction is less often praised for its disinterestedness than blamed for "escapism."

As Lewis points out, "there is a clear sense in which all reading whatever is an escape" (68). This process becomes "escapism" in the morbid sense only when we are guilty of "escaping too often, or for too long, or into the wrong things" (69). Lewis' defense of imaginative escape recalls Tolkien's in "On Fairy-Stories" (which Lewis cites in this same chapter in another connection). Tolkien counters the majority view by praising escape as one of the positive values of literary fantasy. The attempt to escape from banality, ugliness, pain, sorrow, and death may be far from ignoble and even heroic. "Why should a man be scorned if, finding himself in prison, he tries to get out and go home?... The world outside has not become less real because the prisoner cannot see it" (79). Tolkien seems to be implying the Christian doctrine that this fallen world is not our true home. This conjecture is rendered more probable by his discussion of the Incarnation in the Epilogue of "On Fairy-Stories." The "eucatastrophe," the joyous climax, of the fairy tale "may be a far-off gleam or echo of *evangelium* in the real world" (Tolkien, p. 88). The Gospel is a fairy tale that has entered the primary world (the world of "real life," as opposed to the "secondary world" of literature). We are reminded of Lewis' oft-repeated statement that in the life of Christ "myth became fact." Here indeed fantastic fiction has the potential of showing an image of reality "at some more central region."

Tolkien's doctrine of "sub-creation," like Sayers' idea that "creation" is Christianity's unique contribution to aesthetics, seems to directly contradict Lewis' remarks on "creativeness." Yet Lewis displays the highest admiration for Tolkien's essay. The apparent contradiction begins to fade when we notice that Tolkien acknowledges that the maker of a secondary world must borrow all his ingredients from the primary world. Sub-creation, in fact, enables us to view the primary world with new eyes. As Lewis remarks along similar lines, a tale of enchanted woods "makes all real woods a little enchanted" ("Three Ways of Writing for Children" 38). And Tolkien's theory defines the Christian artist as mimetic in a more fundamental sense than any mentioned so far. Just as Sayers believes that the human artist figures forth the Trinitarian nature of the Divine Creator, so Tolkien maintains that our right to create, albeit in a "derivative mode," springs from our being "made in the image and likeness of a Maker" (Tolkien, p. 75). The artist's activity is a mimesis of God's. For the Christian writer, then, fantasy ought to be the highest form of fiction, since it is the most sub-creative. The principle strikingly recalls Sidney's claim that the God-like prerogative of generating "another Nature" is the distinguishing mark of the poet.

Lewis' Epilogue to *An Experiment in Criticism* reiterates his insistence that "we must treat the reception of the work we are reading as an end in itself" (130). If the value of fiction does not reside in its extra-literary effect on the reader, what, then, is it good for? Lewis answers that fiction provides "an enlargement of our being" *Experiment in Criticism,* p. 137). Through literature we enter the consciousness and see through the eyes of others. The first "escape" offered by literature is escape from the limitations of the isolated self; it "heals the wound, without undermining the privilege, of individuality" (140). Primary reality is not broad enough to satisfy this drive: Lewis wishes to participate, not only in what others have experienced, but what they have invented. The sub-creative activity is legitimized. Making stories of what might be, as well as what is (to recall the Devil's words in *Perelandra*), need not be diabolical.

Examination of *An Experiment in Criticism* has thus shown the value Lewis finds in imaginative literature. His earlier works suggest that literature may be one path to the Beatific Vision. The later book shows how literature may be uniquely well-suited to this function, since it enables us to share the Vision as experienced by minds other than our own. Fantastic fiction, moreover, because it embodies a particularly disinterested exercise of the sub-creative faculty, has a special role to play in the process.

## Works Cited

Lewis, C.S. "Christianity and Culture." *Christian Reflections.* Grand Rapids: B. Eerdmans, 1967.

——. "Christianity and Literature." *Christian Reflections.* Grand Rapids: Eerdmans, 1967.

——. *An Experiment in Criticism.* Cambridge: Cambridge UP, 1961.

_____ *The Great Divorce.* New York: Macmillan, 1946.

_____ "Learning in War-Time." *The Weight of Glory and Other Addresses* 1949. Rpt. Grand Rapids: Eerdmans, 1965.

_____ "On Stories." *On Stories and Other Essays on Literature.* New York: Harcourt, 1982.

_____ "On Three Ways of Writing for Children." *On Stories and Other Essays on Literature.* New York: Harcourt, 1982.

_____ *Perelandra.* New York: Macmillan, 1965.

Scott, Nathan A., ed. *The New Orpheus.* New York: Sheed and Ward, 1964.

Tolkien, J.R.R. "On Fairy-Stories." *The Tolkien Reader.* New York: Ballantine, 1966.

# Critical and Fictional Pairing in C.S. Lewis

*Robert Boenig*

In a letter to Arthur Greeves written on 8 November 1916, an exuberant eighteen year old C.S. Lewis lays down the critical theory that was to dominate much of his later professional life:

> What fiddlesticks about Malory being only a translation: I wish you were here that I could have the pleasure of stripping every shred of skin from your bones and giving your intestines to the birds of the air. What do you mean by saying "It" is "an old French legend": the "Morte" includes a hundred different Arthurian legends & as you know the Arthur myth is Welsh. Of course he didn't invent the legends any more than Morris invented the Jason legends: but his book is an original work all the same. Just as the famous "Loki Bound" of Lewis is based on a story in the Edda, but still the poem is original—the materials being re-created by the genius of that incomparable poet (*They Stand Together* 147-48).

The use of one of his original works as a tool for illuminating a critical point plus the brief but serviceable explanation of source criticism is significant, given the direction of Lewis's literary career, for there are certain obvious connections between Lewis's scholarly books and his fiction. *A Preface to Paradise Lost,* written about the same time as *Perelandra,* treats many of the same themes as the novel from a critical viewpoint. Likewise, his books on medieval literature, *The Allegory of Love* and *The Discarded Image,* have certain resonances with the medieval world he created in *The Chronicles of Narnia.* Among his articles, there are similar connections. His "The Vision of John Bunyan" matches nicely with *The Pilgrim's Regress,* while his various articles on Dante illuminate to a certain extent his version of *The Purgatorio, The Great Divorce.*

One pairing that is rather less obvious than these is perhaps the most important. In "What Chaucer Really Did to *Il Filostrato,*" he exercises the critical method he elaborated in his letter to Greeves—the author's creative alteration of his source; it thus pairs best with *Out of the Silent Planet,* his own creative alteration of the H.G. Wells who wrote *The First Men in the Moon*—the novel which best exhibits this critical method transformed into a creative one. In *Out of the Silent Planet,* Lewis adapts Wells as closely as Chaucer did Boccaccio, giving us a novel with two important implications for Lewis as a literary critic. First, it is the paradigm for Lewis's own method of writing, and second, it is a casebook for the medieval literary craft. As such it should be rated with Lewis's best literary criticism, for it is a tool for understanding his own criticism as well as medieval literature.

"What Chaucer Really Did" was originally published in the journal *Essays and Studies* in 1932.[1] As such it represents Lewis's literary criticism at an early stage of his career, for he was only 33 when it appeared, *The Allegory of Love* was in progress, and his influential *A Preface to Paradise Lost* and *English literature in the Sixteenth Century, Excluding Drama* were wholly unconceived. Similarly, his book outlining his new critical theory, *An Experiment in Criticism,* was decades in Lewis's future. Lewis speaks of the genesis of this article in a journal letter to Greeves, sent December, 1929:

> Dec. 23rd—Delighted to get back to my books again and did a good morning's work on Chaucer, mostly textual problems.
> Dec. 27th—Worked at Chaucer all morning. (*Together* 320; 324)

In the interval, curiously, Lewis was also reading Wells:

> Dec. 25th—Afterwards—as a Christmas treat!—I read a modern novel, H.G. Wells' Meanwhile which deals chiefly with the General Strike, and contains very good comic elements. You and I ought to read, think and talk of these things more than we do. (*Together* 321)

This modern interlude over, Lewis went hard at work on Chaucer throughout the winter of 1929-30, specifically tracing down the sources and analogues of passages in *The Canterbury Tales:*

> Thurs [Jan.] 9th—Another day all on Chaucer. What I am actually doing is going thro the parts of the Canterbury Tales which I know least with the aid of several commentators, making copious notes and trying to get really "sound" on them. You see there has been a new edition since my undergraduate days, so that most of my knowledge—it was never very exact—on Chaucer, is out of date. This sounds dull, but in a matter of fact I take great pleasure in it.
>
> What a glory-hole is the commentary of an old author. One minute you are puzzling out a quotation from a French Medieval romance: the next, you are being carried back to Plato: then a scrap of medieval law: then...manuscripts, and the signs of the Zodiac, and a modern proverb..., five smoking room stories, the origins of the doctrine of immaculate conception, and why St. Cecilia is the patroness of organists. So one is swept from East to West, and from century to century, equally immersed in each oddity as it comes up.... (*Together* 330)

Immersing himself thus in the medieval mind, Lewis became convinced that contemporary criticism of Chaucer's *Troilus and Criseyde* was wrong. The source of that poem is Boccaccio's *Il Filostrato,*[2] and since the appearance of W. M. Rossetti's *Chaucer's Troylus and Cryseyde Compared with Boccaccio's Filostrato*[3] critics had been mislead by seeming modernism in the English poet.[4] Lewis comments,

> . . . such studies, without any disgrace to themselves, often leave singularly undefined the historical position and affinities of a book; and if pursued intemperately they may leave us with a preposterous picture of the author as that abstraction, a *pure* individual, bound to no time nor place, or even obeying in the fourteenth century the aesthetics of the twentieth. ("What Chaucer Did" 27)

Lewis here is an early opponent of a form of the criticism which would grow to dominate literary studies in the mid-twentieth century—the so-called New Criticism of Empson and the like,[5] which urged readers to pay close attention to an author's text and abandon extraneous historical, biographical, or interdisciplinary pursuits. For Lewis, Boccaccio, living in an early Renaissance Italy, is a modern while Chaucer, living in a still medieval England, is not; thus Chaucer's creative response to his source is one of conscious "medievalization" (27). The body of Lewis's article is an analysis that proves this point by classifying the various ways Chaucer departs from his source.

First, Chaucer, unlike Boccaccio, gives his *Troilus* the illusion of being a history: "Thus, in I, 141 *et. seq.*, he excuses himself for not telling us more about the military history of the Trojan war and adds what is almost a footnote to tell his audience where they can find that missing part. . . ." (30). Second, Chaucer constantly uses the embellishments of medieval rhetoric in places where Boccaccio does not (31-33). Third, Chaucer is didactic while Boccaccio abandons medieval didacticism (33-35). And fourth, Chaucer, unlike Boccaccio, is interested in Courtly Love (35 passim).

This last point is the one that interests Lewis the most. He had begun serious study of Courtly Love in the late 20s, and this research was beginning to coalesce into the book that would first bring him fame—*The Allegory of Love* (1936). A large section of that book is devoted to Chaucer's *Troilus*, and "What Chaucer Really Did" is the basis upon which the later insights are built. In brief, Lewis's points about Chaucer and Courtly Love are as follows:[6] (1) Chaucer often uses the language of liturgy so common among medieval treatments of Courtly Love where Boccaccio lacks it (38-40). (2) Chaucer eliminates some of the passages in Boccaccio where Troilus is cynical about love (37-38). (3) Chaucer allegorizes (38). (4) Chaucer moralizes about love (38-40). (5) Chaucer emphasizes Boccaccio's contempt for women (40). (6) Chaucer makes Criseyde a figure commanding a respect lacking in Boccaccio (40-43).

The argument of "What Chaucer Really Did" was so persuasive that almost every important study of Chaucer's *Troilus* published since 1932 has either depended on it, argued with it, or tacitly accepted it.[7]

The point I wish to make is that it also holds an important place in literary criticism. We have already seen how Lewis rejected some tendencies of modern criticism in it, but the interesting thing about the article is that Lewis also rejected some of the tendencies of older criticism as well.

When Lewis first joined the English faculty at Oxford, it was in a critical morass, especially with regards to the interpretation of medieval literature. There were, in fact, two groups at odds with each other—those primarily interested in language and those primarily interested in literature. In his valedictory lecture, Lewis's friend, J.R.R. Tolkien, looks back at the situation in 1925 and his conciliatory role in it:

> *Language* and *Literature* appear as "sides" of one subject. That was harmless enough, and indeed true enough, as long as "sides" meant, as it should, aspects and emphases.... But alas! "sides" suggested "parties," and too many then took sides. And thus there entered in *Lang* and *Lit,* the uneasy nest-fellows, each trying to grab more of the candidates' time, whatever the candidates might think.[8]

Tolkien, of course, was a member of the Lang side who "took a liking to Lit," (24) while Lewis became a member of the Lit side who had always been devoted to Lang.[9] Lewis speaks in similar conciliatory terms as Tolkien about his entrance into the English Faculty:

> At my first coming into the world I had been (implicitly) warned never to trust a Papist, and at my first coming into the English Faculty (explicitly) never to trust a philologist. Tolkien was both. (*Surprised by Joy* 216)

The study of the English Language at Oxford then meant identifying dialects in medieval texts to establish the correct line of descent from Old to Modern English. The Oxford English Dictionary Project and the Early English Text Society are the two lasting monuments to this scholarly study of Lang. Lit had a broader range of meaning then than Lang, but nothing nearly so broad as it does now, after the intervening effect of the New Criticism and the recent linguistically-oriented criticisms. Basically, Lit at Oxford in the 20s meant biographical criticism, in which the details of a given author's life were used to illuminate his works, literary history, in which chronological connections between authors and movements were explicated, and source criticism, in which the direct or indirect sources of a given work or part of a work were identified.

The startling fact is that none of these approaches explicate the artistic worth of a piece of literature. *Beowulf* may be a gold mine of dialectical oddities; Malory's *Works* may contain oblique references to his involvement in the War of the Roses; Chaucer's Dream Visions may have an important place in the genre started by *The Romance of the*

*Rose*; and the source of *Andreas* may be a lost Latin translation of a Greek prose hagiographical romance, but all these insights fail to tell us why a piece of literature is moving or enjoyable to read. Tolkien, in his famous lecture of 1936, "*Beowulf:* the Monsters and the Critics," laments this situation:

> ...I have read enough, I think, to venture the opinion that *Beowulfiana* is, while rich in many departments, specially poor in one. It is poor in criticism, criticism that is directed to the understanding of a poem as a poem. (51-52)

Tolkien points out the difficulties of much of the criticism of his day by presenting a parable:

> A man inherited a field in which was an accumulation of old stone, part of an older hall. Of the old stone some had already been used in building the house in which he actually lived, not far from the old house of his fathers. Of the rest he took some and built a tower. But his friends coming perceived at once (without troubling to climb the steps) that these stones had formerly belonged to a more ancient building. So they pushed the tower over, with no little labor, in order to discover whence the man's distant forefathers had obtained their building material. Some suspecting a deposit of coal under the soil began to dig for it, and forgot even the stones. They all said: "This tower is most interesting." But they also said (after pushing it over); "What a muddle it is in!" And even the man's own descendants, who might have been expected to consider what he had been about, were heard to mutter: "He is such an odd fellow! Imagine his using these old stones just to build a nonsensical tower! Why did not he restore the old house? He had no sense of proportion." But from the top of that tower the man had been able to look out upon the sea. (54-55)

The importance of Tolkien and Lewis to us as critics is that they used the old methods for a new purpose—enabling a modern reader to glimpse the sea while reading an old work of literature. The type of criticism we thus see in Lewis's "What Chaucer Really Did" is one step beyond source criticism, for it does not rest in merely identifying a source but develops the analysis of what the author did creatively with that source. It is thus a *via media* between the senseless artifact-digging of the old critics and the historical shortsightedness of the New. In it Lewis uses the old technique combined with the new.

It is not surprising then that when Lewis turned to writing fiction a few years later he would use the technique that he had explicated. Almost every book of fiction that he produces is somehow linked to a literary work, often through the medium of one of his critical studies. Thus, *Perelandra,* published in 1944, two years after *A Preface to Paradise Lost,* may be subtitled, "What Lewis Really Did to Milton." *The Pilgrim's Regress,* published in 1933, reflects the reading Lewis made of Bunyan in 1929-30 which culminated in the BBC Radio talk published much later as "The Vision of John Bunyan." Although his admitted opponent is the Blake of *The Marriage of Heaven and Hell,* Lewis adapted the Dante of *The Purgatorio* more for *The Great Divorce* (1945); it reflects the research for the articles Lewis wrote on Dante in the 1940s, "Dante's Smiles" and "Imagery in the Last Eleven Cantos of Dante's *Comedy.*" The works which lack a published critical partner still reflect Lewis's literary interests. *The Silver Chair* is closely related to the romances of George MacDonald; *Till We Have Faces,* Apuleius; and *That Hideous Strength,* Charles Williams. Even *The Screwtape Letters* may not have been written if Lewis had not read and disliked a book by Valdemar Adolph Thisted (1815-1887) entitled *Letters from Hell.*[10] If *Out of the Silent Planet* may be subtitled, "What Lewis Really Did to Wells," it is in this novel, however, that the connection between title and subtitle is strongest.

Published in 1938 and thus his earliest novel, *Out of the Silent Planet* is Lewis's closest adaptation of a source. As he states in his brief prefatory note,

> Certain slighting references to earlier stories of this type which will be found in the following pages have been put there for purely dramatic purposes. The author would be sorry if any reader supposed he was too stupid to have enjoyed Mr. H.G. Wells's fantasies or too ungrateful to acknowledge his debt to them.[6]

This ambivalence towards Wells is significant, given Lewis's opinion in "What Chaucer Really Did" about Chaucer's ambivalence towards Boccaccio:

> When first a manuscript beginning with the words *Alcun di Giove sogliono il favore* came into his hands, he was, no doubt, aware of a difference between its contents and those of certain English and French manuscripts which he had read before. That some of the differences did not please him is apparent from his treatment.... He certainly thought the story a good story; he may even have thought it a story better told than any he had yet read.... Approaching *Il Filostrato* from this angle, Chaucer, we may be sure, while feeling the charm of its narrative power, would have found himself, at many passages, uttering the Middle English equivalent of "This will never do!" (28-29)

If we substitute the names "Lewis" for "Chaucer" and "*The First Men in the Moon*" for "*Il Filostrato*" and the words "As I sit down to write here amidst the shadows of vine-leaves" for "*Alcun di Giove...*," we have the situation that lead to Lewis's book. Lewis was both attracted and repelled by Wells. We have seen that his work on Chaucer during the winter of 1920-30 was interrupted by the Christmas treat of Wells's *Meanwhile.* Enthusiastic but qualified praise is Lewis's general attitude towards him in his other letters to Greeves:

When one has set aside the rubbish that H.G. Wells always puts in, there remains a great deal of original, thoughtful and suggestive work. . . .(1914)
You will be surprised when you hear how I employed the return journey—by reading an H.G. Wells novel called "Marriage," and perhaps more surprised when I say that I thoroughly enjoyed it; one thing you can say for the man is that he really is interested in all the big, outside questions. . . .(1920)
. . .you will remember that astronomy, fed on H.G. Wells' romances, was almost my earliest love. (1931).[11]

He mentions Wells, moreover, in his criticism, using several quotations from *The First Men in the Moon* as examples in *Studies in Words* (249; 259) and posits Wells's imaginative connections to Dante in both "Dante's Similes" (68) and *A Preface to Paradise Lost* (114). But Wells came to represent to Lewis what was most wrong about the modern, scientific worldview. In *Miracles,* for instance, Lewis writes:

A Naturalist like Mr. H.G. Wells has spent a long life doing so [treating good and evil as illusions] with passionate eloquence and zeal. But surely this is very odd? (37)

Wells, in fact, was the model for the character Jules in *That Hideous Strength*—a pompous little cockney whose "progressive" views on science mask his underlying ignorance of it.

But without Wells, *Out of the Silent Planet* could never have been written.[12] A brief summary of each book will underscore the similarities and some of the significant differences. In *The First Men in the Moon,* a brilliant and eccentric physicist, Cavor, constructs a spherical spaceship in the backyard of a vacation cottage, and with a mercenary and unscientific companion, Bedford, travels to the Moon. While there they encounter first domestic animals and then the Selenites themselves—tall, black creatures similar to ants. Violence ensues, partly because of Bedford's interest in gold; Bedford escapes while Cavor is captured and later killed because he inadvertently reveals something about the cruelty of man. In *Out of the Silent Planet,* a brilliant and eccentric physicist, Weston, constructs a spherical spaceship in the backyard of a vacation cottage, and with both a mercenary and unscientific companion, Devine, and an unsuspecting victim of kidnap, Ransom, travels to Mars—or "Malacandra." While there, Ransom escapes, fearing violence of both the Malacandrians and his companions, and encounters first domestic animals and then members of one of the three races on the planet—tall, black creatures similar to seals. Expecting violence, Ransom is surprised to find a peaceful civilization where violence is almost unheard of. After killing a Malacandrian, however, Weston and Devine are captured and meet Ransom again in a trial before all the races of Malacandra and its ruling spirit. The three are sent back to the earth—

Ransom with the Martians' friendship and his companions with a stern warning never to return.

Ransom's experience while on Malacandra is one of growth from childlike fear of the unknown to spiritual acceptance of a benign universe.[13] Lewis writes of Ransom's childlike state:

> His mind, like so many minds of his generation, was richly furnished with bogies. He had read his H.G. Wells and others. His universe was peopled with horrors such as ancient and medieval mythology could hardly rival. No insect-like, vermiculate or crustacean Abominable, no twitching feelers, rasping wings, slimy coils, curling tentacles, no monstrous union of superhuman intelligence and insatiable cruelty seemed to him anything but likely on an alien world.[14]

What Lewis really does to Wells is take the good story and alter the things over which he doubtless uttered "This will never do." For Wells, the popularizer of science, the universe is blind, cruel, and mindless, completely hostile to man; for Lewis, the Christian apologist, the universe is essentially benign and the evil in it man's alone.

An analysis of two short passages from *The First Men in the Moon* and *Out of the Silent Planet* will bring the alteration into focus. The first glimpse Cavor and Bedford have of the lunar cliffs is significant:

> . . . those spacious, ringlike ranges vaster than any terrestrial mountains, their summits shining in the day, their shadows harsh and deep; the grey disordered plains, the ridges, hills, and craterlets all passing at last from a blazing illumination into a common mystery of black. (*First Men* 42)

The cliffs are vast, "harsh," "disordered," mysterious, and "black"—all words emphasizing the inability of humans to deal with them. Lewis's description of the cliffs of Malacandra is similar yet different:

> Here, he understood, was the full statement of that perpendicular theme which beast and plant and earth all played on Malacandra—here in this riot of rock, leaping and surging skyward like solid jets from some rock-foundation, and hanging by their own lightness in the air, so shaped, so elongated, that all terrestrial mountains must ever after seem to him to be mountains lying on their sides. He felt a lift and lightening at the heart. (53)

The mountains are still huge, and Wells's disorder finds its equivalent in Lewis's "riot," yet Ransom perceives the cliffs as almost human—they play and leap and stand upright when compared to their recumbent terrestrial equivalents. The important word, though, is "perpendicular"—the word used by art historians to describe the architectural style of late medieval English churches and cathedrals[15]—a significant concept considering Ransom's spiritual growth in the novel.

What such source criticism does is that it reveals an author's intentions. If Chaucer alters Boccaccio by developing the theme of Courtly Love, we then know that in a real sense the subject of *Troilus and Criseyde* is Courtly Love. Similarly, if we know that Lewis alters Wells by adding a character who starts out believing in a Wellsian universe of blind violence and ends up believing in one of peace and order, then we know that in a real sense *Out of the Silent Planet* is about conversion.

By doing in *Out of the Silent Planet* what he explicated in "What Chaucer Really Did to *Il Filostrato*," Lewis demonstrates how medieval authors wrote books. The critical insight is that the first step for understanding a medieval book is to read its immediate source. To know Malory's *Quest for the Holy Grail*, for instance, we must read first the anonymous French *Quest*; then we see that Malory is interested more in the state of sinners trying to be righteous than in holiness easily achieved, for Malory alters things in the direction of making Lancelot, not Galahad, his hero. Lewis thus implies a reader strategy for confronting his own books: read Milton before *Perelandra*, Bunyan before *The Pilgrim's Regress*, and Dante before *The Great Divorce*.

## Notes

[1]C.S. Lewis, "What Chaucer Really Did to *Il Filostrato*," *Essays and Studies* 19 (1932), 56-75; rpt. in C.S. Lewis, *Selected Literary Essays*, ed. Walter Hooper (Cambridge: Cambridge UP, 1969), 27-44.

[2]See R.K. Gordon, trans., *The Story of Troilus* (London: Dent, 1934, rpt., Toronto: U of Toronto P, 1978), 25-127.

[3]William Michael Rossetti, *Chaucer's Troylus and Cryseyde Compared with Boccaccio's Filostrato* 2 vols. (London: Chaucer Society, 1875, 1883).

[4]Lewis takes issue especially with Emile Legouis, *Geoffrey Chaucer*, trans., L. Lailavoix (London, 1913), 134. See Lewis, "What Chaucer Really Did," 27, n. 1.

[5]For a brief survey of the New Criticism, see George Sampson, *The Concise Cambridge History of English Literature*, 3rd ed., revised by R.C. Churchill (Cambridge: Cambridge UP, 1941, 1972), 918-923.

[6]Recent critics have detected some flaws in Lewis's treatment of Courtly Love; see, for instance, Henry Ansgar Kelly, *Love and Marriage in the Age of Chaucer* (Ithaca: Cornell UP, 1975, 19ff); and E. Talbot Donaldson, *Speaking of Chaucer* (New York: Norton, 1971), 156-63.

[7]See, for instance, Kelly; Charles Muscatine, *Chaucer and the French Tradition* (Berkeley: U of California P, 1957), 130-262-63; Donald R. Howard, *The Idea of The Canterbury Tales* (Berkeley: U of California P, 1976), 37; and J.S. Bennett, *Chaucer and the Fifteenth Century* (Oxford: Clarendon P, 1947), 61.

[8]J.R.R. Tolkien, "Valedictory Address to the University of Oxford, 5 June 1959," in Mary Salu and Robert T. Farrell, eds., *J.R.R. Tolkien, Scholar and Storyteller: Essays in Memorium* (Ithaca: Cornell UP, 1979), 23.

[9]Lewis's proficiency in learning languages was enormous; William Kirkpatrick, his pre-university tutor, spoke of his feat of mastering Italian in a half term in a letter to his father dated 18 April 1917: "I conceived with the enthusiastic assent

of the pupil, of course, the bold conception of mastering the Italian language in half a term. And we did it. None but a quite exceptional student could have attempted it, much less succeeded in it" (qtd. in Hooper, *They Stand Together*, 178).

[10]See Hooper, 123, 126, 130, 136, 151.

[11]Hooper, 49, 264, 405.

[12]For an analysis of the relationship between Wells and Lewis, see Janice Neuleib, "Technology and Theocracy: The Cosmic Voyages of Wells and Lewis," *Extrapolation* 16 (1975), 130ff; and Robert Boenig," Lewis's Time Machine and His Trip to the Moon," *Mythlore* 24 (Summer 1980), 6-9; cf. Kathryn Hume, "C.S. Lewis' Trilogy: A Cosmic Romance," *Modern Fiction Studies* 20 (1974-75), 505-17.

[13]See Judith Brown, "The Pilgrimage from Deep Space," *Mythlore* 15 (March 1977), 13-15.

[14]Lewis, Out of the Silent Planet; cf. Boenig, 6-7.

[15]Cf. Boenig, 7.

# Works Cited

Bennett, J.S. *Chaucer and the Fifteenth Century. Oxford: Clarendon P, 1947.*

Boenig, Robert. "Lewis's Time Machine and His Trip to the Moon." *Mythlore,* Summer 1980: 6-9.

Brown, Judith. "The Pilgrimage from Deep Space." *Mythlore,* March 1977: 13-15.

Donaldson, E. Talbot. *Speaking of Chaucer.* New York: Norton, 1971.

Gordon, R.K., trans. *The Story of Troilus.* Toronto: U of Toronto P, 1978.

Hooper, Walter, ed. *They Stand Together: the Letters of C.S. Lewis to Arthur Greeves (1914-1963).* New York: Macmillan, 1979.

Howard, Donald R. *The Idea of the Canterbury Tales* Berkeley: U of California P, 1976.

Hume, Kathryn. "C.S. Lewis' Trilogy: A Cosmic Romance." *Modern Fiction Studies,* 1974-1975: 505-517.

Kelly, Henry Ansgar. *Love and Marriage in the Age of Chaucer.* Ithaca: Cornell UP, 1975.

Lewis, C.S. *The Allegory of Love.* London: Oxford UP, 1936.

_____. *Miracles.* New York: Macmillan, 1947.

_____. *Out of the Silent Planet.* New York: Macmillan, 1965.

_____. *A Preface to Paradise Lost.* London: Oxford UP, 1942, 1961.

_____. *Studies in Medieval and Renaissance Literature.* Cambridge: Cambridge UP, 1966.

_____. *Studies in Words.* Cambridge: Cambridge UP, 1967.

_____. *Surprised by Joy.* New York: Harcourt, Brace & World, 1955.

_____. "What Chaucer Really Did to *Il Filostrato.*" In *Selected Literary Essays.* Ed. Walter Hooper. Cambridge: Cambridge UP, 1969.

Muscatine, Charles. *Chaucer and the French Tradition.* Berkeley: U of California P, 1957.

Neuleib, Janice. "Technology and Theocracy: The Cosmic Voyages of Wells and Lewis." *Extrapolation.* 1975.

Rossetti, William Michael. *Chaucer's Troylus and Cryseyde Compared with Boccaccio's Filostrato.* London: Chaucer Society, 1875, 1883.

Sampson, George. *The Concise Cambridge History of English Literature.* Revised by R.C. Churchill. Cambridge: Cambridge UP, 1941, 1972.

Tolkien, J.R.R. "*Beowulf:* the Monsters and the Critics." rpt. in Lewis E. Nicholson, ed., *An Anthology of Beowulf Criticism.* Notre Dame: U of Notre Dame P, 1963, 1971.

———. "Valedictory Address to the University of Oxford, 5 June 1959." in Mary Salu and Robert T. Farrell, eds., *J.R.R. Tolkien, Scholar and Storyteller: Essays in Memoriam.* Ithaca: Cornell UP, 1979.

Wells, H.G. *The First Men in the Moon.* New York: Berkeley, 1967.

# The Polemic Image: The Role of Metaphor and Symbol in the Fiction of C.S. Lewis

*Kath Filmer*

There is no doubt that the reader encounters, in the fiction of C.S. Lewis, a wealth of metaphor and symbol, in which he has encoded arguments for supernaturalism and spiritual individuation. His writing has been called "didactic" and with just cause. It certainly is instructive. But the didacticism of Lewis's work is part of the overall polemic image associated with both the author and the man. Lewis instructs in order to argue, to stimulate within each of his readers the beginning of that lived dialectic by which reason may move them to truth.

Lewis's own personality was one which blossomed in the heady atmosphere of dispute. He was a man "hungry for rational opposition," a man for whom the flash of silver swords of chivalric battle was replaced by the flashing eye, the quick keen wit, and the razor sharpness of his intellect. But Lewis knew that bald argument can be an unlovely thing. Like the ancients he honed into tools the figures of speech, the tropes—metaphor and symbol—so that what was insistently polemical might also be imaginative and pleasing.

In this paper I propose a theory of metaphor and symbol which draws heavily on Lewis's own. It establishes that their role in the polemic of Lewis's fiction is one of intrinsic value as arguments for Lewis's Christian Platonist (or Platonic Christian) world view.

In evaluating the role of metaphor and symbol in the polemic of Lewis's fiction it must first be understood that they are not only rhetorical tools but imaginative constructs, and an understanding of the nature of the imagination in Lewis's thought is basic to this study. For Lewis, the imagination is the image-making faculty of the human mind. To imagine, says Lewis, is to "cause to exist the mental pictures of material objects, and even human characters and events" in the human mind. There are two practical manifestations of the image-making process which must be considered at this juncture: that of creation and that of expression. The imagination provides the nearest approximation to the divine creative process that can be achieved by created beings, and since Lewis was an admitted Romanticist, it is not surprising to find echoes of Coleridge in Lewis's thinking.

Coleridge ascribed an almost divine creative ability to the Imagination, especially to the perceptive faculty or "Primary Imagination" which he described as "a repetition in the finite mind of the eternal act of creation in the infinite I Am." The image-making faculty, or the "Secondary Imagination" Coleridge describes as being

> identical with the primary in the *kind* of its agency, and differing only in *degree*, and in the *mode* of its operation. It dissolves, diffuses, dissipates, in order to re-create; or where this process is rendered impossible, yet still at all events it struggles to idealize and to unify. (516)

The process of "dissolving, diffusing, and dissipating" the elements perceived by the primary imagination is that of image-making, which Lewis achieves in his fiction. Lewis modifies the Coleridgean view by asserting that the human imagination is able only to re-combine elements borrowed from the real universe; it cannot create new elements, such as a new primary colour (*Miracles* 36). This theory of "sub-creation" which Lewis readily adopted was most succinctly formulated by his friend J.R.R. Tolkien, who diverged from Coleridge's notion of evoking in a reader the "willing suspension of disbelief" as a means of participating in the writer's 'creative' imaginative process. To Tolkien, the kind of "literary belief" to which Coleridge's phrase refers is "not...a good description of what happens." Rather, the story-maker becomes the "sub-creator" of a secondary world into which the reader's mind may enter. While the reader is thus "present" in the secondary world, he "believes" in it. Should disbelief arise, Tolkien adds, "the spell is broken; the magic, or rather art, has failed. You are then out in the Primary World again, looking at the little abortive Secondary World from outside (60-61). The belief aroused by a writer's imaginative and artistic skill is a positive state, rather than the negative state suggested by Coleridge.

This theory was the subject of a conversation which influenced Lewis very deeply just prior to his acceptance of Christianity in September, 1931. Applying the notion of the human faculty of subcreation to myths, Tolkien argued that man, whose origins are Divine, draws his ultimate ideals from God, including not only his abstract thoughts but also his imaginative inventions, which must therefore contain elements of eternal truth. As Humphrey Carpenter reports, Tolkien then defined the making of myth, "mythopoeia," as the activity of subcreation, and therefore a fulfilment of God's purpose, a "[reflection of] a splintered fragment of the true light" (142-43).

That Lewis was fully convinced by Tolkien's argument is evident from Lewis's own definition of myth:

> Myth...is not merely misunderstood history (as Euhemerus thought) nor diabolical illusion (as some of the Fathers thought) nor priestly lying (as the philosophers of the Enlightenment thought) but, at its best, a real though unfocused gleam of divine truth falling on human imagination. (*Miracles* 138n)

In Tolkien's view, literary Subcreation is "an aspect of mythology" and not to be taken lightly (51-54). The word "spell," he points out, "means both a story told, and a formula of power over living men" (56); and the power of imaginative subcreation is derived from the simple fact that "we make still by the law in which we're made" (72). In Tolkien's view, Fantasy is a form of literary subcreation, a natural human activity, an expression of the mythopoeic process, and as shown above, the vehicle for truth. Lewis's own ideas are in agreement with Tolkien's. Far from merely "suspending disbelief," Lewis believes that literature should allow us to reach beyond the limits of our own psychology:

> We want to see with other eyes, to imagine with other imaginations, to feel with other hearts, as well as our own. (*An Experiment* 137)

Fantasy as a literary mode can deepen the process of perception and the experience of reality; indeed Lewis writes that "literature admits us to experiences other than our own" (*An Experiment* 139). And for Lewis, the reading of great literature is a quasi-religious experience:

> But in reading great literature I become a thousand men and yet remain myself. Like the night sky in the Greek poem, I see with a myriad eyes, but it is still I who see. Here, as in worship, in love, in moral action, and in knowing, I transcend myself; and am never more myself than when I do. (141)

It is clear, then, that the imaginative faculty has for Lewis a sub-creative function which carries with it the responsibility for passing on, through its expression in literature, "gleams of truth."

When images are formed by the sub-creative process they are available only in the consciousness of individual beings. The images may only be communicated to others by means of language which enables them to construct in their own minds an image roughly similar to that thus described. This process is relatively simple when material objects are involved; but when the imagination deals with concepts which cannot be perceived by the senses, the language by which these concepts are expressed must be "metaphorical." To Lewis, metaphor is a linguistic phenomenon which is an essential component of language which deals with insensibles (*Miracles* 76-77). Metaphor is therefore seen to be an expressive component of the imaginative process.

The word "metaphor" itself derives from two Greek words, uetd meaning "change"; and *pherein*, meaning "to carry." It suggests a change in, and an enlargement of, meaning which is supplied by the contextual linking of concepts which though essentially dissimilar, nevertheless have in common certain analogical aspects. For example, in the sentence, "The car beetled up the hill," a link is established between two dissimilar objects, an automobile and a living insect, which depends on the similarity or analogy which may be drawn between them—their round shape, and their relative speed. By means of the metaphor expressed in the word "beetled," the concept of the "car" is extended by the intrusive image of a small round insect hurrying along the ground.

A further example may be found in Lewis's novel, *Out of the Silent Planet*: "the stars...reigned perpetually, with no cloud, no moon, no sunrise to dispute their sway" (34). This sentence forms part of a description of the view from a space-craft *en route* to Mars and it provides a similar enlargement and complexity of meaning through the use of the metaphorical words "reigned", "dispute" and "sway," by which the inanimate stars are analogically related to earthly monarchs. The metaphor thus created forms part of Lewis's argument for supernaturality, and by providing a metaphorical image of stars as kingdoms Lewis imbues them with a sense of regality, and with an implicit vitality which has metaphysical implications. The potency of these implications is better understood when it is pointed out that they depend upon an antecedent, psycho-physical parallelism in the universe which is emphasized by the operation of the metaphor itself.

It is possible to identify two constituent parts of any metaphor, of which the first is the general drift or underlying idea expressed by the metaphor and the second is the basic analogy which is used to expand the meaning of the underlying concept. To these elements, I.A. Richards has given the respective terms, "tenor" and "vehicle." The word "metaphor" refers to the whole unit; the co-presence of the tenor and the vehicle produces the enlargement of meaning which cannot be achieved without their interaction (96, 100). Thus in the example provided above, the tenor of the metaphor is "the stars," their steady light undisturbed by the vagrancies of earth's atmosphere; while the vehicle is the concept of a living monarch expressed by the words "reign" and "sway." Together the elements provide the "enlarged meaning" of stars as living principalities. The choice of vehicle is therefore of utmost importance in determining the effectiveness of a metaphor in its context generally, and in the fiction of C.S. Lewis in particular.

There is no doubt that the analogy inherent in the vehicle of the metaphor quoted above has a metaphysical import, and it is this aspect of his metaphor which accounts for the power of Lewis's fictional polemic. He admitted that his view of the imagination and of metaphor had these metaphysical implications, but he pointed out that an attempt to write without metaphor also reveals an ontological and ideological stance on the part of an author.[1]

Lewis receives unwitting support from the French writer Alain Robbe-Grillet, who maintains that metaphor represents a kind of order imposed upon language which is linked with a bourgeois ideological system and which corresponds to the assumption of power by the middle classes during the years of developing industrialism in Europe. Because of the kinds of values implicit in metaphorical meanings, Robbe-Grillet states that "metaphor is never an innocent figure of speech" (78). To say, for instance, that a mountain is majestic, is to imply that an inanimate geographical feature has attributes linked with royalty or perhaps deity, an implication which subversively reinforces social and religious values pertaining to the kind of society which Robbe-Grillet finds ideologically unacceptable. By using the word "majestic" of a mountain, for example, a reference is raised to the medieval concept of the Great Chain of Being, or what Lewis termed "the medieval model," which consists of a series of hierarchical orders descending in steps from God, the highest being, through angels, mankind, sentient animals, insects, to inanimate objects. The resulting hierarchical construct allows for analogical transference of meaning between sub-hierarchies of spiritual and physical realities, with members of each sub-order occupying a place or rank corresponding to that occupied by members of other sub-orders.[2] For example, the head of the "master" hierarchy is God; at the head of the human sub-order is the King; and at the head of the sub-order of sentient animals is the Lion.

A lion may therefore be used analogically or symbolically to represent either a King or God because of the correspondence between their respective positions in the "Great Chain"; Lewis employs a Lion in this very sense in his Narnian Chronicles. A real lion would never be mistaken for either a human or a supernatural being. The symbol relies for its potency on the underlying correspondence on which the analogy is based. Since metaphor and symbol depend on analogies and correspondences between objects and beings, they demand metaphysical interpretation, and therefore they function persuasively in literature, and in particular, in Lewis's fiction. Like Robbe-Grillet, Lewis sees metaphor and symbol as polemical tools and it is as such that he employs them. His literary tactic finds support in the writings of past rhetoricians, however: Aristotle said of metaphor, the primary analogical trope, that "it is...in the highest degree instructive and pleasing" (159-61), and sixteenth century writer Henry Peacham believed that "if schemate rhetorical wake the ear, they assist the mind" (qtd. in Tuve 104).

Indeed, in medieval poetic practice, metaphorical images were used not to communicate the personal experiences of the poet or his subjective perceptions of reality, but to express and to illustrate ideas which were commonly accepted and believed, ideas which were derived from contemporary cosmology. The medieval poet wrote about the way in which common beliefs held that the world was arranged so that his verse said, in effect, "this is the way things are" rather than "this is how I feel" (Tuve 41-49). His poetry functioned, as Rosemond Tuve points out, "to make the will reach out toward perfection,... [to move] the will to good" (398). Poetic metaphors, ultimately derived from the analogies afforded by the medieval model or chain of being, were seen as "active agents" with a persuasive function.

The approach which Lewis takes in both his theory of metaphor and the imagination and in his fiction closely parallels that of the medieval poets. Lewis described himself as an anachronism, an example of "Old Western Man," and is critically recognised as a consummate medievalist (Bennett 10). He claimed to read medieval and Renaissance texts like a native, and had made the medieval model his own. It may reasonably be regarded, therefore, as the source of many of the analogies expressed by the metaphors and symbols which are seen to operate with persuasive power in Lewis's fiction. Each aspect of the new worlds which are a product of his imaginative sub-creation is shown so as to highlight its debt to earthly orders and hierarchical systems. For example the system of government in the Narnian Chronicles is monarchical; and in the science-fiction trilogy the monarchical structure is fundamental to the mythic cosmology by which Lewis introduces his readers to his Deep Heaven and its ruler Maleldil. Thus even in the metaphor discussed above, "the stars reigned perpetually," there is at work an antecedent manipulation of the reader's response by means of the subtle analogy drawn between the stars and monarchy and, if the analogy is extended, to deity.

By means of metaphor, Lewis engages in imaginative sub-creation and maintains the traditional links between reality and fantasy, between what is known and what is unknown. When language is used to describe insensibles such as causes, relations, mental states and thoughts, that language, of necessity, is deeply metaphorical. Metaphor instructs, argues, and persuades by analogy, but because of its imaginative function it gives the reader delight and pleasure as well as fulfiling its function of widening his experiential perceptions of unseen realities.

In Lewis's fiction there are two other literary devices which contribute to the polemic image he adopts. The first of these is *simile,* which is closely linked with metaphor for most practical purposes. Nevertheless some aspects of the function of simile in establishing analogies must be distinguished.

The simile performs its analogical function explicitly, linking the tenor and the vehicle of the comparison it is drawing by means of the conjunctions "like" or "as." In other words, the simile explicitly declares that, in certain aspects, one thing is "like" another. In Lewis's *Out of the Silent Planet* there are the following similes:

> Amidst the lake there rose *like* a low and gently sloping pyramid or *like* a woman's breast, an island of pale red, smooth to the summit. (118, emphasis mine)

In this example, the tenor is the island; the vehicles expand the reader's perception of the island's shape by introducing images of a pyramid and of a woman's breast. The first provides the comparison with a pyramid from the flat environment of a desert; the second softens that image by superimposing upon it the image of the gentler contours of a female breast. To the visual image of the pyramid is added the visual, tactile and sensuous images of the breast which enable the reader to participate in the cognitive apprehension experienced by the book's protagonist, Ransom. As with metaphor, simile enriches and extends meaning so that more of the "truth" which attends the vehicle may be imaginatively expressed, and experienced also by the reader.

Although simile draws an analogy by an explicit comparison, the second literary device which Lewis uses in his fiction, the symbol, does so implicitly, calling forth an emotional and ontological response aroused by the objects, ideas or concepts it signifies. A symbol functions basically as a metaphor truncated by the omission of the tenor. It is, in fact, an analogy for something unstated, and it consists of the articulation of verbal elements which possess meanings which lie beyond the reference and limits of its contextual discourse and therefore it embodies and offers a complexity of feeling and thought (Tindall 120-13). A rose, for example, may be a symbol for romantic love, or a flag for a particular country, its ideological stance, its culture and its customs; it is used as a symbol for that country in such international events as the Olympic Games or forums such as the United Nations. A lion may be a symbol for a monarch or for God: the Lion Aslan is a symbol for the second person of the Trinity in Lewis's Narnian Chronicles.

As with metaphor and simile, the primary function of the symbol is to express the imaginative concepts which will enlarge for the reader his experiential knowledge of reality, although the full mythological or literary reference of the symbol may be unknown to him and may therefore pass unrecognised. In such an instance, however, the reader may respond to the inherent potency of the symbol itself—for example, to the power and beauty of a lion rather than to its traditional role as "king of beasts" and as an heraldic device for royalty—and although the reader responds beneath the level of awareness required for full interpretation, he may nevertheless "find himself surprised by an enrichment he cannot account for" (Tindall 15). And indeed Lewis himself observed that "[Symbols] exist precisely for the purpose of conveying to the imagination what the intellect is not ready for."[3]

Because Lewis's polemic depends upon the efficacy of metaphors and symbols to "add to life," to express the imagination's subcreative potency for recombining existing elements to make new images and to draw fresh analogies, and finally to convey truth, their power to function in this way must be established. It is therefore necessary to demonstrate that Lewis, as a rationalist, emphasized the necessity of the dual operation of the imagination and of reason in the apprehension of truth, and in its expression through metaphor and symbol.

Lewis writes that the imagination of itself is not the organ of truth, since some of the images it recreates are inaccurate. For example, human imagination continually provides anthropomorphic images of the incorporeal deity. Whether the metaphorical and analogical nature of these images (for example of God as "King" sitting on a "throne") is perceived or not, the *meaning* derived from the images is essentially true. Lewis observes,

> If we turn to Theology,—or rather to the literature of religion—the result will be...surprising...for unless our whole argument is wrong, we shall have to admit that a man who says *heaven* and thinks of the visible sky is pretty sure to mean more than a man who tells us that heaven is a state of mind. ("Bluspels" 157)

Thus imaginative images, despite their inaccuracy, provide meaning: the imagination is the organ of meaning. Since meaning is, however, the antecedent condition of both truth and falsehood, the imagination cannot be the organ of truth, nor the cause of truth. But when the imagination, working with reason, produces new metaphors and revivifies old ones, it is "the condition of truth." The meanings produced by the imagination, subjected to reason, result in metaphors which function as pointers to truth. Such a view, admits Lewis, implies that there is a kind of truth or rightness in the imagination itself, a truth which depends upon the psycho-physical parallelism in the universe, the nature and composition of which the medieval model is one attempt to explain ("Bluspels" 158). Ultimately, of course, the truth within human imagination and in its various manifestations such as myth and fantasy depends upon the divine origins of, and divine influence upon, the individual imagination, and it is upon this that Tolkien's theory of sub-creation depends.

Lewis believed that all our truth, or at least the greater part of that which we apprehend, is won by metaphor, and therefore the metaphors by which we think are good ones. Conversely, as expressions of truth, the metaphors and symbols we employ most possess a truth-bearing quality and should represent by analogy an underlying reality: reason therefore forms part of the process of determining the suitability of a particular metaphor. The result is a "sacramental" function in accord with Lewis's quasi-religious view of the imagination: metaphors and symbols provide an external sign for an inner, or deeper, reality. As Lewis writes in *The Allegory of Love,* his first critical work which deals with medieval love poetry,

> If ever our passions, being immaterial, can be copied by material inventions, then it is possible that our material world is the copy of an invisible world. As the god Amor and his figurative garden are to the actual passions of men, so perhaps we ourselves and our "real" world are to something else. The attempt to read that something else through its sensible limitations, to see the archetype in the copy, is what I mean by symbolism or sacramentalism...the symbolist leaves the given to find that which is more real. (45)

Here Lewis distinguishes between allegory and symbol. In the first instance, immaterial and abstract concepts such as the human passions of love and lust are given fictional embodiment as material creatures in order to enlarge the reader's cognition of those passions. But if fictional constructs may point to the real passions of man, Lewis reasons, the "real world" as perceived by humankind may point beyond it to some deeper reality. What the symbol does is to represent, especially in literature, realities beyond our sensible perceptions.

Lewis traces the development of symbolism from its use by Plato (whom Lewis calls "the master of meaning") through to its "sacramental" function as recorded in "full grown medieval thought." In the dialogues of Plato, explains Lewis, "the Sun is the copy of the good. Time is the moving image of eternity. All visible things exist just insofar as they succeed in imitating the Forms" (*Allegory* 45). In the middle ages, the spirit of symbolism is expressed in the writings of Hugo of St. Victor, for whom the "external sign" or material element in Christian ritual has nothing arbitrary about it but rests primarily on the pre-existing *similtudo* between the external sign and the spiritual reality. For example, water, *ex naturali qualitate,* was an image of the Holy Ghost long before it became the "external sign" for the sacrament of Baptism (*Allegory* 46). It is frequently used in literature as a symbol for cleansing and restoring and because these are its natural proper ties the symbolic role that water fulfils is an extension, to the metaphysical plane, of those properties. Water as symbol and "sacrament" appear frequently in Lewis's fiction and its choice there, as in most Western literature, is not merely arbitrary but dependent on the *similtudo* between its natural properties and the symbolised spiritual properties, the inner cleansing and regeneration of the soul and spirit. Again, when the lion is used symbolically to represent Christ in the Narnian chronicles, there is an analogical "similarity" between the lion's natural strength and power and the spiritual strength and the power of Christ. These natural attributes of the lion have contributed to its use throughout mythology and literature as an archetypal figure of deity or kingship.

The symbol therefore contributes to that which is symbolised a broadening and deepening of meaning and of the extent to which reality is experienced, because of the intrinsic meaning of the chosen symbol, and because of the additional associations which it calls forth. Symbolic and metaphorical language is required in order to compensate for the inadequacies of literal language: as Lewis points out, even our daily needs of expression drive us to the use of metaphor, and to abandon its use is "to abandon reason itself" (Bluspels" 155) and again, "literalness we cannot have. The man who does not consciously use metaphors talks without meaning" ("Bluspels" 153). Language which deals with the apprehension of truth and reality, with indeed all things other than physical objects is "necessarily metaphorical" ("Is Theology Poetry?" 161). When language endeavours to describe physical objects belonging to or associated with new worlds which are products of the imaginative subcreation, the bridge between the sensible reality and the imagined is also metaphorical and symbolic.

Lewis was fully aware of the difficulties of translating imaginative realities into language. In *Perelandra* the second novel of his science fiction trilogy, he has his protagonist, Ransom, experiencing these very difficulties. Ransom finds himself unable adequately to describe his experiences on the new planet from which he has just returned. The narrator, "Lewis," remarks, "Of course, I realise it's all rather too vague for you to put into words," which elicits from Ransom the sharp response, "On the contrary, it is words that are vague. The reason why the thing can't be expressed is that it's too definite for language" (43). Lewis felt himself to be in a similar position to Ransom. He was trying to describe and argue for realities too great for the language he had at his disposal. They are able only to be hinted at, symbolised, and compared with those realities which can be perceived by the senses.

Metaphor and symbol do more than serve as indications of transcendental truth: they argue for its existence and its validity. Indeed, the comparative and analogical tropes, metaphor and simile, are listed among the *topoi* or topics for arguments provided by Aristotle. More recently, Manuel Bilsky and others in a discussion of the topoi, observed that "it could be plausibly asserted that all comparison [including metaphor and symbol] are used, in varying degrees, for argument. Hence we will not go far wrong if we treat them as arguments" (214). Comparisons and analogies rest as arguments on the question of similarity or dissimilarity between two cases so that argument can proceed, "if in this case then also in that." Bilsky et al. agree with Lewis when they point out that analogies and comparisons facilitate the apprehension of meaning, and they quote from the rhetorician Whately, that analogy may be used not only "to *prove* the proposition in question, but to make it more *clearly understood*" (214). What Lewis achieves in his fiction is an analogy between his fictional worlds and the region of the human spirit so that the struggles undergone by his characters are compared with the moral and spiritual struggles of the individual reader. By analogy, the solutions Lewis offers in his fiction also apply to the situation of the reader in real life: the solutions Lewis presents are variations upon the theme of self-surrender.

Edward P.J. Corbett notes that analogy is so commonly used for the purposes of exposition and argument that the tendency to use it is as natural to man as is his tendency to definition. Primitive man, in his attempt to make sense of the bewildering world about him and the cosmos beyond, must surely have turned to comparison for the purposes of understanding his environment and to construct from it a scale of values. From the familiar he was able to explore the unfamiliar; by comparing one thing with another he was able to distinguish between the "more" and the "less" (116).

Recent studies indicate that in human language metaphor is pervasive because the whole conceptual system by which we think and act is fundamentally metaphorical in nature (Lakoff 3). Modern man relies for his interpretation of reality upon a conceptual model which has several characteristics in common with the medieval model which provides the vehicles for many of Lewis's metaphors and symbols. This conceptual model is itself metaphorical (as indeed is its medieval counterpart) and therefore the way we think, what we experience, and how we act each day is of necessity "very much a matter of metaphor." How we apprehend reality influences our thoughts and our actions. Metaphors which deepen and extend the human perception of reality have the ability to influence our thoughts and our actions. In other words, they function as arguments.

That metaphors have shaped meaning from man's earliest history and continue to do so may be shown by contrasting some meanings which are conceptually linked with the words "up" and "down." If, for example, "things are looking up," the outlook is good; if a person is "on the up and up," his progress is favourable. He is awake and alert if he "wakes up"; he possesses enviable status is he belongs to the "upper echelons"; if he is "upright", he is virtuous. All these positive concepts rely for their meaning on the basic understanding that "up" is also associated with spiritual realities. Its mystical and spiritual associations are seen in such phrases as, "up in the air" and "in the clouds," and its paradisal connotations are evident in references to happiness as "being on Cloud Nine."

The concept of descent and of "down" is, by contrast, negative, and associated with poverty: "down and out"; depression: "feeling down"; with failure and diminished status: "coming down in the world," "being taken down a peg," "being sent down." It refers to the material and concrete rather than to immaterials and abstractions: "down to earth," "down to tin tacks" (Lakoff 5). Here is evidence for modern acceptance of the notion of the cosmological and metaphysical psycho-parallelism for which Lewis argues. Its relevance for the potency of Lewis's metaphors as arguments lies in the degree to which such concepts, metaphorical in themselves, shape human thoughts and behaviour and enhance the receptivity of human consciousness to the metaphorical concepts and arguments which are available in his fiction. Certainly Lewis bases many of his metaphors on the good—up, bad—down equations and he exploits to the fullest the cognitive and emotive power they afford him. In the final Narnian Chronicle, *The Last Battle,* therefore, Heaven is reached by moving "further up and further in," a refrain frequently iterated in the closing chapters. The "heaven" of the story is ultimate reality—the reality perceived in the physical world only by symbol and metaphor. Lewis also shows that the conceptual equation of good and up has long been entrenched in human consciousness by having his character Lord Digory mutter, "It's all in Plato, all in Plato" (161).

The conceptual basis for Lewis's metaphors, then, is not outmoded or obsolete. It is as much a part of modern human consciousness as it was of medieval thought. For that reason alone Lewis's metaphors and symbols have a real potential for argument and persuasion. This potential is considerably enhanced, however, by Lewis's insistence on the additional "sacramental" and quasi-religious significance which may be summed up by reference to metaphor and myth and symbol made by the unseen speaker in *The Pilgrim's Regress.* The voice is apparently God's own, and he addresses the pilgrims in Tolkienesque terms:

> Child, if you will, it *is* mythology. it is but truth, not fact: an image, not the very real. But then it is My mythology...this is my inventing, this is the veil in which I have chosen to appear even from the first until now. For this end I made your senses and for this end your imagination, that you might see My face and live...was there any age in any land when men did not know that corn and wine were the blood and body of a dying and yet living God? (217)

When Lewis uses metaphor and symbol, then, he is obviously striving for more than "the willing suspension of disbelief." He is apparently conscious of using them as a kind of divinely inspired polemic designed to have a lasting and profound effect upon his readers' consciousness and indeed upon their will.

The metaphors and symbols by which Lewis argues most cogently for transcendent realities are not all encapsulated within the phrases of his fiction. Often they encompass an entire novel, as with the metaphor of the "silent planet" in the first of the space trilogy. The full significance of the metaphor is apparent only in the unfolding "myth of Deep Heaven" which the protagonist, Elwin Ransom, uncovers in his visit to Malacandra, when he compares the innocence and peace of Malacandrian society with the social, moral and cultural depravity among humans upon the earth. Earth's "silence" is a metaphor for its spiritual "death," brought about by the fall and consequent influence of its tutelary spirit. *The Great Divorce* (between good and evil) is another instance of a metaphor which is fully explicated only in the complete text of the novel and which symbolises the choice which faces individual beings, between self (hell), and something which transcends and fulfills the self (heaven). The theme of this novel has elements in common with that of *Till We Have Faces,* the title of which forms the basis for a sustained metaphor which again develops through the entire narrative: the "faces" of the title symbolising the surrendered and spiritually individuated self.

The Narnian Chronicles each symbolise aspects of the Gospel narrative, although within each text particular symbols derive their meanings from widely ranging cultural and literary sources. *The Lion, the Witch and the Wardrobe* has as its model redemption through the passion, death, and resurrection of Christ; while *The Voyage of the "Dawn Treader"* draws upon the notion of the way-faring and war-faring Christian of Milton's *Paradise Lost* and his *Areopagitica,* and of Bunyan's *The Pilgrim's Progress.* There is a parallel development of the theme found in *The Great Divorce* and *Till We Have Faces,* the loss of personality suffered by an individual who permits himself to be enslaved by evil.

*The Magician's Nephew* draws on models available in *Genesis, Paradise Lost,* and Tolkien's *The Silmarillion* (which was extant in manuscript form at the time Lewis wrote this story) for its treatment of the creation myth; and *The Last Battle* is an imaginative re-interpretation of Scriptural eschatology. *The Horse and His Boy* is a further account of a spiritual quest and has several elements in common with *The Pilgrim's Regress.* Indeed, the Narnian Chronicles may be seen as a series of parables. The parable is a form of extended or sustained metaphor in which human experiences are particularised and compressed and related as events in the lives of a particular fictional character or group of characters; it possesses a moral purpose. Lewis's parables are set in an imaginary world, but there is clearly an analogy between Narnian and earthly experiences which operates persuasively throughout the series.

Whether Lewis's metaphors are encapsulated in short passages or whether they are sustained throughout the length of his narratives, he uses them to argue for the transcendent realities and truth in which he believes. In doing so he seeks also to deepen his readers' own imaginative insights and to increase their apprehension of reality; but he uses them not only to instruct but to delight. That metaphor had an aesthetic as well as a mechanical function is recognised by Aristotle and rhetoricians from successive ages. The metaphors in Lewis's fiction provide delight by awakening a sensuous appreciation in the reader for the new worlds available to him, and by allowing the reader to feel such a sense of participation in the imaginative apprehension of these new worlds Lewis's writing occasionally approaches the sublime.

Lewis fully intended that his new worlds should offer the reader delight and enjoyment, and because they do so, the force of his polemic is enhanced and rendered more acceptable to the casual reader. As Lewis observed in a letter to his friend Dom Bede Griffiths in which he was discussing his novel *Perelandra*

> Although the theme has serious implications, it is primarily a "yarn" and most of the scenery was meant to be enjoyable—or to have a spiritual meaning only in the v. (sic) general sense of suggesting perfect sensuous happiness.[4]

This allusion to the aesthetic value of metaphor serves also as a warning for a too-zealous dismantling of Lewis's texts in search of Christian "meanings." There is no doubt that the function of Lewis's imaginary worlds involves more than merely the provisions of a backdrop for diadacticism and polemic. They are there to be enjoyed and to be seen as an integral part of the narrative. Writing to the science-fiction author Arthur C. Clarke, Lewis wrote, "What's the excuse for locating one's story on Mars unless 'Martianity' is through and through *used*. . . emotionally and atmospherically *as well as* logically."[5] If in a novel material is introduced, it must be used. Lewis maintained that "whatever in art is not doing good is doing harm," and he therefore worked to ensure that his "other worlds" contributed to his narratives an imaginative appeal which adds to their aesthetic as well as to their value as fantasy.

Lewis depicts his fictional "worlds of the spirit" by means of a skillful use of the comparative tropes which allows for the reader a sense of participation in the sub-creative process. Indeed on occasion it is possible that the reading experience may approach what Longinus termed "the sublime," when a passage may work to "uplift our souls; we are filled with a proud exhaltation and a sense of vaunting joy, just as though we had ourselves produced what we had heard" (107). One passage which may produce the experience of the sublime is that which describes the funeral of the hross in *Out of the Silent Planet* from the point of view of the protagonist, earthman Elwin Ransom who records his reactions to the song of the Malacandrian creatures:

> A sense of great masses moving at visionary speeds, of giants dancing, of eternal sorrows eternally consoled, of he knew not what and yet what he had always known, awoke in him with the very first bars of the deep-mouthed dirge, and bowed down his spirit as if the gate of heaven had opened before him. (148)

The reader is invited to create this experience within his own consciousness and to feel the emotional impact of the Malacandrians' grief. Lewis woos his readers with evocative and poetic images (the images of "masses moving at visionary speeds," "of giants dancing," and the "deep-mouthed dirge," for example) which compel the reader's imagination to form the new concepts expressed in the passage and to appeal to that spiritual *Sehnsucht* which Lewis believed tantalized the imagination of every human being. But this quality of sublimity which may be experienced in Lewis's fiction does not destroy the powerful polemic which characterises it. It too has a rhetorical purpose and operates persuasively by an appeal to the emotion and to the imagination. Lewis's polemic is directed at the whole being, the reason, the imagination, and the will, and its quality of sublimity links it with Renaissance and medieval poetry which also had a didactic purpose (Tuve 41-44), drawing its images from the same hierarchical cosmology and the same classical heritage. The link is not entirely fortuitous, for Lewis was, as well as a medievalist, a poet, albeit a somewhat inhibited and frustrated one. His poetry nevertheless demonstrates his understanding, achieved at an early age, of the rhetorical power of verse, and of the power of metaphor and symbol as rhetorical artifacts. In his first published work, *Spirits in Bondage*, the twenty-year-old Lewis carries on a self-conscious dialectic arguing at once for the existence of an evil god and for an empyrean "far country" as the fulfilment of his spiritual *Sehnsucht*. The work was commended by critic Sir Arthur Quiller-Couch for "its rich metaphor" (qtd. in Como xxix). The place of metaphor and symbol in polemic literature had long been established in Lewis's thinking.

It is not surprising that Lewis should have transferred his poetic techniques to his prose. Indeed, his friend the poet Ruth Pitter writes that "his poetry...is...most evident in his prose,"[6] and indeed Lewis's fiction has that imaginative, "magical" quality that he failed to express in his poetry. It enabled him to catch his readers "unprepared," as it were, with the power of his polemic.[7] That Lewis has succeeded is evident from the great number of people, some of them famous, who acknowledge the impact and influence of Lewis's fiction upon their lives. By approaching his mythopoeic art with an understanding of the power of language, and of metaphorical and symbolic language in particular, Lewis has imbued his polemic with magic, and raised its persuasive power to the level of sacrament, always pointing to the greater realities for which he was so able a spokesman.

## Notes

[1]See C.S. Lewis, "Bluspels and Flalansteres." *Rehabilitations and Other Essays* (Oxford: Oxford UP, 1939), 158.

[2]See C.S. Lewis, *The Discarded Image: An Introduction to Medieval and Renaissance Literature* (Cambridge: Cambridge UP, 1967).

[3]C.S. Lewis, "To Sister Penelope, C.S.M.V." Unpublished letter dated March 25, 1943, in Marion E. Wade Collection (Wade: CSL/L-Penelope/21-T-B).

[4]To Dom Bede Griffiths." Unpublished letter dated May 26, 1943, in Marion E. Wade Collection (L-Griffiths/18-W/Wade).

[5]"To Arthur C. Clarke." Unpublished letter dated January 20, 1954, in Marion E. Wade Collection (CSL/L-Clarke/7-B/Wade), emphasis Lewis's.

[6]Ruth Pitter, note with correspondence from C.S. Lewis in Bodleian Library, Oxford, MS Eng. lett C220/3, 63.

[7]"To Holmes." Unpublished letter dated February 17, 1959, in Marion E. Wade Collection (CSL/L-Holmes/W/Wade).

## Works Cited

Aristotle. *The Rhetoric of Aristotle: An Expanded Translation with Supplementary Examples*. Trans. and Ed. by Lane Cooper. Englewood Cliffs, NJ: Prentice Hall, 1960.

Bennett, J.A.W. *The Humane Medievalist: An Inaugural Lecture*. Cambridge: Cambridge UP, 1965.

Bilsky, Manuel, McCrea Hazlitt, Robert E. Streeter, and Richard Weaver. "Looking for an Argument" *College English*, January 1953: 214.

Carpenter, Humphrey. *The Inklings: C.S. Lewis, J.R.R. Tolkien, Charles Williams and Their Friends*. London: Unwin, 1981.

Coleridge, Samuel Taylor. *Biographica Literaria,* Chapter XIII in *The Portable Coleridge*. Ed. I.A. Richards. Harmondsworth: Penguin, 1977.

Como, James T., Ed. "Introduction: Within the Realms of Plenitude" *C.S. Lewis at the Breakfast Table*. London: Collins, 1980.

Corbett, Edward P.J. *Classical Rhetoric for the Modern Student*. New York: Oxford UP, 1971.

Lakoff, George and Mark Johnson. *Metaphors We Live By*. Chicago: U of Chicago P, 1980.

Lewis, C.S. *The Allegory of Love: A Study in Medieval Tradition*. London: Oxford UP, 1958.

—— "De Descriptione Temporum." *They Asked for a Paper: Papers and Addresses*. London: Geoffrey Bles, 1962.

—— *An Experiment in Criticism*. Cambridge: Cambridge UP, 1961.

—— "Bluspels and Flalansteres." *Rehabilitations and Other Essays*. Oxford: Oxford UP, 1939.

—— *The Discarded Image: An Introduction to Medieval and Renaissance Literature*. Cambridge: Cambridge UP, 1967.

—— "Is Theology Poetry?" *They Asked for a Paper: Papers and Addresses*. London: Geoffrey Bles, 1962.

—— *The Last Battle. London:* Fount Lions, 1980.

—— *Miracles: A Preliminary Study*. Glasgow: Fount, 1975.

—— *Out of the Silent Planet*. London: The Bodley Head, 1938.

—— *Perelandra*. London: The Bodley Head, 1943.

—— *The Pilgrim's Regress: An Allegorical Apology for Christianity, Reason and Romanticism*. Glasgow: Fount, 1977.

—— "Sometimes Fairy Stories Say Best What's to be Said." *Of This and Other Worlds*. Ed. Walter Hooper. London: Collins, 1982.

_____ *Spirits in Bondage: A Cycle of Lyrics.* London: Heinmann, 1919. (Published under the nom-de-plume of Clive Hamilton.)

_____ Unpublished letter to Dom Bede Griffiths dated May 26, 1943, in Marion E. Wade Collection (L-Griffiths/18-W/Wade).

_____ Unpublished letter to Holmes dated February 17, 1959, in Marion E. Wade Collection (CSL/L-Holmes/W/Wade).

_____ Unpublished letter to Sister Penelope, C.S.M.V. dated March 25, 1943, in Marion E. Wade Collection (Wade: CSL/L-Penelope/21-T-B).

Longinus. "On the Sublime." *Classical Literary Criticism.* Trans. with Introduction by T.S. Dorsch. Harmondsworth: Penguin, 1965.

Peacham, Henry. *The Garden of Eloquence.* London, 1953. Quoted in Rosemond Tuve. *Elizabethan and Metaphysical Imagery: Renaissance Poetic and Twentieth Century Criticism.* Chicago: U of Chicago P, 1947.

Pitter, Ruth. Note with correspondence from C.S. Lewis in Bodleian Library. Oxford, MS Eng. lett. C220/3: 63.

Richards, I.A. *The Philosophy of Rhetoric.* Oxford: Oxford UP, 1939.

Robbe-Grillet, Alain. *Snapshots/Towards a New Novel.* Trans. Barbara Wright. London: Calder and Boyars, 1965.

Tindall, William York. *The Literary Symbol.* Bloomington: Indiana UP, 1967.

Tolkien, J.R.R. "On Fairy Stories." *Essays Presented to Charles Williams.* Ed. C.S. Lewis. Grand Rapids: Eerdmans, 1981.

Tuve, Rosemond. *Elizabethan and Metaphysical Imagery: Renaissance Poetic and Twentieth Century Criticism.* Chicago: U of Chicago P, 1947.

# The Affair of Jane's Dreams: Reading *That Hideous Strength* as Iconographic Art

*Joe McClatchey*

I find the method or formula for this reading of C.S. Lewis' novel in his critical book published posthumously, *Spenser's Images of Life*. Lewis says he finds six forms of iconography that Spenser verbalized in *The Faerie Queene:* (1) pageant proper, (2) tournament pageantry, (3) masque, (4) traditional images of gods, (5) hieroglyphs and emblems, and (6) philosophical iconography.[1] Lewis notes that the Florentine Platonists of the 15th century, including Marsilio Ficino and Giovanni Pico della Mirandola, believed that "all myths and hieroglyphs hide a profound meaning" and that "this ancient pagan under-meaning is really in agreement with Christianity" (9). Speaking of Botticelli's use of iconography, Lewis says that "accepting traditional images, he loads them with wisdom from the philosophers and disposes them in divine compositions. And so, in my opinion, does Spenser" (11). And so, in my opinion, does Lewis.

Lewis sees iconographical art as a statement of life: "an accompaniment, rather than a criticism" of it. "Or, if you wish, life itself, in another mode. The planets . . . , the Virtues, the Vices, the Liberal Arts, the Worthies, are *thus.*" Lewis adds what we might take as an approach to a similar study of his own work: "If now we were to use a similar art, it would be full of figures symbolizing the atom, evolution, relativity, totalitarianism, democracy, and so on."[2] Taking such a approach, Lewis concludes, helps us accept Spenser's "propensity for mingling the Christian and the pagan" (12). When we think about Lewis' similar propensity in *That Hideous Strength,* we shall be quickened to the poetic power of its compelling iconographic imagery.[3]

The "obvious" iconography in *That Hideous Strength* includes, first, the dream-symbolic pictures of Jane's dreams, in which she sees Filostrato with the soon-to-be-guillotined Alcasan, Merlin waking from burial, and the murder of Hengist:

The death of Hengist in itself meant nothing to her. She had met him only once and she had accepted from Mark the view that he was a disagreeable old man and rather a snob. But the certainty that she herself in her dream had witnessed a real murder shattered at one blow all the consoling pretenses with which she had begun the morning. It came over her with sickening clarity that the affair of her dreams, far from being ended, was only beginning. The bright, narrow little life which she had proposed to live was being irremediably broken into.[4]

Another breaking into Jane's life can be seen in her vision (much later in the novel) of the coming of the Earth-Venus to the stone lodge, along with all those "ridiculous little men: fat dwarfs in red caps with tassels on them, chubby, gnome-like little men, quite insufferably familiar, frivolous, and irrepressible" (304), who mess everything up, tossing bed-clothes and pillows through the air, turn somersaults, and laugh at her.[5] It reminds Dr. Dimble of a mythological picture by Titian (314).

Then, almost before she can turn around, Jane has what she calls a "vision of the universe." It had a

curiously stormy quality about it. It was bright and darting, and overpowering. Old Testament imagery of eyes and wheels for the first time in her life took on some possibility of meaning. And mixed with this was the sense that she had been manoeuvered into a false position. It ought to have been she who was saying these things to the Christians. Hers ought to have been the vivid, perilous world brought against their grey formalized one; hers the quick, vital movements and theirs the stained-glass attitudes. That was the antithesis she was used to. This time, in a sudden flash of purple and crimson, she remembered what stained glass was really like (316).

A scene very like a masque is the descent of the gods Jove-Glund, Saturn-Lurga, Mercury-Viritrilbia, Mars-Malacandra, and Venus-Perelandra in Chapter 15.

But two of the most striking iconographical scenes concern Mark in his crucial experiences with Professor Frost to prepare him to become an initiate before the Head. The idea of the Straight or Normal occurs to Mark in the Objectivity Room as he thinks about its illusions, lop-sidedness, irregularities, "calculated obscenities," and "built and painted perversities," "making him aware, as he had never been aware before, of this room's opposite" (299):

He had never before known what an Idea meant: he had always thought till now that they were things inside one's own head. But now, when his head was continually attacked and often completely filled with the clinging corruption of the training, this Idea towered up above him—something which obviously existed quite independently of himself and had hard rock surfaces which would not give, surfaces he could cling to (310).

At this point Frost introduces Mark to a new exercise, the conscious abuse of a large wooden crucifix, which lay on the floor of the Objectivity Room. Frost orders him to insult the carved image, but Mark, confused by its realism and his new knowledge of the Straight, hesitates to make a move:

> With the introduction of this Christian symbol the whole situation had somehow altered. The thing was becoming incalculable. His simple antithesis of the Normal and the Diseased had obviously failed to take something into account. Why was the crucifix there? Why were more than half the poison-pictures religious? He had the sense of new parties to the conflict—potential allies and enemies which he had not suspected before (335).

He decides *not* to move, no matter what Frost may do to him. Then he notices the wooden helplessness of the crucified figure before him. Frost presses him harder, and Mark realizes his imminent danger; he might not now get out of Belbury alive:

> He was himself, he felt, as helpless as the wooden Christ. As he thought this, he found himself looking at the crucifix in a new way—neither as a piece of wood nor a monument of superstition but as a bit of history. Christianity was nonsense, but one did not doubt that the man had lived and had been executed thus by the Belbury of those days. And that, as he suddenly saw, explained why this image, though not in itself an image of the Straight or Normal, was yet in opposition to crooked Belbury. It was a picture of what happened when the Straight met the Crooked, a picture of what the Crooked did to the Straight—what it would do to him if he remained straight. It was, in a more emphatic sense than he had yet understood, a *cross*.... Christianity was a fable. It would be ridiculous to die for a religion one did not believe. This Man himself, on that very cross, had discovered it to be a fable, and had died complaining that the God in whom he trusted had forsaken him—had, in fact, found the universe a cheat. But this raised a question Mark had never thought of before. Was *that* the moment at which to turn against the Man? If the universe was a cheat, was that a good reason for joining its side? Suppose the Straight was utterly powerless, always and everywhere certain to be mocked, tortured, and finally killed by the Crooked, what then? Why not go down with the ship (336-37)?

The cross, then, is clearly the informing metaphor of this novel.[6]

In *Spenser's Images of Life,* the major categories of images that Lewis draws are (1) the False Cupid, (2) Antitypes to the False Cupid, (3) Forms of Human Adult Civilized Love, (4) Forms of Natural Appetite, (5) the Image of Evil, (6) the Image of Good, and (7) the Story of Arthur. All of these, I believe, are to be found in *That Hideous Strength.* By the False Cupid Lewis intends a cruel Cupid who is the traducer of married love. In *The Faerie Queene* his work is chiefly polite adultery; in *That Hideous Strength* it is a whole array of practices, the chief being birth control. "Opposed to the image of the false Cupid are several antitypes, images that embody different aspects of love in its true form" (*Spenser's Images* 36). In *The Faerie Queene* these include Venus/Amoret and Diana/Belphoebe, along with the Temple of Venus and the Garden of Adonis, places related to those figures. Lewis emphasizes what he calls the "cosmic activity of generation," as seen in Venus' love for Adonis (53).

Images of love as a social form include the House of Busyrane (bad) and the Temple of Venus (good), while images of love as natural appetite appear as the Garden of Adonis (purely and simply natural) and the Bower of Bliss (artificial). Images of evil are manifested as "solemn, solitary, silent and sterile (as in the House of Busyrane); or bogus, provocative, and inactive (as in the Bower of Bliss); or very expensive (as in both)" (64). Lewis notes that whereas in Milton, Shakespeare, and Marlowe, "evil is portrayed as involving immense concentrations of will," that is, evil appearing as energy—"lawless and rebellious energy, no doubt, but nevertheless energy, abounding and upsurging"; in Spenser there is only one instance in which evil is represented as "upsurging energy" (56-66, 73). Lewis shows five different forms evil takes in *The Faerie Queene:* (1) "the various paynim knights," e.g., Pyrochles, "a picture of frenetic anguish"; (2) "images of disease and defect," e.g., Maleger, Malbecco, and the Seven Deadly Sins, "every one of them...either diseased or deformed or both"; (3) "the form of the disgusting," e.g., the monster Errour; (4) "the form of a temptation to relax, or to fall asleep, or to die," e.g., St. George's temptation by Despayre; and (5) "the Waste House," e.g., the House of Busyrane, the House of Orgoglio, and the Cave of Mammon (68-72).

In contrast, Lewis finds the images of good as "spontaneous, shameless, and fertile, like those of the Garden of Adonis; or ordered, arduous, and active, like those of the Temple of Venus" (64). He points to their characteristic as being the "veiled, mysterious, even hidden" (79). He says that throughout *The Faerie Queene* "veiling and unveiling are actions of key significance" (81). "The effect of this frequent veiling and unveiling is to make us distrustful of outward show" (82). Good is also seen as "fun, as a romp" (84). "Good may be portrayed as the ingenuous, more or less unconscious, unspoiled, and humble. It is often accompanied by gaiety and fun" (86). Another image of good is the "order and ceremony of the house" of Coelia. "The good hermitage entertains, offering homely fare, it is true, but with 'entire affection.'" "The repeated images of greenery give a strong conviction of growth and natural vigour. As with Coelia's house, the good life is shown as explicitly a life of religion." "...the theme of Order is entwined with that of Fertility" (86-88). If evil in Spenser is "pompous and flashy and expensive," then good is "humble, unconscious and spontaneous, and may be inarticulate, naive and clumsy" (93). Evil is usually seen as inactive, empty, silent, and immobile, while good is active—dancing, revelling, making love, and romping—"full of figures in joyous motion" (94).

Finally, there is the story of Arthur. What Lewis says about Spenser's Arthur is, perhaps not surprisingly, suggestive of the Pendragon and his court in *That Hideous Strength:*

> Arthur is the figure in whom the Christianization of Paganism or the Paganization of Christianity...is most intense.... Platonically considered, Arthur is the purged philosophical soul, smitten with a spiritual *eros* for the One, the First Fair.... There is also, however, a level of Christian meaning.... Arthur, as the soul whose gaze is fixed beyond the world, is the knight who saves others when all their own efforts have failed.... He is the "prince of grace," it seems, in a more than chivalric sense. Clearly some close relation obtains between rescuer and redeemer, between Arthur and a liberating faith in the person of Christ (133-35).

The foregoing should not only clarify Lewis' own reading of *The Faerie Queene* but also provide the categories for our reading of his novel.[7]

### Images of Demonic Forms of Natural Appetite and Human Adult Civilized Love: "The False Cupid"

*That Hideous Strength* opens on Jane Studdock musing and moping about marriage.[8] It has not answered her hopes; Mark seems, she surmises, oblivious to her real self, caring chiefly for her person. She wants to be appreciated as a budding scholar instead. Marriage must not suffer her career to languish. She and Mark have been practicing birth control, putting off having children, if they ever have any at all. But when Mrs. Dimble asks if anything is wrong, Jane bristles, thinking, " 'She's dying to know whether I'm going to have a baby. That sort of woman always is' " (3). She triumphantly tells her that she is not going to have a baby, but she cannot deny her loneliness.

Mark has noticed that Jane has become increasingly defensive in their love-making. The rare occasions when she has not been defensive have "tended, in his experience, to be followed next day by inexplicable quarrels" (44). He fails to puzzle through his bewilderment in the face of the unnaturalness of their marriage.[9] She resents the entanglements of marriage and especially fears being invaded by a possible pregnancy: "One had one's own life to live" (73).[10]

Correspondent both negatively and positively to Jane's birth control is the image of Diana in the moon, "the huntress, the untameable virgin, the spear-head of madness" (194). Jane feels the "wildness" of it. At St. Anne's Ransom thinks Jane is chaste, but Merlin knows better. He says:

"know well that she has done in Logres a thing of which no less sorrow shall come than came of the stroke that Balinus struck. For, Sir, it was the purpose of God that she and her lord should between them have begotten a child by whom the enemies should have been put out of Logres for a thousand years...be assured that the child will never be born, for the hour of its begetting is passed.... For a hundred generations in two lines the begetting of this child was prepared; and unless God should rip up the work of time, such seed, and such an hour, in such a land, shall never be again" (278-29).

Ransom acquaints Merlin with the general practice of birth control, relating "the barren beds" (293) to the world-wide madness, falsehood, and poison characteristic of the age of machines.

At Belbury the N.I.C.E. pursues barrenness or sterility as if it were a virtue.[11] Filostrato holds forth on his pet project of abolishing organic life. He wants to rid the earth of all plants and animals, to " 'shave the planet' " (172).[12] He abhors even the human body. He sees the next step in evolution as chemically-fed brains reproduced without copulation. He concludes: " 'There will never be peace and order and discipline so long as there is sex. When man has thrown it away, then he will become finally governable' " (173). Already at Belbury the Head is an unsmiling image of Filostrato's dream. When the initiates enter its sterile apartment they must strip naked.

Appropriately, the moon's brightness corresponds to the increasing unearthiness of the sterile Belbury Conditioners. Mark feels an instinctive dislike for the moonlit faces of Filostrato and Straik, and well he might, for (as Ransom tells Merlin at St. Anne's) on the moon, or Sulva, " 'dwell an accursed people, full of pride and lust.' " It seems that there " 'the womb is barren and the marriages cold' ":

"There when a young man takes a maiden in marriage, they do not lie together, but each lies with a cunningly fashioned image of the other, made to move and to be warm by devilish arts, for real flesh will not please them, they are so dainty (*delicati*) in their dreams of lust. Their real children they fabricate by vile arts in a secret place" (273-74).

This same Sulva shines cold on the Studdock house, similarly empty of love and children, where Jane and Mark, like male and female birds, strut and posture, feeding each other's vanity.[13]

### Images of Apocalyptic Forms of Love: "Antitypes of the False Cupid"

Full as it is of marriages, matings, and mock-marriages, this novel almost could be called a prose epithalamium. When Jane describes her vision of the voluptuous Earth-Venus to Ransom, he warns her that if she continues to repress her responses to Mark, she will fall prey to the Earth-Venus. He holds up Mother Dimble as a model and corrective for her. Paradoxically, Mrs. Dimble, unable to bear children, is a friend of the very mythological world of the Earth-Venus, but she has baptized it. She is a Christian wife. Ransom tells Jane sternly:

> "And you, you know, are not. Neither are you a virgin. You have put yourself where you must meet that Old Woman and you have rejected all that has happened to her since Maleldil came to Earth. So you get her raw—not stronger than Mother Dimble would find her, but untransformed, demoniac. And you don't like it. Hasn't that been the history of your life?" (314)

Jane has been refusing both Christian and Pagan erotic love. Now it occurs to her that if she really hopes for any improvement in her marriage she will have to become a Christian, like Mother Dimble—Mother Dimble, who would never practice birth control; who unblushingly yet ritually prepares the bed for Ivy and Tom Maggs; who though she would never countenance literary talk about such indelicacies as codpieces, which Jane indulges in, "seemed to join hands with some solemn yet roguish company of busy old women who had been tucking young lovers into beds since the world began with an incongruous mixture of nods and winks and blessings and tears" (301). Mother Dimble practices real marriage.[14]

Like a parenthesis, at Belbury Wither and Frost embrace in a horrific mockery of love, slavering and locked together in a perversion of lovers trying to eat each other: "And as they swayed and scrabbled with hand and nail, there arose, shrill and faint at first, but then louder and louder, a cackling noise that seemed in the end rather an animal than a senile parody of laughter" (243). This scene rivals Dante's picture of Ugolino and Ruggieri and Browning's vision of Guido and Judas Iscariot, in *The Ring and the Book*. But it is symptomatic of mock-marriages at Belbury. Fairy Hardcastle is doubtless a lesbian and mistreats the girls on her police force.

On the night Venus descends upon St. Anne's to take Ransom back to Perelandra, Mrs. Dimble, Jane, Ivy, and Camilla Denniston dress for dinner in magnificent robes of state that they find in the room called the Wardrobe. The robes, archetypal of their wearer's true natures, reveal Mother Dimble as Eve, Camilla as Guinevere, Ivy as Morgan le Fay, and Jane as Mary. It is all credible; it is all without demeaning self-consciousness; it is all exactly right.[15]

Then Perelandra comes and all *eros* breaks out with matings galore of animals and humans.[16] Mr. Bultitude finds a she-bear, and Ransom blesses her with the laying-on-of-hands and a " '*Urendi Maleldil.*' "[17] He also gives his blessing to Ivy, whom he sends to Tom, just returned from jail. A pair of hedgehogs squeal and squeak their own merriment.

Suddenly two elephants appear and dance a ceremonial minuet of giants in the garden. MacPhee, always sceptical, is astonished:

> "In the name of Hell where's all them beasts coming from?" he said. "They are the liberated prisoners from Belbury," said the Director. "She comes more near the earth than she was wont to—to make Earth sane. Perelandra is all about us and Man is no longer isolated. We are now as we ought to be—between the angels who are our elder brothers and the beasts who are our jesters, servants and playfellows" (378).

Among those set sane are Jane and Mark. Mark, on his way to St. Anne's from the now smoking Belbury, has, for the last several hours, been learning a new humility, "the humility of a lover." He realizes—all too late, he fears—Jane's real worth and his own clumsy and stupid boorishness toward her sacrosanctity. He now loves her and intends to release her from her vows. Just then he comes to "a doorway in a wall" and sees standing there an almost gigantic woman:

> It was not human, though it was like a woman divinely tall, park naked, part wrapped in a flame-coloured robe. Light came from it. The face was enigmatic, ruthless he thought, inhumanly beautiful. It was opening the door for him. He did not dare disobey ("Surely," he thought, "I must have died"), and he went in: found himself in some place of sweet smells and bright fires, with food and wine and a rich bed (382).

He has come to the very lodge where Jane encountered the Earth-Venus.[18]

Now as Mark has indeed "died" to his old pride and complacency, Jane also must descend the "ladder of humility" to him. Ransom tells her that she is waited for and at her hesitation sends her with his blessing. She says: " 'Then I will go, Sir. But—but—am I a bear or a hedgehog?' 'More. But not less. Go in obedience and you will find love. You will have no more dreams. Have children instead. *Urendi Maleldil*' " (379-80). Her going to Mark promises surprises for them both.

## *Images of Evil*

### *"The various paynim knights"*

The first of the "paynim knights" is Wither, with his Elasticity. His face is "rather vague and chaotic" (52), yet he insists that it is " 'so important to make everything *clear*' " (237). For all his inhumanity, Wither betrays Lewis' deft handling of humor.

Next is Straik, an apostate clergyman who espouses a Radical Eschatology. He preaches to Mark about the coming Kingdom of the Lord Jesus on earth. He uses New Testament language like "resurrection" and "life everlasting" to describe the plans and goals of the N.I.C.E.[20] The ironic import of his eschatology is stupendous; it is as big as the 20th century:

> "It is all going to happen, here in this world, in the only world there is. What did the Master tell us? Heal the sick, cast out devils, raise the dead. We shall. The Son of Man—that is, Man himself, full grown—has power to judge the world—to distribute life without end, and punishment without end. You shall see. Here and now" (128).

This amounts in itself to a kind of prophecy of the Body of Christ's opposite number: a sort of anti-Christ or anti-Body. It is the New Man Filostrato talks about. Straik says of the Head: " 'This is real Man at last, and it claims all our allegiance' " (177). " 'It is the beginning of Man Immortal and Man Ubiquitous.... Man on the throne of the universe. It is what all the prophecies really meant' " (178). When at St. Anne's Dr. Dimble learns about the Head, he exclaims, " 'The emergence of the Bodiless Men!' " (197). Ransom himself ponders the meaning of this step in the abolition of man:

> The time was ripe. From the point of view which is accepted in Hell, the whole history of our Earth had led up to this moment. There was now at last a real chance for fallen Man to shake off that limitation of his powers which mercy had imposed upon him as a protection from the full results of his fall. If this succeeded, Hell would be at last incarnate. Bad men, while still in the body, still crawling on this little globe, would enter that state which, heretofore, they had entered only after death, would have the diuturnity and power of evil spirits. Nature, all over the globe of Tellus, would become their slave; and of that dominion no end, before the end of time itself, could be certainly foreseen (203-04).

Frost, who associates himself with Objectivity, is a third "paynim knight."[21] He thinks social relations are merely chemical phenomena. He tries to be objective about the "organisms" he calls the *macrobes*, the "species" he knows to be the real force operant through the Head; but he may be unaware of their infernal nature.

Fairy Hardcastle is the "knight" of Disturbance. She engineers the riot her own police will quell. Feverstone is the knight of Theology. With hilarity for the reader, Lewis puts God-talk into his mouth—him of all people. His inevitable response to any statement he thinks bathetic or boring is the expletive, " 'God!' " When Jules blathers that " 'modern research shows the temple at Jerusalem to have been about the size of an English village church,' " he cannot stand it. " 'God!' said Feverstone to himself" (338). His everlasting theological remarks rise to a fitting high level of humor when, witnessing the massacre at Belbury after the banquet, he says to himself, " 'Well, I'm damned!' " (356) Minutes later, in his car intending to drive away from the debacle, he discovers that the car is driving itself madly down an old Roman road. "'Here! What the devil am I doing?' thought Feverstone" (357). He ends in a quaking, heaving, Gehenna-like "valley [that] seemed to have turned into Hell," as he falls into a cataract and is completely, deeply, buried alive (367).

Our amusement grows with the False Merlin, the tramp, who outwits the best wits of Belbury; and Jules, the figure-head director of the N.I.C.E., who postures and waddles like a duck. The clergyman Busby and Father Doyle add to the fun. The third glass of wine revives the parson in Busby "after thirty years' apostacy" (37). Father Doyle is Stone's assistant in Belbury's search for Merlin and merely proves that unbelief is no warranty against stumbling incompetence. Jules cannot stand ministers of any sort and on the night of the banquet accuses Wither of turning the N.I.C.E. "into a kind of seminary" (342).

These sometimes ludicrous and almost huddibrastic knights form less a Table Round than an Inner Ring, the striking image that Lewis develops throughout the novel and on which he wrote an essay.[22] It chiefly concerns Mark, who all his sordid life has made it his every work and will to get the eye, ear, and confidence of those in exclusive circles.[23] Once in, he has taken on the color and candor of the insiders and their often cruel prejudices toward outsiders. He has managed to penetrate the inner ring of Bracton College and now of Belbury. But he wakes up eventually to the cost he has paid at every step along the way. He has, since childhood, crassly sacrificed friends and enjoyment, and doing what most surely would satisfy his heart in order to get into each successive, ever-more-inner ring. It has now all come down to initiation to the Head. But as their ends illustrate it, the ultimate inner ring of Belbury has no real fellowship or cohesion. At the fearful close it is still, and now dreadfully and pitiably so, every man for himself.

### *"Images of disease and defect"*

Vivisection at Belbury, like Filostrato's hatred of the organic, suggests a kind of anti-plenitudinousness characteristic of evil in this novel. Belbury carries out such a policy when its N.I.C.E. aliens overrun the town of Edgestow.

### *"The form of the disgusting"*

Lewis' images of the diabolic and hellish are particularly striking.[24] The figures of Wither and Frost suggest the Unman of *Perelandra.*[25] Wither, as Fairy Hardcastle explains to Mark, cannot abide making things clear. " 'That's not how he runs the place. And mind you, he knows what he's about. It works, Sonny. You've no idea yet how well it works' " (97). By a process of glimpses the reader finds out what Wither's Unmannish shelf is like. His office is extremely hot. He himself seems to be almost ubiquitous, much to Mark's dismay, whose escape is blocked with a Wither at every route. His body, or rather, corpse, performs its acts quite automatically, as though his mind or soul is far removed in dreams, or "spreading and dissipating itself like a gas through formless and lightless worlds, waste lands and lumber rooms of the universe" (188).

Moreover, "it may be that the continual appearance of Wither which at almost all hours haunted so many rooms and corridors of Belbury was...a ghost" (213). Certainly he is not known to take time for sleep, and when he speaks, it is in "an antidiluvian tone" (207). Once Fairy Hardcastle has the feeling that he is a "mere mask of skin and flesh" (239).

Frost is a lesser Unman, or more accurately, he is becoming one. One day Mark suddenly realizes that Frost would terrify any child or dog. "Death itself did not seem more frightening" (248). Frost has been in continual intercourse with the Macrobes and knows they might have unpredictable "effects on his psychology." "In a dim sort of way, the possibility of complete destruction was never out of his thoughts" (333).

Wither insists upon a certain unity of his organization. It is " 'like a family, or even, perhaps, like a single personality,' " he tells Mark (120). But this unity really means a devouring of individuals like Mark. Wither complains to Frost that they " 'have not succeeded so far in bringing many people in—really *in.*' " They " 'are under orders to supply' " their superiors a " 'hard unchangeable core of individuals really devoted to the same cause' " as themselves (242):

> "Of course," said Wither, "nothing is so much to be desired as the greatest possible unity.... Any fresh individual brought into that unity would be the source of the most intense satisfaction to—ah—all concerned. I desire the closest possible bond. I would welcome an interpenetration of personalities so close, so irrevocable, that it almost transcends individuality.... I would open my arms to receive—to absorb—to assimilate this young man" (243).

This sounds very much like a Hell. It is not only a unity and a family but also a brotherhood. Filostrato counsels Mark that the Head demands a total commitment from him, including his wife Jane: " 'He will have all of you, and all that is yours' " (175). Wither confides to him: " 'We regard ourselves here as being so many brothers and—er sisters' " (209). To pressure Mark into bringing Jane to Belbury he warns him that the Head feels a "fatherly" concern for him: " 'You must look upon this as your *home,* Mr. Studdock.... We all now feel that you are really one of us in a deeper sense... Unity, you know. The family circle' " (212). It appears that confirmation in the brotherhood of this Hell depends upon something like a parody of Christian conversion, for Wither explains to Frost that he believes that Mark should have " 'a real change of heart' " in order to make him bring Jane (240).

But the N.I.C.E. is more than a brotherhood; Fairy Hardcastle calls it an army. When Mark sees the procession of refugees fleeing Edgestow, he is introduced to the results of battle. Feverstone tells him that Edgestow " 'is a conquered and occupied city' " (219). In time he will learn just how serious this war is. He does not know at this point that Bragdon Wood has, thanks to the N.I.C.E. forces, been turned into a Pandemonium and become a place of "clangings, thuddings, hootings, shouts, curses, and metallic screams" (121).

Behind the unity or family or brotherhood or army of Hell is that "central fear," the Head, which, it turns out, is itself an image of the devouring most-inner-ring of Macrobes, mostly likely servants-in-fear to Satan himself.

### *"The form of a temptation to relax, or to fall asleep, or to die"*

Lewis pictures damnations in Wither, Frost, and to a limited extent, Mark. Mark fails to notice how his desire to be an insider subtly undermines his integrity: "it all slipped past in a chatter of laughter, of that intimate laughter between fellow professionals, which of all earthly powers is strongest to make men do very bad things before they are yet, individually, very bad men" (130). Mark will get much worse before he gets any better. But after his experience in the Objectivity Room with the wooden Christ he will be able to begin to repent.

Wither and Frost, however, are too far gone into the depths ever to decide to change their souls' direction. Wither's final moments when Belbury falls bring a predictable conclusion to the logic of his life: He "had long ceased to believe in knowledge itself." He had refused "everything that was in any degree other than himself.... He had willed with his whole heart that there should be no reality and no truth, and now even the imminence of his own ruin could not wake him":

> The last moments before damnation are not often...dramatic. Often the man knows with perfect clarity that some still possible action of his own will could yet save him. But he cannot make this knowledge real to himself. Some tiny habitual sensuality, some resentment too trivial to waste on a blue-bottle, the indulgence of some fatal lethargy, seems to him at that moment more important than the choice between total joy and total destruction. With eyes wide open, seeing that the endless terror is just about to begin and yet (for the moment) unable to feel terrified, he watches passively, not moving a finger for his own rescue, while the last links with joy and reason are severed, and drowsily sees the trap close upon his soul. So full of sleep are they at the time when they leave the right way (353).

Frost's damnation holds more immediate terror for the reader. He has long believed that the mind is an illusion, a mere by-product of the body's functions. Now in his last hour his mind—the self he has always denied, calling it a chemical phenomenon—watches helplessly while his body commits suicide. He is unable to stop it from making a pile of flammables in the Objectivity Room, locking the door, removing the key beyond reach, and setting fire to the pile. His mind screams in protest, but his body, schooled to ignore all feeling, cannot respond. What his philosophy really meant all along surprises him with an ungentlemanly, unphilosophical cruelty. He has bought with his mindless coin more than he ever guessed he was paying for; the Macrobes, his real mentors, watch him die with a silent objectivity of their own:[26]

> Not until then did his controllers allow him to suspect that death itself might not after all cure the illusion of being a soul—nay, might prove the entry into a world where that illusion raged infinite and unchecked. Escape for the soul, if not for the body, was offered him. He became able to know (and simultaneously refused the knowledge) that he had been wrong from the beginning, that souls and personal responsibility existed. He half saw: he wholly hated. The physical torture of the burning was not fiercer than his hatred of that. With one supreme effort he flung himself back into his illusion. In that attitude eternity overtook him as sunrise in the old tales overtakes [trolls] and turns them into unchangeable stone (358).

### *"The waste house"*

The symbol of the N.I.C.E., ironically enough, is "a muscular male nude grasping a thunderbolt," presumably the god Zeus, suggesting, of course, *Deus*, god, or even God.[27] This figure stands for the Belbury Conditioners, who intend to apply science to social problems with all the force of the state. They will take charge of man, manipulate his brain, and make him do what they wish. They will experiment on animals and men, without regard to public or private views about vivisection of timed sentences for crimes. Lewis links Mark's academic specialization, sociology, to the Conditioners' goals and methods. He shows graphically how sociology is applied when Mark and Cosser set to work uprooting and remodelling the once placid and contented village of Cure Hardy. The Conditioners mean to make it over in their own image of Belbury.

Belbury means confusion, for Belbury obviously is Babel. The novel's epigraph announces it in capital letters:

> THE SHADOW OF THAT HYDDEOUS STRENGTH
> SAX MYLE AND MORE IT IS OF LENGTH.
> (Sir David Lyndsay: from *Ane Dialog*.
> describing the Tower of Babel)

At Belbury the hierarchy is confused. Jules is the ostensible Director, but Wither, the Deputy Director, actually gives the orders—although Frost, without official title, seems his equal in authority; nevertheless, the Head is higher still and is recognized by such as Fairy Hardcastle, who apparently does not know about the Macrobes, who are really in charge. Yet when the tramp comes, seemingly gives orders, and is mistaken for Merlin, he is obeyed implicitly—although Wither would have consulted the Head had he had the time; since Jules, undeceived about all this confusion, was coming and all would have to be "dancing attendance on him until midnight" (332). Of course, by midnight it would be too late to undeceive themselves about the tramp. In pulling down Deep Heaven on their heads, they will also drag down their whole hierarchical structure in one awful crash.

Doubtless the best image of this "waste house" is the confusion of tongues at the banquet. It is a scene at once archetypal of the Genesis Babel and Odysseus' slaughter of the suitors, a master-stroke of literary humor, and a sobering reminder of the significance of language.[28]

### *Images of Good*
### *"Spontaneous, shameless, and fertile"*

Lewis relates goodness and plentitude.[29] When Mark drives with Cosser to Cure Hardy, he is temporarily awakened, in spite of himself, to earth and sky; the air is filled with the loud calling of rooks. When Jane takes the train down from St. Anne's after her first visit with Ransom, she sees the multifarious everyday world with new eyes:[30]

> She saw from the windows of the train the outlined beams of sunlight pouring over stubble or burnished woods and felt that they were like the notes of a trumpet. Her eyes rested on the rabbits and cows as they flitted by and she embraced them in heart with merry, holiday love (152).

The many animals in the novel attest to this plentitude and vitality, from Mr. Bultitude to Ransom's mice that eat up the crumbs from his meals of bread and wine to a certain "very fine jackdaw" to Pinch the Cat to the many maltreated beasts great and small at Belbury, including the terrible tiger and serpent and the avenging elephant.[31]

It should be noted in passing that the descriptions and accounts of Mr. Bultitude take up and develop what Ransom calls "Barfield's 'ancient unities' " (261). His is a prose-less life, whose even simple wants are "quivering and ecstatic aspirations which absorbed his whole being, infinite yearnings, stabbed with the threat of tragedy and shot through with the colours of Paradise" (306). His furry mind suggests the "pre-Adamite" impulses, the mythological thinking, of the first stage in the evolution of consciousness.[32]

This fullness, or "packed reality" (320), also includes the Oyeresu of the planets—the diversity of Heaven—who descend upon St. Anne's with their awesome powers: Viritrilbia/Mercury, Perelandra/Venus, Malacandra/Mars, Lurga/Saturn, and Glund/Jupiter.[33] They are the heavenly archetypes, "resonant, dogmatic, flaming, and unanswerable."[34]

And of course the Manor at St. Anne's itself is an image of the good.[35]

*"Ordered, arduous, and active"*

Probably the best image of good as ordered, arduous, and active is the play of language at St. Anne's, both in the Great Tongue known only to Professor Dimble, and later in the descent of Viritrilbia. Ransom has Dimble practice for his possible meeting with Merlin:

> great syllables of words that sounded like castles came out of his mouth...it was as if the words spoke themselves through him from some strong place at a distance—or as if they were not words at all but present operations of God, the planets, and the Pendragon. For this was the language spoken before the Fall and beyond the Moon and the meanings were not given to the syllables by chance, or skill, or long tradition, but truly inherent in them as the shape of the great Sun is inherent in the little waterdrop. This was Language herself, as she first sprang at Maleldil's bidding out of the molten quicksilver of the star called Mercury on Earth, but Viritrilbia in Deep Heaven (229).

When Mercury comes to the Manor everyone is filled and inspirited with the gift of archetypal language.[36] Several of the Company are gathered in the kitchen for tea and suddenly break forth into loud, delighted talk. Their eyes dance; they make extraordinarily witty puns, "plays upon thoughts, paradoxes, fancies, anecdotes, theories...such eloquence, such melody...such toppling structures of double meaning, such skyrockets of metaphor and allusion" (321).

> For Ransom, whose study had been for many years in the realm of words, it was heavenly pleasure. He found himself sitting within the very heart of language, in the white-hot furnace of essential speech. All fact was broken, splashed into cataracts, caught, turned inside out, kneaded, slain, and reborn as meaning. For the lord of Meaning himself, the herald, the messenger, the slayer of Argus, was with them: the angel that spins nearest the sun, Viritrilbia, whom men call Mercury and Thoth (322).

This is all suggestive of Barfield's primal unity, glossolalia, and the language spoken before Babel, not to mention the Word become Flesh.

*"Order and ceremony of the House"*

The archetypal Oyeresu are, for all their monumental majesty, part of a great hierarchy. Everyone, no matter how great, is assigned his fitting place and function. Jane learns obedience to Mark by submitting first to Ransom, the Director. Also in submission to Ransom in their proper order are the jackdaw and the bear. When the gods descend all feel themselves "taking their places in the ordered rhythm of the universe, side by side with punctual seasons and patterned atoms and the obeying Seraphim" (325). For this hierarchy is one and the same with the Great Dance.[37] When Jove-Glund comes they dance in earnest. "It seemed to each that the room was filled with kings and queens, that the wildness of their dance expressed heroic energy and its quieter movements had seized the very spirit behind all noble ceremonies" (325). It is all ceremony, all courtesy, all humility, all dance, all game, all obedience, all perfect and precise matching of persons and functions.

*"Veiled, mysterious, hidden"*

In contrast to the highly publicized N.I.C.E., the Company at St. Anne's on-the-Hill are relatively obscure. Even the location is at the railroad's terminus, "and the end of everything" (50). Once there Jane encounters a mysterious collection of persons: Grace Ironwood, tall, imperious, and scholarly; Camilla, like Jane, a university professor's wife; the Dimbles; Ivy; Andrew MacPhee, crotchety, rationalistic, and agnostic; Arthur Denniston, Camilla's husband; and, of course, Ransom.[38] It seems that they have all been drawn together by some unseen authority. Except for MacPhee, they are all Christians. Ransom considers MacPhee necessary to the Company, however; he has his function to fill.

The Company are, of course, Belbury's opposite at almost every point of comparison. Besides those suggested above, such as hierarchy, function, and freedom, one need only mention temper, the gaiety and laughter of the Company over against the morbidity of the Conditioners. Furthermore, as they prepare for battle, they develop a loyalty to each other that shows the "unity" desired by Wither for his organization to be involuntary, at best. When Malacandra/Mars descends among them, the archetypal warrior, they feel heroic and all laugh together. "Their love for one another became intense. Each, looking on all the rest, thought, 'I'm lucky to be here. I could die with these' " (324).[39]

Perhaps the most striking instance of the hiddenness of the Company derives from a report Fairy Hardcastle makes to Wither and Frost about three possible enemies, Lancaster, Lyly, and Dimble, all associated with Northumberland College. She says the first two are dangerous because they "are the sort of people who get things done." They are men experienced in organizations that wield power by virtue of their organizational structure. She dismisses Dimble—the only one whose arrest might have eventuated in the discovery of the Company, her very purpose in this investigation—as a harmless, impractical scholar. She herself makes the mistake of relying upon organization to get things done and therefore assumes that Belbury's enemies would do the same. She lets Dimble get away, allowing the Company to remain veiled in mystery.

Worth mentioning in concluding this section on the images of good are first, the quiet, hidden, intimate conversions of Jane and Mark;[40] and second, the "unknown couple" who give Jane a necessary lift to the Manor at St. Anne's. This couple plays a vital but anonymous role in the larger drama.

*The Story of Arthur*

When Jane first visits the Dimbles in their home, Dr. Dimble starts talking about the Arthurian legend.[41] He brings it in in such a way that it appears to do the same thing for this novel that the pageantry and tableaux do for the *Faerie Queene*.[42] It gives a colorful background and realistic depth that transcends the present, both connecting the surface narrative with the early stages of European history and also hinting at something outside the story, the whole eschatological and chiliastic tapestry of the last generation.[43]

Dimble even helps us see it this way by acting as a sort of Master of the Pageants. But actually he is just doing what he would do as a teacher of English literature; this is just his way of seeing things—pointing out a pronounced antithesis of "two sets of characters," as he puts it:

> "There's Guinevere and Launcelot and all those people in the center; all very courtly and nothing particularly British about them. But then in the background—on the other side of Arthur, so to speak—there are all those *dark* people like Morgan and Morgawse, who are very British indeed and usually more or less hostile though they are his relatives. Mixed up with magic. You remember that wonderful phrase, how Queen Morgan 'set all the country on fire with ladies that were enchantresses.' Merlin too, of course, is British, though not hostile. Doesn't it look very like a picture of Britain as it must have been on the eve of the invasion?" (31).

Of course, Lewis as well as Dimble is setting the stage and in the process making his contribution to modern retellings of Malory's book.

Dimble carries the dichotomy he has introduced even further by juxtaposing "Logres" and "Britain."[44] He says that Logres haunts Britain. Arthur and Milton and Sidney characterize Logres; Mordred, Cromwell, and Cecil Rhodes, Britain. He aligns Belbury with Britain and St. Anne's with Logres, thereby making a credible realm for Merlin, the Fisher King, and the Pendragon.

The figure of Merlin appears as early as Jane's first dream as "a sort of ancient British, druidical kind of man, in a long mantle" (15).[45] Merlin is convenient for Lewis' purposes because of the mystery surrounding his interment, supposedly while he was yet living; so that his revival is a waking, not a resurrection.[46] Then too, Merlin is brought back so that his soul may be saved, Ransom tells him. He serves nicely as a link between Britain and Logres, since he is British in blood, yet associated with the Christians, and a Druid, yet familiar with the Grail.[47] Dimble muses that he may "represent the last trace of something the later tradition has quite forgotten about—something that became impossible when the only people in touch with the supernatural were either white or black, either priests or sorcerers" (32).

By having Dimble, the Dennistons, and Ransom associate Merlin with "the last vestiges of Atlantean magic" (201), claiming for him a kind of magic different from and superior to that of such occultists as Faust and Paracelsus, Lewis deftly lends him a realism; by placing Merlin's myth against a backdrop of still another myth (Atlantis), he makes him seem less mythical, more immediate.[48] Merlin is not only the last relic of the "Atlantean Circle," he is also the "Darkness" of the Dark Ages, a Pre-Roman, Pre-British creature familiar with the realities behind the "elves and ogres and wood-wooses of the later tradition" (265, 232-33). He embodies "all that age" of the powerful and fearsome Druids who ritually mixed the mortar for house-building with babies' blood (233). The Belbury forces think he comes from pre-glacial periods.

Lewis makes much of Merlin as the corporeity of an ancient, out-of-doors Nature that was wet, decaying, full of old trees and dead leaves; in short, Merlin as almost a beast, but not in any pejorative sense. "Merlin was like something that ought not to be indoors. Bathed and anointed though he was, a sense of mould, gravel, wet leaves, weedy water, hung about him" (287). Nevertheless, his is not the sensuality often associated with animality, but rather its sagacity. Merlin is left obscure enough that at first neither Belbury nor St. Anne's knows whose side he is on. He and his magical powers are rendered acceptable to the modern reader by the long series of speculations about him that the other characters make before he actually comes into the story personally.[49]

For Lewis' Fisher King, Ransom serves admirably. He seems to be much younger than the middle-aged man he is; he sustains a continually bleeding heel wound he received in mortal combat; he holds court in the Manor at St. Anne's; and he subsists on a diet of bread and wine.[50] Camilla tells Jane that he calls himself Mr. Fisher-King because his sister, a Mrs. Fisher-King, had offered to leave him a large fortune at her death if he would assume the name and an attendant role. That role was to be the headship of a company of folk who would gravitate to him and place themselves voluntarily under his authority for the purpose of combatting a greater danger that Mrs. Fisher-King and her mentor, a certain Indian Christian mystic called the Sura, believed would soon come upon the earth, specifically, upon England.[51]

At first Jane rebels at the idea of a Mr. Fisher-King assuming authority over her, discounting what Camilla and Arthur tell her as a fairy tale. Angrily she remembers something she had read in her childhood: "'And so the king promised that if anyone killed the dragon he would *give* him his daughter in marriage'" (117). Least of all she wants to meet "this Fisher-King man and [get] drawn into his orbit" (124). Therefore she is taken by surprise when she first senses him in one of her special dreams, although she does not know it is he:

And immediately she had the picture of someone, someone bearded but also (it was odd) divinely young, someone all golden and strong and warm coming with a mighty earth-shaking tread down into that black place.... Jane had an impression that she ought to courtesy to this person (136-37).

When at last Jane consents to meet him face to face, she is still sceptical, and even the "bright and golden" autumn sunlight falling on the carpet and walls does not prepare her for the confrontation with him: "Jane looked; and instantly her world was unmade" (142).[52] He appears to be a twenty-year-old boy, but the "gold hair and the gold beard of the wounded man," the manifest strength of his arms and shoulders that "could support the whole house," and the impression that she is standing before a mighty ruler in a throne room, all serve to dispel her doubts (142). "How could she have though him young? Or old either? It came over her, with a sensation of quick fear, that this face was of no age at all" (143). Suddenly she realizes that this man is different from all her contemporaries, that he is someone of another order:

But that was because she had long since forgotten the imagined Arthur of her childhood—and the imagined Solomon too. Solomon—for the first time in many years the bright solar blend of king and lover and magician which hangs about that name stole back upon her mind. For the first time in all those years she tasted the word *King* itself with all linked associations of battle, marriage, priesthood, mercy and power (143).

When he speaks she thinks again of sunlight and gold. "Like gold not only as gold is beautiful but as it is heavy" (143). His majesty overwhelms her. "For her world was unmade: anything might happen now.... All power of resistance seemed to have been drained away from her and she was left without protection" (143-44).

Much later Camilla explains to Jane that Mr. Fisher-King's endless youth is due to his experiences on Perelandra, where " 'Paradise is still going on' " (194). He would never grow a month older as long as he lived on Earth. She tells Jane that someday he would be taken back into Deep Heaven.

By making Ransom the Fisher King, Lewis accomplishes at least two important things: he enhances Ransom's suggestiveness of the Lord in a way similar to the Christ-likeness of Spenser's Prince Arthur, and he lends profundity and dignity to the person who would convert Jane to faith in Christ. Ransom's heel wound is reminiscent of the prophecy concerning Christ in Genesis 3:15: "And I will put enmity between thee and the woman, and between thy seed and her seed; it shall bruise thy head, and thou shalt bruise his heel."[53] Of course, Lewis also nicely weaves together Ransom's name with this and the other elements of the old legend that combine to suggest Christ: the bread and wine diet, the twelve knights in his attendance (Ransom himself has twelve attendant "knights," if one counts the eight humans plus the bear, cat, and jackdaw at the manor; but alas! one must not include the mice), and the questions put to him by Merlin. The dissimilarities do not concern us here.

Ransom as Mr. Fisher-King is mentioned always with reference to Jane or when Jane is somehow the center of attention; otherwise he is called by other titles. Jane comes to him as a modern unbeliever whose knowledge of literature far outweighs her knowledge of theology. Her conversion has to come about, if at all, by meeting a person who enacts, out of literature, as it were, Christ.

One of Ransom's other titles is the Pendragon.[54] Lewis nicely makes the lineage from Arthur to Ransom not necessarily a blood line. Dimble explains to the Company that

> "Ransom was summoned to the bedside of an old man then dying in Cumberland.... That man was the Pendragon, the successor of Arthur and Uther and Cassibelaun. Then we learned the truth. There has been a secret Logres in the very heart of Britain all these years; an unbroken succession of Pendragons. The old man was the seventy-eighth from Arthur: our Director received from him the office and the blessings; tomorrow we shall know, or tonight, who is to be the eightieth" (369).

Very probably the next Pendragon will be Arthur Denniston, who has not been doing very much throughout the narrative. His name bespeaks it, and he is the last one with Ransom at the end, Ransom having dismissed all the others. At any rate, Lewis unifies the several strands of the story of Arthur to his long novel's credit and the reader's satisfaction.[55]

# Notes

[1]*Spenser's Images of Life*, ed. Alastair Fowler (Cambridge: Cambridge University Press, 1967) 3; hereafter references are in the text.

[2]In a letter to Mr. Kinter, dated July 30, 1954, Lewis says: "I think *That Hideous Strength* is about a triple conflict: Grace against Nature and Nature against Anti-Nature (modern industrialism, scientism, and totalitarian policies)."

[3]See Kathryn Hume, "C.S. Lewis' Trilogy: A Cosmic Romance," *Modern Fiction Studies*, 20 (1974-75), 505-17. Professor Hume argues convincingly for the Ransom trilogy as a praiseworthy, artistic cosmic romance, "a work which expands the bounds and interests of the genre to higher spiritual levels than any romancer since Spenser at least has attempted in English" (517).

[4]C.S. Lewis, *That Hideous Strength* (New York: Macmillan, 1968), 83. All further page references appear in the text.

[5]Eugene Warren shows that this goddess has the same attributes as Venus in Lewis' *The Four Loves*; see "Venus Redeemed," *Orcrist*, 6 (1971-72), 14.

[6]Cf. Richard Purtill, "*That Hideous Strength:* A Double Story," in *The Longing*

*for a Form: Essays on the Fiction of C.S. Lewis,* ed. Peter J. Schakel (Kent State UP, 1977), 91-102. Purtill believes that the novel's structure is like the contrast of the cities of God and man in St. Augustine, that "the dialectic of the theme is echoed by the dialectic of the tale," and that "the finer structure of the story also displays an intricate and detailed opposition of scenes and character" (91). See also Charles Moorman, *The Precincts of Felicity: The Augustinian City of the Oxford Christians* (Gainesville: U of Florida P, 1966): "*That Hideous Strength* is...Lewis' best novel, since in it he has discovered a set of images and characters which can convey his theme far better than could the 'silent planet' myth" (75). Purtill thinks *That Hideous Strength* "is, if you like, a sermon, preached against certain dangers of our times...and like all sermons its purpose is to make us repent and change our ways. That it is addressed to our condition is proved by the kind of opposition it has aroused" (102). Patrick J. Callahan disagrees with this view. He argues that Lewis' concern is not theological, "much less an apology for church orthodoxy," but moral. He says that Lewis is doing what Jonathan Swift did in *Gulliver's Travels*: "Although Lewis has as acute a Christian consciousness as had Swift, he, like Swift, refrains from preaching. He renders his morality into the image, symbol, and dramatic situation of art." For a study of the garden archetype, see Callahan's article, "The Two Gardens in C.S. Lewis' *That Hideous Strength,*" in *SF: The Other Side of Realism: Essays on Modern Fantasy and Science Fiction,* ed. Thomas D. Clareson (Bowling Green, Ohio: Popular Press, 1971), 147, 149. Judith Brown, in "The Pilgrimage from Deep Space," *Mythlore,* 15 (1977), supposes that Lewis' *Pilgrim's Regress* "might be a prototype for *That Hideous Strength.*" She says that for "nearly every member of the N.I.C.E. there is a pilgrim from St. Anne's going towards the mountains" (15). For the origin of the Ransom trilogy, see Roger Lancelyn Green and Walter Hooper, *C.S. Lewis: A Biography* (London: Collins, 1974), 164, 174-75, 179. Of course, Lewis says in his Preface to *THS* that he intended it to illustrate his argument in *The Abolition of Man.* See Clyde S. Kilby, *The Christian World of C.S. Lewis* (Grand Rapids: Eerdmans, 1964), 104-15; and *Images of Salvation in the Fiction of C.S. Lewis* (Wheaton, Ill.: Harold Shaw, 1978), 107-23, for balanced commentaries.

[7]For negative reactions to *THS,* see Chad Walsh, *The Literary Legacy of C.S. Lewis* (New York: Harcourt 1979); and William Luther White, *The Image of Man in C.S. Lewis* (Nashville: Abingdon). Walsh says that *THS* "is, for a literary critic, a more troubling book than the two other space fantasies. The fundamental question is whether Lewis tried to pack too much into it, and whether the final chapters lose strength and cogency because of this. The problem is one of pacing. How much intensity and catastrophe can a reader absorb before his capacity to respond is dulled? The book is also intellectually overstuffed. It is as though Lewis has taken a series of convictions dear to his heart, and forced them between the covers of one book" (118). White thinks *That Hideous Strength* "fails to give the 'new and sharper insight into reality' [quoting Rudolf Schmer] which readers have a right to expect of fantasy.... The complexities and improbabilities of the material detract from the impact of the work" (134).

[8]Edward G. Zogby, S.J., sees *THS* as "a movement from archetype to anagoge, from speculation on the universal truth to that same truth brought into contemporary personal experience.... That which moves this story...from archetype to anagoge is the story within the story, the failing marriage of Jane and Mark Studdock.... That anagogic level of the story is thus located in the reordering of the archetype within the self of both Jane and Mark so that the Presence which gives the archetype power to reconcile coinciding opposites without destroying their particular

individuality can deal life to them"; cf. "Triadic Patterns in Lewis' Life and Thought," in *The Longing for a Form* (26; 27).

[9]For incisive comment on Jane and Mark's desperate moral need to jettison their hell-worthy sophistication for "the real ancient business of marriage": ordinariness, see Thomas Howard, "The 'Moral Mythology' of C.S. Lewis," *Modern Age*, 22 (1978), 391-92.

[10]Fr. Zogby notes: "Polarities yield trinities; this is what the imagination knows. This the Feminine knows as it stands before the Masculine. When polarities remain simply two poles without a relationship of coinciding opposition, no marriage or union is possible. Without the imagination impressed by God's grandeur, one is condemned to a sterile, barren marriage bed; such was the problem facing Jane and mark Studdock in *That Hideous Strength*" (36).

[11]Gilbert Meilaender, in his impressive book, suggests that one of the things the N.I.C.E. is doing is what we call "genetic engineering"; *The Taste for the Other: The Social and Ethical Thought of C.S. Lewis* (Grand Rapids: Eerdmans, 1978), 219.

[12]Filostrato's ideal is a dystopia. See Chad Walsh, *From Utopia to Nightmare* (New York: Harper, 1962), 139.

[13]For a wrongheaded approach to *THS*, see Robert Plank, "Some Psychological Aspects of Lewis' Trilogy, in *Shadows of Imagination: The Fantasies of C.S. Lewis, J.R.R. Tolkien, and Charles Williams*, ed. Mark R. Hillegas; new ed. (Carbondale: Southern Illinois University Press, 1979). Plank thinks that not only does Lewis mean to identify the Studdocks's practice of birth control with the "golemistic practices" on Sulva, but also that he "included the Merlin-Jane episode to provide a belated rationale for his golem fantasy; and that it is this fantasy that really matters to him" (33)!

[14]For a discussion of the idea that sex in *THS* has a "spiritual validity," see Corbin S. Carnell, *Bright Shadow of Reality: C.S. Lewis and the Feeling Intellect* (Grand Rapids: Eerdmans, 1974), 124-27. See Meilaender, 148-59, for a careful delineation of the centrality of marriage in *THS*.

[15]See Howard's reminder of the moral idea behind "the traditional, ancient ordering of hierarchy": "It is when the gods are enthroned in their heavens that you find all heroes and noble heroines as figures in the stories. In Greek tragedy, in Nordic saga, in Shakespearean tragedy, and in thirteenth century figures of the Madonna crowned with gold, you find the paradox: those noble and blissful images of humanity emerged, not from the emancipated late centuries of human history, but straight from the ages when we saw ourselves as walking under authority, robed in the splendor that had been given us in the ordering of things, and bearing the burden of obedience" (*Modern Age*, p. 389).

[16]Lewis wrote to E.R. Eddison on 30 December 1942 for information about "Arcturogamie or bears-bridal": "Sir, if you knowe/ought of the nuptiall practices and amorous/carriages of beares, fayle not to let me knowe,/for I have brought in a beare in the book I/now write and it shal to bedde at the end/with the others."

[17]At least one writer presumes that *Urendi Maleldil* means *Dominus vobiscum;* cf. R.J. Reilly, *Romantic Religion: A Study of Barfield, Lewis, Williams, and Tolkien* (Athens: U of Georgia P, 1971), p. 135. This appears in his discussion of the numinous in *THS*.

[18]Warren thinks this tall lady is the "redeemed" Venus, named Perelandra (Venus Redeemed," p. 15).

[19]In a letter to Miss Montgomery, dated June 10th, 1952, Lewis explains: "Oh,

I just 'made up' all those things in *That Hideous Strength*; i.e. I took existing. . . tendencies and produced them (in the geometrical sense—Produce the line AB to the point X) to show how dreadful they might become if we didn't take care."

[20]Perhaps the most celebrated attack on the novel (and its author) was made by J.B.S. Haldane in his essay, "Auld Hornie, F.R.S.," *The Modern Quarterly* (Autumn 1946); rpt. in *Shadows of the Imagination*, 15-25. Haldane was one of several critics who have expressed uneasiness about the implication of the N.I.C.E. for Lewis' attitude toward science. Haldane sounds like Straik in the conclusion of his essay: "I would state my case briefly as follows. I agree with Mr. Lewis that man is in a sense a fallen being. . . . But I disagree with him in that I also believe that man can rise again by his own efforts" (24). In "A Reply to Professor Haldane," *Of Other Worlds: Essay and Stories*, ed. Walter Hooper (New York: Harcourt, 1967), Lewis says that if *THS* could be reduced to a proposition it would certainly be "not 'scientific planning will certainly lead to Hell,' but 'Under modern conditions any effective invitation to Hell will certainly appear in the guise of scientific planning'—as Hitler's regime in fact did" (80). In a letter to Mr. Clarke, dated Dec. 7 [1945], Lewis says: "I agree Technology is *per se* neutral: but a race devoted to the increase of its own power by technology with complete indifference to ethics *does* seem to me a cancer in the universe. Certainly if he goes on his present course much further man can *not* be trusted with knowledge." Chad Walsh, in his earlier book, *C.S. Lewis: Apostle to the Skeptics* (New York: Macmillan, 1949), recalls a conversation with Lewis on this topic: "Somehow the subject of N.I.C.E. came up once when I was with Lewis and I asked him whether he was against science. He answered—with unusual warmth—that he was not. " 'Science is neither an enemy nor a friend,' he said. 'Science is not a *person*!' " (129). And in a letter he wrote to Mr. Canfield on 28 February 1955, Lewis urges him: "note that what is attacked in my story is not scientists but (what is growing in the real world) a kind of political conspiracy using science as its pretext. All tyrants avail themselves of whatever pretext is most popular in their age. As earlier tyrants made religion their pretext, of course modern ones make science theirs. The only real disinterested scientist in my book (Hingest) has to be murdered by the conspirators. The best scientist (Filostrato) is not in the inner circle. Jules is only a novelist."

[21]See Paul L. Holmer, *C.S. Lewis: The Shape of His Faith and Thought* (New York: Harper and Row, 1976), for a discussion of *THS* as it relates to modern language philosophy and phenomenology. Holmer believes that the "tragedy at Belbury is that Frost has to destroy everybody else's subjectivity so that his alone governs. Somehow he wants to believe that by saying that all value is subjective he at least has made a claim compatible with the facts. But he has only fooled himself" (p. 57). Holmer calls this "the fact-value bifurcation" (p. 58). "Lewis will not concur with the notion that the language of science is uniquely objective. Furthermore, he rejects categorically the view that there is only one literal language that reproduces the structure of the world" (p. 59).

[22]"The Inner Ring," in *The Weight of Glory and Other Addresses* (Grand Rapids: Eerdmans, 1965 [1949]), pp. 55-66. In his "Reply to Professor Haldane," Lewis says that the desire of men to be in the inner ring is "the chief theme" of *That Hideous Strength (Of Other Worlds*, p. 79).

[23]Holmer says, "Lewis would have us all remember that the more we identify with the modern age and the spirit of the times, the less likely we are to be clear about ourselves" (*op. cit.*, p. 79(.

[24]In a letter to Mr. Evans, dated 26th September 1945, Lewis remarks: "I'm glad

you recognized the N.I.C.E. as not being quite the fantastic absurdity some readers think. I hadn't myself thought that any of the people in contemporary rackets were *really* dabbling in Magic; I had supposed that to be a roma tic [sic] addition of my own. But there you are. The trouble about writing satire is that the real world always anticipates you, and what were meant for exaggerations turn out to be nothing of the sort."

[25]Kathryn Hume (514-15) shows that the N.I.C.E. is linked "ineluctably" with the chief symbols of evil in *Out of the Silent Planet* and *Perelandra*—the hnakra and Weston, the Unman.

[26]Cf. Mark R. Hillegas, *The Future as Nightmare: H.G. Wells and the Utopians* (Carbondale: Southern Illinois UP, 1967), for his interpretation of *THS*. Hillegas says that by "showing the dark *eldila* of earth as aiding the men of the N.I.C.E. so to create the New Man, Lewis presented a grotesque and sinister caricature of the vision so often identified with Wells. No anti-utopia exists which is more counter-Wellsian that *That Hideous Strength*"(144). Hillegas says that Wells appears in the novel as Horace Jules, the D.D. of the N.I.C.E. (136). But Green and Hooper sharply deny it (*Biography*, 164).

[27]See Robert Scholes, *Structural Fabulation: An Essay on Fiction of the Future* (Notre Dame: U of Notre Dame P, 1975), for a scathing criticism of Lewis. Scholes compares him unfavorably with Ursula le Guin, author of the earth-sea fantasies: "Where C.S. Lewis worked out of a specifically Christian set of values, Ursula le Guin works not with a theology but with an ecology, a cosmology, a reverence for the universe as a self-regulating structure. This seems to me more relevant to our needs than Lewis, but not simply because it is closer to the great pre-Christian mythologies of the world and also closer to what three centuries of science have been able to discover about the nature of the universe" (82). "In C.S. Lewis's universe, which is the traditional Christian universe, God...[distorts] the natural balance of the universe. God accepts the blame for man's sin without accepting the responsibility, leaving the world forever unbalanced, with man forever burdened by a debt that cannot be repaid" (85).

[28]Chad Walsh thinks that "the realistic elements in the narration are invariably successful. The fantasy gives rise to problems. The final triumph of goodness and God's forces leaves a number of troubling questions in the reader's mind" (120). Plank says he has "the impression of Lewis endlessly gloating over all the spilled blood" at Belbury (35). He thinks Lewis has a "gusto for violence" (34). But other critics would not agree. Ed Chapman in his unusual essay, "Toward a Sacramental Ecology: Technology, Nature, and Transcendence in C.S. Lewis's Ransom Trilogy," *Mythlore*, 3 (1976), 10-17, shows that with "fitting irony the N.I.C.E. is destroyed in part by ecological disasters which the Institute has helped to create" (15). Corbin S. Carnell likens the fall of Belbury to Armageddon (*Bright Shadow*, 99), and Fr. Zogby also thinks of this novel as a picture of the eschaton ("Triadic Patterns," 26). Professor Kilby sees the final judgment on Belbury as "shockingly complete." He says, "I suspect that he [Lewis] had at least partly in mind Second Thessalonians 1:7-8, where we are told that the Lord 'shall be revealed from heaven with His mighty angels, in flaming fire taking vengeance on them that know not God' " (*Images*, 122). Charles Moorman, who sees Belbury as the *Civitas Terrena* as over against St. Anne's as the *Civitas Dei*, lends support to this view (cf. *Precincts*, 76-874).

[29]Chapman argues: "Ecological sanity is embodied in St. Anne's in contrast to the sterility images and the worship of technology represented by Belbury.... But St. Anne's symbolizes more than mere ecological sanity; it represents a movement

back to a sacramental consciousness of nature, and a sacramental relationship with nature" (15). Chapman says Merlin has this consciousness and relationship.

[30]Callahan sees the archetype of the garden as the "symbolic center of the novel" (p. 149). He relates the garden at St. Anne's to the Garden of Adonis in *The Faerie Queene*, order, and fertility. For a better study of the garden archetype in *THS* see Nancy-Lou Patterson, "Anti-Babels: Images of the Divine Center in *That Hideous Strength*," *Mythcon II Proceedings*, ed. Glen GoodKnight, 6-11.

[31]For a thoughtful discussion of the place of animals in community, see Meilaender, *Taste*, 84-86.

[32]For Barfield's thinking on the evolution of consciousness, see Owen Barfield, *Romanticism Comes of Age* (Rudolf Steiner Press, 1966), 184-204; and *Evolution of Consciousness: Studies in Polarity*, ed. Shirley Sugerman (Middletown, Conn.: Wesleyan UP, 1976), p. 3-28. For his writing on "primal unity," see *The Rediscovery of Meaning and Other Essays* (Middletown: Wesleyan UP, 1977), 11-21; and *Poetic Diction: A Study in Meaning*, 3rd ed. (Middletown: Wesleyan UP, 1973), 86-87.

[33]In *The Allegory of Love*, Lewis notes the word *Oyarses* in Bernardus Sylvestris and relates it to planetary intelligences (362). In *The Discarded Image* he explains the medieval view of planetary intelligences "that each sphere, or something resident in each sphere, is a conscious and intellectual being, moved by 'intellectual love' of God.... These lofty creatures are called Intelligences. The relation between the Intelligence of a sphere and the sphere itself as a physical object was variously conceived. The old view was that the Intelligence is 'in' the sphere as the soul is 'in' the body, so that the planets are, as Plato would have agreed,—Celestial animals, animate bodies or incarnate minds." In a letter he wrote to Sister Penelope, dated January 31, 1946, Lewis comments on the Oyeresu from another perspective: "*That Hideous Strength* has been unanimously damned by all reviewers. About Holst's *Planets*, I heard Mars and Jupiter long ago and greatly admired them but have heard the complete work only in...the last 6 weeks. But his characters are rather different from mine, I think. Wasn't his Mars brutal and ferocious?—in mine I tried to get the *good* element in the martial spirit, the discipline and freedom from anxiety. On Jupiter I am closer to him: but I think his is more 'jovial' in the *modern* sense of the word. The folk tune on which he bases it is not regal enough for my conception. But of course there is a general similarity because we're both following the medieval astrologers." Among those who find fault with *THS* is Wayne Shumaker in "The Cosmic Trilogy of C.S. Lewis," *Hudson Review*, 8 (1955), 240-54; reprinted in *The Longing for a Form*, 51-63. Shumaker criticizes Lewis for permitting "disembodied spirit" "to take matters out of the hands of the human agents." He thinks it is seriously unfortunate, "for it is not on Mars or Venus, but on Earth, that the real test of the Christian world view must come," he says (63). Somewhat stronger are Haldane's remarks. As a scientist, humanist, and Marxist, Haldane attacks Lewis on several fronts, occasionally damning him with faint praise, as when he compares him with Dante and Milton, but then adds a mordant satire: "Christian mythology incorporated the cosmological theories current eighteen centuries ago. Dante found it a slight strain to combine this mythology with the facts known in his own day. Milton found it harder. Lewis finds it impossible" (p. 16).

[34]Lewis uses these adjectives in *Surprised by Joy* to describe certain great artists he became capable of appreciating (198).

[35]Moorman, who sees St. Anne's as an image of the city, finds this image in *THS* serving three functions—"as a transition stage between life and death, as an opposition of the Cities of God and Earth, and as the basis for a theory of history

[the redemption of man]" (*Precincts,* 82). Callahan says that "St. Anne's symbolizes the life-giving female body" and contrasts it with Belbury's "perversion and sterility" symbol, Fairy Hardcastle (152).

[36]Professor Kilby observes that one "familiar with Acts 2 may find a number of parallels between the coming of the Oyeresu and the glorious visitation of the Holy Spirit at Pentecost" (*Images,* 119). One critic who has found them is William White (*Image of Man,* 133). See also Brian C. Bond, "The Unity of Word: Language in C.S. Lewis's Trilogy," *Mythlore,* 2 (1972), 13-15.

[37]See Howard (390) for a splendid evocation of the Great Dance in modern terms. Leanne Payne, in *Real Presence: The Holy Spirit in the Work of C.S. Lewis* (Westchester, Ill.: Cornerstone Books, 1979), says that the Key to the Great Dance is obedience: "Not only must we listen in the presence of the Father, but we must let the Son and Holy Spirit respond in obedience through us" (87).

[38]In a letter to Father Peter Milward, dated 4/7/55, Lewis says of Ransom: "I'm afraid I made him a philologist chiefly to render his rapid mastery of Old Solar more plausible. His friends in *THS* are a literary critic (Dimble), a Doctor (Miss I.), an unspecified scientist (MacPhee), a scholar's wife, a charwoman, and a bear! It is v. important that there are 2 untainted scientists in the book (MacPhee & Hingest), as many of the Belbury group are not scientists at all." Purtill thinks that Grace Ironwood does not succeed: "This is one of the few instances...where Lewis has painted himself into a corner from a literary point of view." "But in order to give St. Anne's this initially unsympathetic face, Lewis created a somewhat unsympathetic character, Grace Ironwood, who is a slight embarrassment to him in later scenes" (98).

[39]Richard Purtill, in *Lord of the Elves and Eldils: Fantasy and Philosophy in C.S. Lewis and J.R.R. Tolkien* (Grand Rapids: Zondervan, 1974), makes the following astute observation of Lewis' achievement: "Indeed, I suspect that part of the indignation some moderns feel about Lewis—their accusations that he writes "propaganda' or, absurdly, "a formal apology for Christianity'—is that he applies one of their own techniques in reverse. The modern temper has been fed to some extent on works in which the pleasant characters represent science, progress, political leftism, and so on, and the unpleasant characters represent religion, absolute ethical values, tradition, and so on. H.G. Wells is a vintage source of this kind of technique. But in Lewis the allocations of virtue and vice are reversed. No one in his right mind would want to be a part of the 'society' at Belbury, and it requires very strong prejudices indeed not to be attracted by the company at St. Anne's. But whereas people like Wells did almost seem to be saying that 'progressives' are Nice People and 'reactionaries' are Nasty People, Lewis is not saying that Christians are Nice People and scientists are Nasty People. He is saying that morally good people, people who *act* on the Christian principles of love and justice—even if, like MacPhee, they are honest unbelievers—are people it is good to be among; and morally evil people, whose lives are based on self-love and hatred of others—even if, like Straik, they use the language of religion—are people it is bad to be among, and this is true as a matter of experience, even if it were not almost true by definition."

[40]Professor Kilby notes that in Jane and Mark "the symbol of final spiritual awareness is the wish to read childhood stories, a strong echo of our Lord's remark that childlikeness is a mark of the Kingdom of Heaven" (*Images,* 121). See also Charles J. Nolan, Jr., "The Child Motif in *That Hideous Strength,*" *New York C.S. Lewis Society Bulletin,* 5 (1974), x, 5-7.

[41]For the standard discussion of *THS* as a modern retelling or adaptation of

Arthurian romance, see Nathan Comfort Starr, *King Arthur Today: The Arthurian Legend in English and American Literature, 1902-1953* (Gainesville: U of Florida P, 1954), 142, 143, 181-87. Starr concludes: "*That Hideous Strength* deserves an honored place in the Arthurian legend, for it is a highly original restatement of old truths applied to our violent, distraught world, and it is conceived in terms of vaulting imagination" (187).

[42]For a different view, see Gunnar Urang, *Shadows of Heaven: Religion and Fantasy in the Writing of C.S. Lewis, Charles Williams, and J.R.R. Tolkien* (Philadelphia: Pilgrim Press, 1971). Urang thinks that "the satiric and grotesque elements tend to overwhelm the mythic ones. The myth itself seems synthetic and contrived. Lewis has been left with the mythical apparatus from the earlier books which has to be made relevant to the new earthly setting and has to be integrated with the Arthurian material he now wishes to introduce. The welding does not hold, the machinery creaks and groans, and the result has neither the haunting simplicity nor the focused intensity required for mythopoeic power" (27).

[43]For possibly the finest analysis of the Arthurian elements in *THS* in the context of the Ransom trilogy, see Charles Moorman, *Arthurian Triptych: Mythic Materials in Charles Williams, C.S. Lewis, and T.S. Eliot* (Berkeley: U of California P, 1960). Moorman believes that Lewis uses the Arthurian myth to take the place of the "silent-planet myth" (112). "What Lewis seems to see in the Arthurian myth is a metaphor that will fit within the overall scheme of the silent-planet myth and at the same time reinforce his general scheme by expressing it in yet another and more overtly literary set of terms" (114).

[44]See Carnell, 97-102, who explains that "Logres is perceived in Britain always when men respond to that which comes from 'without,' inspiring awe, mystery, and awareness of something holy. Logres represents the impingement of the supernatural, not in any simple two-story world but rather in a world where the two kinds of reality 'co-inhere'. Thus for Lewis as for Charles Williams (and for Plato) the real is not *ganz anders* but the archetype of the Phenomenal" (100-01). See also Meilaender, 102-104.

[45]Lewis, in the previously cited letter to Mr. Evans, says: "About Merlin: *don't know much more than you do....* But the blessing about Merlin (for you and me) is that 'very little is known'—so we have a free hand."

[46]Green and Hooper muse that "something of [the] grander Yeats [whom Lewis knew early in his career] may have helped to create Merlin in *That Hideous Strength*" (67).

[47]Walsh fears that Merlin "comes close to being a *deus ex machina*" (*Legacy*, 119).

[48]Green and Hooper fear that the "introduction of Merlin with the tantalizing hints about the Circle of Logres, Numinor and 'the last vestiges of Atlantean magic', must strike many readers as the least successfully achieved strand in the whole web" (176).

[49]Margaret Hannay, "Arthurian and Cosmic Myth in *Thad Hideous Strength, Mythlore*, 2 (1970), 7-9, argues that the cosmic myth and Arthurian elements are tied together by the riddle game in which Merlin questions Ransom (9).

[50]Walsh thinks that of the major characters, "only Ransom himself...is a shade ghostly, almost as though he were pure spirit temporarily caught in the confines of a body" (*Legacy*, 120).

[51]Dr. Hannay believes that the justification offered for Ransom's "mythical function" as Fisher-King is weak, "a bit far-fetched" (9).

[52]Kathryn Hume says that Ransom, in his fight against the Unman on Perelandra had received "the transpersonal force which Neumann labels Higher Cultural Masculinity, a benevolent embodiment of the archetypal First Father, which works toward harmony, organization, social stability, and spiritual enlightenment" (507). She notes that "Ransom passes from what Northrop Frye identifies as the active to the contemplative, penseroso stage and becomes the figure of Higher Cultural Masculinity to whom lesser mortals must learn to ally themselves" (513).

[53]Moorman observes: "The wounded heel also suggests, of course, the vulnerable heel of Achilles which in that myth also functions as a symbol of the hero's humanity" (116-17). "The wounded heel becomes a symbol of the hero's humanity" (116-17). "The wounded heel becomes a symbol of Mr. Fisher-King's heritage both as a Keeper of the grail and as a man among men, and by transferring the wound from thigh to heel, Lewis involves both myths" (117).

[54]Moorman says: "Lewis views the Arthurian myth from Williams' vantage point; thus, he thinks of Arthurian Britain as the ideal secular civilization awaiting a reconciliation with its religious counterpart. By making the triple identification, Ransom-Fisher-King-Pendragon, Lewis completes Williams' pattern by joining the Grail (Mr. Fisher-King) with the ideal Kingdom (the Pendragon) with Deep Heaven (Ransom the voyager). The menage of Mr. Fisher-King represents, within this novel, a microcosm of the Arthurian court. . . ." (117-18).

[55]Moorman says that in his selected use of Arthurian materials "Lewis is able by indirection to imply the whole history of the Table and through this implication to suggest a comparison between Logres and modern England. . . . Through the Arthurian myth, Lewis conveys the impression that we are dealing not merely with the moral struggles of Jane and Mark Studdock, but with issues of momentous importance, issues that once split the kingdom and destroyed the civilization whose unification could have brought about the Second Coming. The presence of the Arthurian materials thus suggests the gravity of the issue. . . . It would have been impossible to suggest a theme of such grandeur and magnitude in terms of the battle between Bracton College and Belbury. . . . But to place the battle within the Arthurian context magnifies and gives meaning to the theme. . . . The Arthurian myth, in short, gives to the fictional situation of *THS* the full meaning and power inherent in its own structure" (125-26).

# Part IV:

# C.S. Lewis and His Critical Milieu

# C.S. Lewis: The Natural Law in Literature and Life

*Kathryn Lindskoog and*
*Gracia Fay Ellwood*

The human race is haunted by the idea of doing what is right. In the first five chapters of Mere Christianity, C.S. Lewis discusses the fact that people are always referring to some standard of behavior that they expect other people to know about. People are always defending themselves by arguing that what they have been doing does not really go against that standard, or that they have some special excuse for violating it.

What they have in mind is a law of fair play or a rule of decent behavior. Different people use different labels for this law—traditional morality or the Moral Law, the knowledge of right and wrong, or Virtue, or the Way. We choose to call it the Natural Law. This law is an obvious principle that is not made up by humans but is for humans to obey. Lewis claims that all over the earth humans know about this law, and all over the earth they break it; he further claims that there is Something or Somebody behind this Natural Law.

According to Lewis, we find out more about God from Natural Law than from the universe in general, just as we find out more about a person by listening to his conversation than by looking at a house he built. We can tell from Natural Law that the Being behind the universe is intensely interested in fair play, unselfishness, courage, good faith, honesty and truthfulness. However, the Natural Law does not give us any grounds for assuming that God is soft or indulgent. Natural Law obliges us to do the straight thing no matter how painful or dangerous or difficult it is to do. Natural Law is hard: "It is as hard as nails" (*Mere Christianity* 23).

This last sentence also appears as the central thought in Lewis's moving poem "Love." In the first stanza he tells us how love is as warm as tears; in the second, how it is as fierce as fire; in the third, how it is as fresh as spring. And in the final stanza he tells us how love is as hard as nails.

Love's as hard as nails,
  Love is nails;
Blunt, thick, hammered through
The medial nerve of One
Who, having made us, knew
The thing He had done,
Seeing (with all that is)
Our cross, and His. (*Poems* 123).

In Lewis's first chronicle of Narnia, *The Lion, The Witch and The Wardrobe,* this hardness of the love of God was predicted by the lion Aslan when he promised to save Edmund from the results of treachery. He said "All shall by done. But it may be harder than you think" (104). When he and the White Witch discussed her claim on Edmund's life, she referred to the law of that universe as the Deep Magic. Aslan would not consider going against the Deep Magic; instead, he gave himself to die in Edmund's place, and the next morning came back to life. He explained to Susan that though the Witch knew the Deep Magic, there is a far deeper magic that she did not know. This deeper magic says that when a willing victim is killed in place of a traitor, death itself would start working backwards. The deepest magic worked toward life and goodness.

In Narnia, and in this world as well, if the universe is not governed by an absolute goodness all our efforts and hopes are doomed. But if the universe *is* ruled by perfect goodness, says Lewis, we are falling short of that goodness all the time; we are not good enough to consider ourselves allies of perfect goodness (*Mere* 4). In Narnia Edmund fell so far short of goodness that he finally realized with a shock of despair that he needed forgiveness.

At the end of the chapter entitled "Right and Wrong As A Clue to the Meaning of the Universe" in *Mere Christianity,* Lewis claimed that until people repent and want forgiveness, Christianity won't make sense. Christianity explains how God can be the impersonal mind behind the Natural Law and yet also be a Person. It tells us how, since we cannot meet the demands of the law, God Himself became a human being to save us from our failure.

Lewis was of course aware that the presence of natural and moral evil in the world makes the governance of the world by absolute goodness seem questionable, to say the least. He understood Housman in his bitter complaint against "whatever brute and blackguard made the world." But Lewis asks by what standard the creator is judged a blackguard. The very lament for Moral law or rejection of Moral Law itself implies a Moral Law.

Lewis was deeply concerned about the fact that many people in this century are losing their belief in Natural Law. He spoke about this in the Riddell Memorial Lectures given at the University of Durham, published in 1947 as *The Abolition of Man.*

In *Abolition* he used "the Tao" as a shorthand term for the Natural Law or First Principle. This choice of label is perhaps unfortunate. It is hard to believe that he read, received (to use his own language) and savored the *Tao Te Ching,* Taoism's scripture, and came away with the sense that "Tao" is the most accurate and succinct term to use for the moral law. Although the Tao is finally ineffable, according to the *Tao Te Ching,* it can best be described with words such as "the Flow," "the way things change," "the Life," "the Source." To follow the Tao is indeed to live morally, for it requires respect for the lowly and avoidance of oppression or pride. However, the Tao is ultimately a way of accepting what is, whether good or evil. Lewis might have done better in *Abolition* to stay with the term Moral Law or Natural Law, or if he wished to use Chinese thought, "the Will of Heaven."

Lewis claimed in *Abolition* that until quite recent times everyone believed that objects could merit our approval or disapproval, our reverence or our contempt. It was assumed that some emotional reactions were more appropriate than others.

This conception is vividly represented in *The Lion, The Witch and the Wardrobe*; Edmund had inappropriate emotional responses from the very beginning. When his brother and sisters imagined pleasant creatures they would like to meet in the woods, he hoped for snakes. When the children met the wise old professor, Edmund laughed at his looks. When Edmund met the White Witch, his initial fear quickly turned to trust; and when she gave him a choice of foods, he stuffed himself with Turkish Delight candy. His attitude toward his sister Lucy was resentful and superior; he was even suspicious of the good Robin and Beaver who came to guide the children to safety. Instead of noticing the Beaver's house, he noticed the location of the Witch's castle in the distance. When the name Aslan was first spoken to the four children, they all had wonderful feelings except Edmund; he had a sensation of mysterious horror. Later events would educate Edmund to respond as the others did.

Lewis pointed out that according to Aristotle the aim of education, the foundation of ethics, was to make a pupil like and dislike what he ought. According to Plato, we need to learn to feel pleasure at pleasant things, liking for likeable things, disgust for disgusting things, and hatred for hateful things. In early Hindu teaching righteousness and correctness corresponded to knowing truth and reality. Psalm 119 says the law is "true." The Hebrew word for truth here is "emeth," meaning intrinsic validity, rock-bottom reality, and a firmness and dependability as solid as nature.

This meaning is reflected in the final book of Narnia, *The Last Battle,* where Lewis introduced a young man named Emeth who had grown up in an oppressive country where people worship an evil god named Tash. In spite of his upbringing, Emeth was a man of honor and honesty who sought what was good. He died worshipping Tash and found himself in the presence of Aslan instead. He responded with reverence and delight. All that he though he was doing for Tash could be counted as service to Aslan instead. He was one of Aslan's friends long before he knew it because he liked what was likeable and hated what was hateful.

Lewis was alarmed by all the people in our day who deny that some things are inherently likeable, debunking traditional morality and the Natural Law, thinking that there can be innovation in values. Some of them try to substitute necessity, progress or efficiency for goodness. But in fact necessity, progress or efficiency have to be related to a standard outside themselves to have any meaning. In many cases that standard will be, in the last analysis, the preservation of the person who thinks of himself as a moral innovator, or the preservation of the society of his choice. Such people direct their scepticism toward any values but their own, disparaging other values as "sentimental" (*Abolition* 19).

But Lewis's analysis shows that if Natural Law is sentimental, *all* value is sentimental. No factual propositions such as "our society is in danger of extinction" can give any basis for a system of values; no observations of instinct such as "I want to prolong my life" give any basis for a system of values. Why is our society valuable? Why is my life worth preserving? Only the Natural Law, asserting that human life is of value, gives us a basis for a coherent system of values.

"If nothing is self evident, nothing can be proved," Lewis claimed. "If nothing is obligatory for its own sake, nothing is obligatory at all" (27). He means that if we do not accept Natural law as self-evident and obligatory for its own sake, then all a person's conceptions of value fall away. There are no values that are not derived from Natural Law. Anything that is judged good is such because of values in the Natural Law. The concept of goodness springs from no other source.

Thus, modern innovations in ethics are just shreds of the old Natural Law, sometimes isolated and exaggerated. If any values at all are retained, the Natural Law is retained. According to Lewis, there never has been and never will be a radically new value or value system. The human mind has no more power of inventing a new value than of inventing a new primary color.

Admittedly, there are imperfections and contradictions in historical manifestation and interpretations of Natural Law. Some reformers help us to improve our perceptions of value. But only those who live by the Law know its spirit well enough to interpret it successfully. People who live outside the Natural Law have no grounds for criticizing Natural Law or anything else. A few who reject it intend to take the logical next step as well: they intend to live without any values at all, disbelieving all values and choosing to live their lives according to their whims and fancies.

Lewis's poem "The Country of the Blind," published in *Punch* in 1951, presents an image of people who have come to this. He describes what it would be like to live as a misfit with eyes in a country of eyeless people who no longer believe that vision ever existed.

This poem tells of "hard" light shining on a whole nation of eyeless men who were unaware of their handicap. Blindness had come on gradually through many centuries. At some transitional stage a few citizens remained who still had eyes and vision after most people were blind. The blind were normal and up-to-date. They used the same words that their ancestors had used, but no longer knew their meaning. They spoke of *light* still, meaning an abstract thought. If one who could see tried to describe the grey dawn or the stars or the green-sloped sea waves or the color of a lady's cheek, the blind majority insisted that they understood the feeling the sighted one expressed in metaphor. There was no way he could explain the facts to them. The blind ridiculed such a person who took figures of speech literally and concocted a myth about a kind of sense perception that no one has ever really had.

If one thinks this is a far-fetched picture, Lewis concluded, one need only go to famous men today and try to talk to them about the truths of Natural Law which used to stand huge, awesome, and clear to the inner eye.

One of those famous men is B. F. Skinner, who answered in his book *Beyond Freedom and Dignity* that the abolition of the inner man and traditional morality is necessary so that science can prevent the abolition of the human race. Lewis had already exclaimed in *Abolition*, "The preservation of the species?—But why should the species be preserved?" (40) Skinner does not provide an answer, but welcomes Lewis's scientific "Controllers" who aim to change and dehumanize the human race in order more efficiently to fulfill their purposes.

Lewis satirized this kind of progress in his poem "Evolutionary Hymn," which appeared in *The Cambridge Review* in 1957. Using Longfellow's popular hymn stanza form from "Psalm of Life," Lewis exclaimed: What do we care about wrong or justice, joy or sorrow, so long as our posterity survives? The old norms of good and evil are outmoded. It matters not if our posterity turns out to be hairy, squashy, or crustacean, tusked or toothless, mild or ruthless. "Goodness is what comes next." His conclusion is that our progeny may be far from pleasant by present standards; but that matters not, if they survive.

Lewis has often been carelessly accused of being against science. In fact, he gives us an admirable scientist in Bill Hingest in *That Hideous Strength*. Significantly, Hingest was murdered by order of the supposed scientists who directed the NICE. The enemy is not true science, which is fueled by a love of truth, but that applied science whose practitioners are motivated by a love of power. In Lewis's opinion the technological developments that are called steps in Man's Conquest of Nature in fact give certain men power over others. Discarding Natural Law will always increase the dangers of having some people control others. Only Natural Law provides human standards which over-arch rulers and ruled alike. Lewis went so far as to claim, "A dogmatic belief in objective value is necessary to the very idea of a rule which is not tyranny or an obedience which is not slavery." (*Abolition* 46).

*The Magician's Nephew*, the tale of the creation of Narnia, gives us two characters who exemplify the Controllers—Jadis and Uncle Andrew Ketterly. Both claimed to be above Natural Law; they had "a high and lonely destiny." Jadis was a monarch and Uncle Andrew was a magician, but both were strongly suggestive of modern science gone wrong. They both held that common rules are fine for common people, but that singular great people must be free—to experiment without limits in search of knowledge, to seize power and wealth. The result was cruelty and destruction. In contrast, the wise men of old had sought to conform the soul to reality, and the result had been knowledge, self-discipline, and virtue.

Two examples from Lewis's verse illustrate this traditional wisdom. The 1956 poem "After Aristotle" praises virtue, stating that in Greece men gladly toiled in search of virtue as their most valuable treasure. Men would willingly die or live in hard labor for the beauty of virtue. Virtue powerfully touched the heart and gave unfading fruit; virtue made those who love her strong.

A second example is "On a Theme from Nicolas of Cusa," published in the *Times Literary Supplement* in 1955. In the first stanza Lewis notes how physical foods are transformed by our bodies when we assimilate them; in the second, he points out that when we assimilate goodness and truth they are not transformed, but we are.

At the end of *Abolition* Lewis implores his readers to pause before considering Natural Law only one more accident of human history in a wholly material universe. To "explain away" this transcendent reality is perhaps to explain away all explanations. To "see through" the Natural Law is the same as not to see at all.

The idea that some things are inherently good and others are not is also the basis for Lewis's approach to literature in *An Experiment in Criticism*. His thesis is that the work of art, and particularly the literary work, is to be *received* for its own sake, not *used* for other purposes. Each detail is to be savored and, if good, enjoyed. We are to look *at* the work, not to use it as a mirror to reflect ourselves and our own fantasies or as a lens through which we look at the world.

This principle is a particular application of the Natural Law. We approach a work of literature, as we might a person or flower, with the assumption that here is something good for its own sake, something worth attending to. After we have looked at it attentively, objectively, either our efforts will have been rewarded or we may decide it is not of much value after all; but in any case we will have given it a fair try, done it justice.

In *Experiment* Lewis contrasts the principle of the inherent value of works of literature with the habits of people who use literature (and thus misuse it), who prostitute the work to some other purpose.

The unliterary read a work only for the excitement they can get from the plot (as in an adventure story), for the provocation and satisfaction of their curiosity (as in a detective story), or for vicarious emotional fulfillment (as in a love story). Such readers use literature much as a child uses a toy, or a worshipper a crucifix: as a starting point for a journey inward or beyond. Unlike the child or the worshipper, who cherish their object and use it many times over, the unliterary usually use a story only once; then it is used up, discarded.

There are also users among the literary. There are the status seekers, who read the academically fashionable literature in order to impress themselves and others. There are the self-improvers—whose concern with their mental enrichment takes the place of a focus on the work itself.

And there are the wisdom-seekers, who value a work for the Statement about Life that it presents. But, says Lewis, works of art do not give us adequate world views. Too much selection is involved. In life, suffering is not often grand and noble and attributable to Tragic Flaws; matters do not end at points of satisfying finality, but go drizzling on. Works of literature may in fact make us wiser, but that is really incidental to their true function; and the wisdom we think came from a particular Great Work may in fact have come largely from within ourselves. Wisdom-seeking is carried to absurdity in a particularly keen group he calls the Vigilants (he is surely referring to F.R. Leavis and friends) who will place their stamp of approval only on those few works that express their own conception of how life should be lived. They form a kind of Committee of Public Safety, lopping a new head every month.

By contrast with the users, the receivers surrender to a work of literature, getting themselves out of the way, attending closely to each part and its relationship to other parts, for the time being taking the author's viewpoint as their own. Their refusal of a subjective reading enables them to enlarge the narrow prison of the self and see with others' eyes. The temporary annihilation of the self that takes place actually serves to heal the loneliness of the self. Lewis overtly compares the process to what happens in the pursuit of knowledge, or of justice, or the experience of love: we temporarily reject the facts as they are for us in favor of the facts as they are. In the work of literature we are experiencing the (morally) good or evil data, the (aesthetically) good or poor data, that really are out there and really possess the qualities we perceived. Lewis does not deny that our perception and judgment are sometimes flawed. But good and bad are real.

Lewis's aesthetic provides a necessary and refreshing corrective to rigorously dutiful approaches that have ruined the enjoyment of literature for many from student days onward. For those Christians to whom literary pleasures have seemed frivolous or dangerous temptations that might lead away from the Straight Path, Lewis affirms their goodness. He also exposes the sort of single-issue criticism that darkens counsel by words without knowledge. Unless we can put ourselves to one side for a time and see what is actually in the text, we ought not to say anything about a work; and in many instances we might be better off not reading it at all.

Having gratefully accepted Lewis's basic aesthetic enterprise, we must express a few reservations. Of course it is true that any work of imaginative literature is too selective to present an adequate philosophy of life. But much the same could be said of any essay or multi-volumed work in discursive prose. Any time we want to speak of the whole, of universals (or the absence thereof), we must be selective. Most formal treatises on Being, Becoming or Causality leave out the terror and the joy of the world. The supposedly universal human experience of Reality discussed in nearly all of theology turns out to be male reality. Humans are limited; we may intend the universal, but any reflection upon it is bound to be limited.

The need for selectivity does not prohibit a work of literature from being intended, or taken, as a dramatized world view. This is particularly evident when a work gives support to oppressive social structures. For example, a story whose few Jewish characters are rapacious schemers or (if admirable) are baptized, may well give generous minds such as Lewis's the enlarging experience of finding out what it is like to be antisemitic. Unfortunately, it will also cause certain readers to come away with sharpened convictions that the Jewish Conspiracy is the fountainhead of the world's evil. Likewise, a work whose achieving and admirable characters are all male, with its females frothy, manipulative, passive, victimized, and/or marginal, is saying something about the relative value of male and female.

Lewis in fact acknowledges, in an exchange of letters in *Theology* (1939-1940), that there are (morally) bad books that corrupt people by making false values attractive (*Christian Reflections* 30-35). He does not refer specifically to fiction, nor does he exclude it. Surely, then a (morally) bad work of literature can be bad because it presents a dangerously false view of life, quite possibly by its selections. In contrast, a (morally) good work of literature can present true values. There is no reason why we cannot receive such a work with diligent and delighted care, and also use it as a parable. Surely what is objectionable is, in Kant's language, to make the work a means only and not an end also. It is ironic that Lewis should have rejected the concept of the literary work as a parable, in view of the fact that his own novels (especially the Narnian tales) are parables of such enormous power and wisdom.

This, of course, is not to say that every work of literature offers a world view. The comedy is not necessarily saying that life is finally a joke, nor is the whodunit perforce telling us that the ills of the world have a neat and gratifying solution right at hand, if we could only be perceptive enough to see. Even Freud realized that sometimes a cigar is just a good cigar.

We have affirmed, with minor reservations, Lewis's reasoning that a work of literature possesses value in itself. Now we turn back to his thesis of intrinsic value as applied to all of life, his corrective to a totally relativistic value (or rather nonvalue) system. Sensitive persons who have felt their meaning-world collapse around them know how dehumanizing felt meaninglessness is. Lewis knew whereof he spoke. (People who experience this collapse without pain are even more dehumanized.) As to the end result of consistent subjectivism, the world of the Controllers, Lewis's portraits of Jadis and the directors of the NICE tell us more vividly than his discursive prose just how nightmarish such a world would be.

Within the context of a basic agreement, once more we offer a qualifier. Consistent and total subjectivism we certainly do not want, and we know why. But subjectivism and relativism can be good things sometimes; they can be freeing. People with a sharp and absolute vision are not often as broad in mental sympathies and as rich in charity as Lewis; they tend more towards psychological imperialism. Many of us, Lewis included, would rather live among people who hold firmly that "Love thy neighbor as thyself" is the only universally binding principle in personal morality,—leaving to the individual's own judgment this rule's application to sexual ethics, the role of women, or to political allegiance—than among people who know in detail God's will for other private lives as well as for their own and are busy trying to bring about theocracy. Theocracy is one of our oldest banes, and one that Lewis particularly detested. But we have far more pressing worries today.

In conclusion, Lewis's teaching about Natural Law has acquired unique urgency today. He published *Abolition* in 1947; since then there has been a radical shift in the locus and imminence of threat to the world. The danger of nuclear armaments was obvious in 1947, but there were not enough in existence then to destroy all life on earth. Since then there has been a cancer-like proliferation of nuclear weapons that only part of the public foresaw. Now we face not only the danger of sudden massive destruction of human life (and our libraries and literary heritage), but also catastrophic biological after-effects from probable destruction of the ozone layer and a nuclear winter that would likely end all plant and animal life on earth. This scenario sounds like the end of the world as foretold in the Norse mythology that Lewis found so compelling.

Such a cataclysm is as likely to be triggered by an American president who sincerely intends to do the will of God as by a Soviet premier whose professed intent is only to protect sovereign Soviet airspace. (This is not to imply that the quality of life in the two systems is the same.) The very idea of life on earth lasting long enough for Controllers to take over begins to have a certain appeal! Alive under their rule, we might still have hopes of wresting power back out of their hands some day. Those in power may be consistent or confused in their ethics, absolute or relative in their values; but the most crucial factor today is whether they show that, whatever they profess, they value human life.

Lewis sensed, by 1955, the way death technology was heading in our world. In *The Magician's Nephew* Jadis decided to use the Deplorable Word, a weapon she had paid a terrible price to obtain. A moment later every living thing in her world was dead. She did this in outright defiance of Natural Law. That is Lewis's commentary on possible use of today's arsenal.

In 1956 Lewis published *The Last Battle,* in which the land of Narnia died away more gradually than the land of Charn, ending in ice. "Yes, and I *did* hope," said Jill, "That it might go on forever. I knew *our* world couldn't" (160). Lewis always assumed that our earth has to die eventually.

In Aslan's beautiful everlasting country Peter found that Lucy was crying because of the death of Narnia, and he tried to stop her. But Lucy appealed to the law in all our hearts and said she was sure it was not wrong to mourn the death of the world they dearly loved. And Tirian, last king of Narnia, affirmed her. "It were no virtue, but grave discourtesy, if we did not mourn" (160).

The Natural Law teaches us to fight to save our world from death, and, should it die, to mourn its destruction. But C.S. Lewis predicted that the Natural Law itself will outlast all worlds. And he promises us a new life that will be the Great Story which goes on for ever, in which every chapter is better than the one before. (184). And all who live that story will be receivers.

## Works Cited

Lewis, C.S. *The Abolition of Man.* New York: Macmillan, 1947.
_____. *Christian Reflections.* Grand Rapids: Eerdmans, 1967.
_____. *The Last Battle.* London: The Bodley Head, 1956.
_____. *The Lion, the Witch and the Wardrobe.* New York: Macmillan, 1950.
_____. *Mere Christianity.* New York: Macmillan, 1953.
_____. *Poems.* New York: Harcourt, 1964.

# C.S. Lewis and G.K. Chesterton: Conservative Defendants as Critics

*Alzina Stone Dale*

Although they never met nor corresponded, a comparison of the lives and literary careers of G.K. Chesterton and C.S. Lewis reveals that the two men had a great deal in common. Chesterton is commonly seen as a jolly journalist and polemical Roman Catholic, whose conversion subverted his intellectual judgment; and Lewis is known as a highly literate professor to whose Irish Protestantism Chesterton's idea of "Rome" was anathema. But inspite of these obvious differences, their public roles as "Defenders of the Faith" reflect a basic intellectual resemblance between them. The source of these similarities lie in their lives, in their literary careers, and, finally, in their common roots.

Not only did they have similar personal experiences, but they also had similar intellectual and imaginative outlooks: half analytical, half creative. They were so similar that Chad Walsh's comment that, "One half of Lewis's mind functions easily within the rational framework of exposition and argument. The other half turns to highly imaginative ways of saying things indirectly. The two halves present the same ultimate intuition of reality, but the strategies by which they storm the reader's guard are very different..." (187) may also be said about Chesterton.

In their literary criticism, both showed a rational commonsense—declaring a book to be an object with a real existence—together with a hearty appetite for debate. Both loved good argument, but both were also enthusiastic, not disparaging, critics who saw themselves as literature's "defendents" in the Chestertonian sense that:

> If the world is good we are revolutionaries, if the world is evil we must be conservative. These essays...seek to remind men that things must be loved first and improved afterwards... A Defendent is chiefly required when worldlings despise the world. (Chesterton, *The Defendent* 6-7)

Their literary tastes were not always the same (Chesterton adored detective stories and Lewis was a devourer of fantasy and myth) but both enlisted in the fight against what critic George Steiner has called "organized (literary) amnesia," which made them warriors fighting to preserve

Western civilization itself. Both men recognized the fact that this culture was based upon Christian foundations, so that in their work it is impossible to cut apart the seamless garment of their adult beliefs and critical commentary, but a similar belief is not necessary to understand or accept their literary conclusions. What is required is a willingness to allow intellectual integrity to men like these who have publically confessed their Christian faith and defend it with rational arguments.

In describing their similarities, it is important that both Lewis and Chesterton were born and bred Englishmen, even if Englishmen of somewhat different political varieties, because there is a particular, definable insularity bred in Englishmen. The British Empire had begun to fade in Chesterton's youth and as a 19th century Liberal, he has not taught to admire painting the map red. Lewis, on the other hand, was born and bred an Englishman in Ireland's Protestant Pale, which made him at once more aggressively "English" than Chesterton and less tolerant of Celtic subcultures and "lesser breeds without the Law." Their shared "mere Englishness" was shown in such things as their somewhat self-consciously unkempt appearance, their public, boyish exuberance, and their fondness for masculine companionship, with its love of talk, pubs, and tobacco.

Ironically for a pair of self-confessed "dinosaurs," both were products of the Industrial Revolution's broadening of the English social base, and it was Belfast and London which provided the source of their families' prosperity. Proud as he was that his mother's family went back to a Norman knight whose bones lay at Battle Abbey, it was only with Lewis's father that his family entered the "professional" class, while Chesterton was the third generation of prosperious middle-class London real estate agents. The consciousness of one's social origins is never far below the surface of English life, so that despite his lack of a university education, it was Chesterton, more secure in his roots, who demonstrated a stronger distaste for caste and was able to commit the ultimate social solicism of becoming a Roman Catholic convert.

Both families religiously followed the English path of upward mobility by using their increasing wealth to buy better private education for their sons. Their fathers went to good secondary schools and were apprenticed to professional trades but their sons went to real "public" schools. Both families also were remarkably literate. Lewis described his home as jammed with books while Chesterton happily teethed on his father's library. Not only were there many books about, but they were accessible to the boys, something not at all common in English families unless they were professional educators. For Lewis and Chesterton, reading was a family habit, so that both grew up assuming the world was full of "ordinary readers" who were not necessarily professors or professional critics.

Although it was their fathers' books that they read, initially it was their mothers who read to them. In their happy homes, both men could take it for granted that a mother's role was the intellectual nurturing of the young. It was their mothers and nursemaids who introduced them to the sustaining myths of their childhoods, fairytales, and to their "mutual" fairy godfather, George MacDonald. Both men later paid tribute to the way such stories teach children what the universe is all about, and both are quoted by Dr. Bruno Bettleheim, saying:

> Literary critics such as G.K. Chesterton and C.S. Lewis felt that fairy stories are 'spiritual explorations' and hence 'the most life-like' since they reveal human life as seen or felt, or divined from the inside. Fairy tales...direct the child to discover his identity and calling, and they also suggest what experiences are needed to develop his character further. Fairy tales intimate that a rewarding, good life is within one's reach despite adversity—but only if one does not shy away from the hazardous struggles without which one can never achieve true identity. (24)

To both men, the "ethics of Elfland" were first made manifest in these old stories, so it was their mothers who taught them those virtues Lewis later called "the Tao."

The two men's fathers, although very different, were equally important in their psychological and intellectual development. Both fathers were strongly-felt presences in their sons' lives in a manner again atypical of the English who kept their children virtually unseen and unheard in the nursery until sent off at an early age to school from whose spartan atmosphere there was usually no appeal. But Lewis did appeal successfully, while Chesterton was never sent away to school at all.

Chesterton's father, "Mister Ed," was a genial, even-tempered amateur hobbyist magnificently equipped to educate his sons in English literature. Through his early retirement he succeeded their mother in the role of chief playmate; and it was Mister Ed who was Chesterton's original "Clavigor," or Key Bearer, whose toy theatre introduced his son to "joy." All his life he continued to be his sons' greatest supporter.

He was nothing at all like Lewis' mercurial and moody father, whose odd devotion to routine ended by estranging his sons. Mister Ed, however, was no racconter nor debater like Lewis's father, despite the fact that both Chesterton and Lewis were famous for their fondness for argument and their conviviality, which, as adults, made them the bellweathers of their flocks whose friendship was sought by everyone.

In both families, it might be said that their fathers' real "religion" was politics because it was the subject of most serious family conversation and the source of both men's apprenticeship in debate. Chesterton responded to this concern by taking a "religious" approach to political issues, that is, all his life he argued the issue of means and ends and dealt with individual liberty inside the social scene. Lewis publically denied an interest in "politics" because of the boredom he had felt as a youngster listening to his father and his friends, but it can be demonstrated that he, too, talked about the individual in a society, not in isolation from mankind even in Outer Space. Superficially, Chesterton has been seen to argue social issues from a "medieval" position and Lewis to be concerned only with individuals, but both not only wrote political fantasies describing utopias that have a very real, modern message, but they also defended individual liberty within the historical context of "Christendom," that is, Western Civilization, which is the cultural concept Chesterton meant when he talked about "the Church."

Despite the charm and comfort of their lives, full of time to devote to their own creative pursuits, both men had childhoods drastically destroyed by tragedies. As a result the boys also grew up with an "existential anxiety," which had a tremendous effect on their view of the world. By nurture, therefore, neither was naive or optimistic.

In Chesterton's case, his older sister Beatrice died suddenly when he was three. Not only was he inconsolable but his otherwise sane and balanced father acted like a maniac, forbidding any mention of her very name. This loss was the source of Chesterton's abiding recognition that

> I felt and feel that life itself is as bright as the diamond, but as brittle as the window-pane; and...I was afraid that God would drop the cosmos with a crash. (*Orthodoxy* 15)

as well as his more celebrated comment that we must "contrive to be at once astonished at the world and yet at home in it..." which reflects his joy in the birth of his brother Cecil. (15)

Lewis' childhood loss of his mother meant that he was shortly packed off to school, souring his relationship with his father, while cementing it with his adored older brother Warren. Her death also destroyed Lewis's universe:

> with my mother's death, all settled happiness, all that was tranquil and reliable, disappeared from my life. There was to be much fun, many pleasures, many stabs of Joy; but no more of the old security. It was sea and islands now; the great continent had sunk like Atlantis. (*Surprised By Joy* 21)

The emotional slack in both men's lives was taken up by their adored brothers, who remained their best friends and fellow-subcreators until they died. In Lewis's case it was his older brother Warren who was mentor, protector, instructor, and admirer; while Chesterton himself was the mentor, protector, and admirer of his younger brother Cecil for whom, in a manner not unlike Warren Lewis, he rearranged his adult life to assume Cecil's professional responsibilities.

For both men the only way they enjoyed their remaining childhood was as the small "sub-creators" of their own literary worlds, first built with the help of their brothers. In Chesterton's case he later was to share this relationship with his best friend at school, E.C. Bentley, and still later, with Hilaire Belloc, who like Lewis's university colleague and friend, J.R.R. Tolkien, has a reputation for a far more critical approach to men and books than either Chesterton or Lewis. Both the J.D.S. and the Inklings were groups begun from common literary interests.

Lewis and Chesterton found "boyhood" itself a bad time. Lewis was the better student, but both were totally disinterested in the English preoccupation with games. For them "real" life began again in adolescence, when they grew out of what Lewis called that "alien territory in which everything. . . has been greedy, cruel, noisy and prosaic, in which the imagination slept," and Chesterton described as "the mysterious transformation that produces that monster, the school boy. . . " (*Surprised* 17; *Autobiography* 57).

Their salvation came from finding like-minded friends, fond of literature and debate, with an existential concern about the meaning of life. Bentley was Chesterton's chief confidant as Arthur Greeves was Lewis's. However, much as they felt alienated from prevailing school norms, their upper-class education (Oxford and St. Paul's School) gave both Lewis and Chesterton a shared, but largely unconscious assumption of equality with other similarly educated men. They could remain urbane in the face of intellectual criticism because they had no hidden emotional agendas; they had none of the need to prove themselves by exhibiting the "chronological snobbery" that was typical of those who came from less socially acceptable backgrounds, like G. B. Shaw, H. G. Wells, or C. P. Snow. This lack of "caste-consciousness" on the part of two very bright boys who were school misfits also came from their passion for the past, or, as Chesterton put it, their dislike for the undemocratic habit of disenfranchising one's ancestors.

Adolescence for both was a time of troubles, but both also appreciated the return of their capacity to feel and to imagine that had been lost during boyhood. It meant a return to their "childhood" world where "joy" and "wonder" were to be found. Their adolescence also laid the emotional groundwork for their adult allegiance to Christianity, which grew out of personal debates with believers and from the witness of the written word.

One very interesting philosophical difference remains, which is reflected in their choice of careers as well. For Lewis as adolescent the triggering response-joy-came from "Northerness." This enthusiasm translates roughly into a passion for the 19th century's Teutonic mythology, which so influenced Nietszche, Wagner, Ibsen, and Shaw, and brought to England their ideals of the Welfare State and its governing class of Supermen. For Chesterton, no philosophy was less productive of reason or revelation: he abominated its elitist orientation, which he labeled "Prussianism," renouncing all its works, among which he included racism, eugenics, plutocracy, and imperial pretentions. Chesterton also recognized and fought against "Prussianism's" disparagement of Rome as the progenitor of Western culture, the fixer of her true boundaries, and the real source of their common European heritage. Since "Oxbridge" was the intellectual home of the English version of this "zeitgeist", Chesterton always mistrusted these universities themselves nearly as much as Lewis loved them.

This disagreement represents the most crucial intellectual difference between the portly, "working journalist" and the eccentric English don. Lewis, for example, divides his "ordinary reader into the "few and the many," or "sheep and goats," in a way that Chesterton would never do. If anything, Chesterton erred on the side of attributing mind and heart and spirit to everyone, including the well-defined misfits society did not accept. With all his delicate distinctions among readers such as "professionals," "status seekers," or even "Puritans" (a term which Lewis uses in the very Chestertonian meaning of an intolerant, self-righteous dispiser of pleasure) Lewis is still talking about a more consciously literate group than Chesterton, who says he is writing for "the ordinary modern outsider and inquirer. (*St. Francis* 11-12; *Experiment* 3). (Chesterton would have suggested it was his university education and his subsequent teaching career that confirmed Lewis in this kind of "elitism" in which the individual appears to be a variety of student.) This distinction cannot be pushed too far, however, for Chesterton's "common man" is also something of a literary creation, not based on great contact with the masses. As adults both became popular writers and "men of letters." (Chesterton at thirty was asked to stand for one of the first professorships in English Literature and much of what he wrote was a variety of literary criticism.) But then their worldwide readership made them automatically "suspect" in intellectual circles. Their equivocal position was only enhanced by the fact that both men also became star performers on the BBC.

Their adult domestic lives were equally undramatic and even bourgeois, while their quite different wives shared some important characteristics. Both women grew up in intellectual urban communities, where they were expected to express educated opinions, but where there was also great pressure to conform to the prevailing progressivism. In a phrase which might have been used about Joy Davidman Lewis, Cecil Chesterton accused his sister-in-law Frances with being "a conservative rebel against the unconventional" (98).

By the time they met their future husbands, each had a strong, articulated belief in Christianity. Paradoxically, however, while Joy Lewis "caught" Christianity from reading her future husband's works, Frances Chesterton was the chief person to "carry" Christianity to hers. These women also shared their husbands' knowledge of and appreciation of literature; both were qualified to be their husband's critics; and both suffered, too, from the jealousy of their husbands' male friends, who gave them a bad press, ignoring the fact that both men would have been incomplete and less effective persons without them.

As writers and critics both Chesterton and Lewis worked extremely hard, developing remarkable powers of concentration. Each produced a great deal of work in a variety of genres from essays and reviews, to fiction, poetry, and apologetics. A number of their books can also be paired because they are so similar in intent, if not in style. Among the more obvious examples are: *Orthodoxy* and *Surprised by Joy* as twin spiritual autobiographies; *The Ball and the Cross* and *Out of the Silent Planet, The Man Who Was Thursday* and *That Hideous Strength* as pairs of SF-fantasies; and *What's Wrong with the World* and *The Abolition of Man* as paired philosophical works. In addition, Chesterton's *The Everlasting Man,* and Lewis's *The Allegory of Love,* and *The Oxford History of English Literature: English Literature in the Sixteenth Century* all are woven from the same historical perspective. Stylistically, however, Chesterton, the working journalist, wrote with a flourish whose convolutions owed much to the manners but not the mores of Oscar Wilde, while Lewis was famous for his crispness and clarity which appealed to the non-intellectual. Paradoxically, it seems that the professor wrote like a journalist; the journalist like a professor.

Both men began as poets and ended their prolific careers disapproved of as an "eclectic" writer who would not stay in one genre (Lewis) or the "master without a masterpiece" (Chesterton). As literary critics, both men are seen as reactionaries who only found value in older writers, older opinions, and older worlds because their critics do not accept as intellectually valid Chesterton's remark that, "real development is not leaving things behind, as on a road, but drawing life from them, as from a root" (*The Victorian Age* 11-12). Critics are almost equally unwilling to see value in the fact that they also showed a "correspondence in spirit.... Anyone who has spent much time reading either author will have noticed the gusto, the spirited enthusiasm for whatever subject is under consideration, and the zest for life itself...they are warm and friendly, even when they chide.... Each fights savagely against the spirit of the age, but each fights fairly and with a courtesy...they never condescend; never speak with disdain or scorn" (Daniel 12).

Recently some literary critics have begun to take Chesterton seriously again. A great admirer of Chesterton's satiric verse, W.H. Auden's final judgment on Chesterton was that he was a "writer's critic":

> Our day has seen the emergence of two kinds of literary critics, the documentor and the cryptologist...both such critics will no doubt dismiss Chesterton's literary criticism as out-of-date, inaccurate and superficial, but if one were to ask *any living novelist or poet which kind of critic he would personally prefer to write about his work,* I have no doubt as to the answer. Every writer know that certain events in his life, most of them in childhood, have been of decisive in forming his personal imaginative world, the kinds of things he likes to think about, the qualities in human beings he particularly admires or detests.... This Chesterton understands...Chesterton literary criticism abounds in insights into [particular authors] which, once they have been made, seem so obviously true that one cannot see why one had not seen them for oneself.... But Chesterton was the first critic to see these things. As a literary critic, therefore, I rank him very high... (398-400; italics mine)

Auden's comment supports another critic, Garry Wills's explanation of why Chesterton's "cameo" insights are often neglected: they are too witty to be properly academic. This problem is brilliantly shown in Chesterton's statement that:

> the usual way of criticising an author who has added something to the literary forms of the world is to complain that his work does not contain something which is obviously the speciality of someone else. Thus the right thing to say about Cyrano de Bergerac is that it shows a certain wit and spirit, but it really throws no light on the duty of middle-aged married couples living in Norway. (*Robert Browning* 138-39).

Wills considers most of Chesterton's vast body of work to be:

> literary criticism, in which a profound unity informs all [its] judgments, no matter how scattered or occasional... Contained in them, assumed throughout them, is a philosophy of criticism far in advance of Victorian moralism and decadent aestheticism. The basis of this criticism was laid in Chesterton's first book of essays, *The Defendent.* Chesterton insists, in his defense of penny dreadfuls and of detective stories, that literature is an object, good or bad...[he] arrived at [this] awareness by...an existential insight which kept BOTH the word's meaning AND its mode of existing operative, in a state of tense struggle and reinforcement" (57)

Wills also shows that Chesterton had method in his madness when he deliberately wrote books like his study of Browning with few facts and misquoted lines. It was not because Chesterton could not help it or because he wanted to shock. He quoted from memory both by temper and on principle because "that is what literature is for; it ought to be a part of a man" (*The Daily News*).

In 1913 just before the Marconi Trial and World War I broke his world in half, Chesterton wrote what is perhaps his best book of literary criticism, *The Victorian Age in Literature*. It was prepared for the Home University Library, established for the ordinary, self-educated reader, but in a typical Chestertonian scenario, the editors became panic-stricken at Chesterton's approach and disclaimed any responsibility for the book's contents. But Wills and more recent critics like Lawrence Clipper have agreed that not only is this book a superb guide to Victorian literature, but

> *The Victorian Age* is marked by great caution and fairness: Dickens, Browning, Stevenson, and Chesterton's other heroes are discussed with full consciousness of their faults, while even Wilde and Beardsley are praised for what is strong in both men. The extracts often quoted from this little volume are even more misleading than such isolated citations normally are; the book is a masterpiece of arrangement, of suspension and counter-tension, whereby names are lifted in large webs of inter-reacting influence.... (77-79)

A good example of those extracts which demonstrate the value and wit of Chesterton's criticism is his masterly remark about Mathew Arnold who was "undoubtedly serious and public-spirited in intention.... But kept a smile of heart-broken forbearance, as of the teacher in an idiot school, that was enormously insulting" (*The Victorian Age* 7-9).

The underlying thesis of Chesterton's whole study is that:

> It is useless for the aesthete (or any other anarchist) to urge the isolated individuality of the artist, apart from his attitude to his age. His attitude to his age is his individuality: men are never individual when alone. (*The Victorian Age* 9-10)

This is Chesterton's answer to the modern heresy of "organized amnesia" in which texts themselves have more or less disappeared as objects of analysis or appreciation, as in the extreme Deconstructionalist positions of Derrida and Fish, with their gnostic disregard for the reality of an author, his book, or his period. In rebuttal, Chesterton would recommend using common sense, and making the obvious assumption that there do exist particular men writing particular books in particular places worthy of study. To him, any "existential" approach which denies the reality of both book and reader is nothing more than the inordinate pride of the creature who assumes he is the creator. He also knows, like Lewis, that such godlings easily lose touch with outer reality and become nothing to themselves as well.

In view of their essential similarity of approach, it is interesting to recall that Lewis' first encounter with Chesterton was on a literary basis, as novice to master craftsman. Not many first readers ignore GKC's amusing verbal facility to grasp his inner meaning and purpose, but Lewis's comments demonstrate that as he read Chesterton in an army hospital, he was practicing himself what he would later preach: reading the text itself. Lewis's own professional approach to literature as a fact instead of a subjective construct or piece of propaganda was so close to Chesterton's own method that it seems obvious either Lewis had read Chesterton or that they began at the same starting point. Both points seem to be true.

Lewis's comment about Chesterton was:

> I first read a volume of Chesterton's essays. I had never heard of him and had no idea of what he stood for (but)...liking an author may be as involuntary and improbable as falling in love. I was by now a sufficiently experienced reader to distinguish liking from agreement.... His humor was of the kind which I like best—not "jokes" imbedded in the page like currants in a cake, still less...a general tone of flippancy and jocularity, but the humor which is not in any way separable from the argument but is rather (as Aristotle would say) the "bloom" on dialectic itself...for the critics who think Chesterton frivolous or "paradoxical" I have to work hard to feel even pity;... I liked him for his goodness [because] "Smug" and "smugness" were terms...which had never had a place in my critical vocabulary. I lacked the critic's nose...or bloodhound sensitivity for hypocrisy or Pharisaism. (*Surprised by Joy* 190-91)

This is the statement of one man of letters upon another, a literary judgment about the nature and purpose of the other's style, and at the same time, a commentary on the twin issues of the appropriate stance of the critic and the moral purpose of literature itself. Like Chesterton, Lewis was aware of the fact that every work has a moral purpose, whether articulated as such or not, a recognition only now being taken seriously again by such "serious" critics such as the late John Gardiner or Wayne Booth. Lewis also described the essential elements of Chestertonian commentary, from the balancing humor he used to make his points to the fact he saw himself as a fighter engaged in battle for men's minds, not as a clown capering about in motley to amuse them.

Lewis, of course, never lost his first insight into Chesterton. It was he who much later defended Chesterton against the charge that he was "dated" in an essay with an unmistakably Chestertonian tone of voice, where Lewis first dismissed the charge of Chesterton's being too "public" a poet (i.e. popular, then, in words Chesterton might have used, added:

> The truth is that the whole criticism which turns on dates and periods, as if age-groups were the proper classification of readers, is confused and vulgar...it lumps together the different ways in which a man can be 'of his period'.... A man is likely to become 'dated'...precisely because he is anxious not to be dated...to move with the times.... On the other hand a man may be 'dated' in the sense that the forms, the set-up, the paraphernalia, whereby he expresses matter of permanent interest are those of a particular age. In that sense the greatest writers are often the most dated." ("Period Criticism" 115).

There is a startling similarity here to Chesterton's comment in *The Victorian Age in Literature* that:

> the critic who wishes to move onward with the life of an epoch must be always running backwards and forwards among its mere dates...[because of] the difficulty of keeping the moral order parallel with the chronological order. For the mind moves by instincts, Associations, premonitions, and not by fixed dates or completed processes. Action and reaction will occur simultaneously, or the cause actually be found after the effect...thus Newman took down the iron sword of dogma to parry a blow not yet delivered that was coming from the club of Darwin. For this reason none can understand tradition, or even history, who has not some tenderness for anachronism. (178)

In this same critical essay Lewis makes what to many is his unbelievable, or unacceptable, comparison between Chesterton and Franz Kafka, in which he suggests that "while both give a powerful picture of the loneliness and bewilderment which each one of us encounters in his (apparently) singlehanded struggle with the universe Chesterton, attributing to the universe a more complicated disguise, and admitting the exhilaration as well as the terror of the struggle, has got in rather more: is more balanced; in that sense *More Classical, More Permanent* (116; italics mine), Interestingly, too, Lewis also shows that he had read not only Chesterton's theological works, but also his fiction, for he passionately describes the timelessness of *The Flying Inn's* portrait of a modern English politician.

Lewis recognized and rebuked the same spirit of the age that Chesterton had described earlier when he said that criticism seems more intellectual "when it permits any writer to emphasize doubts...but no man to emphasize dogmas" (*Charles Dickens,* xv). In his *An Experiment in Criticism* Lewis remarked that "I have sometimes discovered [in my students] a belief that [a tragedy] is valuable, is worth witnessing or reading chiefly because it communicates something called the tragic 'view' or 'sense' or 'philosophy' of life [but] the real story does not end...real sorrow ends neither with a bang nor a whimper" (77-78).

Like Chesterton, Lewis clearly stood in the literary camp of those to whom the text is real; to them books are some of the very building blocks that make Western culture itself. If Lewis was somewhat more exclusive in those whom he chose to call "mature readers," "the few for whom the first reading of some literary work is...an experience so momentous that only experiences of love, religion, or bereavement can furnish a standard of comparison" (*Experiment* 3), still the fact remains that Chesterton himself was a Lewis reader. Paradoxically, he was also one of Lewis's "many." He read and reread many writers from Macaulay to Dickens, but he was also known for his ability to go through a book once and have its heart out; in fact, the book itself usually appeared to have been through the wars. Lewis, when all is said and done, is thinking of his reader in a quasi-academic setting while Chesterton is really writing more for the man in the street.

As a critic Lewis also focused on the text itself, trying to help its reader see it as fresh and whole as Chesterton could wish, and bring to its appreciation the sense of wonder Chesterton would stand on his head to achieve. Neither one used the close readings popular with New Critics, nor was either vastly curious about secondary sources as a trail through the wilderness, for that smacked too much of faddism and "period criticism." They liked to follow a sane and balanced *via media* which they saw as an intellectual reflection of the cardinal virtues. Both would have seen as the ultimate nonsense, or solipsistic sin of pride, the concept that a book is nothing more than the sum of the emotions of its reader, who is also defined as a bundle of reactions rather than a person.

In terms of what they both said to their readers, however, Chesterton shared with his "literary" godson the strong feeling that, as Chesterton expressed it, "English history had moved away from English literature" (qtd. in *G.K. Chesterton An Anthology* 147). Lewis proves his Chestertonian birthright by his own "re-writing" of that same history to show that the Renaissance never happened in England...or that if it did, it had no importance" (Walsh 187). Both men were speaking here as "Old Western Men" in defense of "Christendom."

Whether as critics in arms or as Christians, the ultimate characteristic shared by both men was that neither set up to be a common scold. They loved literature and wanted nothing more than to be the good fairies present at the birth of a happy reader, and both exerted themselves wholeheartedly to share and shape their reader's childlike (not childish) enthusiasm for what he read. The enjoyment both radiated as they talked about literature was based—in the end—upon their common spiritual attitude towards the Creator, His Creation, and its subcreators, among whom they modestly included themselves. It is this inate similarity which makes this cheerful daydream of Jerry Daniel's whimsical, but realistic portrait of our two critics alive in a world in which

> life is a dance.... The best literature is that which...allows us to see, however dimly, a portion of the dance...when I think of the Old Testament story of David dancing around the ark of the covenant, in my mind's eye he is a bouncy fat man, wearing pince-nez, and with tousled hair and shaggy moustache. Near him, dancing slower and with a little more dignity, but with plenty of energy, is a ruddy, pipe-smoking professor with thinning hair and a tweed jacket. (13)

## Works Cited

Auden, W. H. "The Gift of Wonder." *G. K. Chesterton, A Centenary Appraisal.* London: Paul Elek, 1974.

Bettelheim, Bruno. *The Uses of Enchantment.* New York: Vintage Books Edition, 1977.

Chesterton, Cecil. *G. K. Chesterton, A Criticism.* London: Alton Rivers, 1908.

Chesterton, G. K. *Autobiography.* London: Hutchinson & Co., 1936.

—— *Charles Dickens.* London: Metheun, 1906.

—— *The Daily News,* 28 Sept. 191.

—— *The Defendent.* London: Brimley Johnson, 1901.

—— "Milton and Merrie England." In *G. K. Chesterton: An Anthology.* D. B. Wyndham Lewis, ed. London: Oxford UP, 1957.

—— *Orthodoxy.* New York: Dodd, Mead & Co., 1908.

—— *Robert Browning.* London: Macmillan, 1904.

—— *The Victorian Age in Literature.* New York: Henry Holt, 1913.

Clipper, Lawrence J. *G. K. Chesterton.* New York: Twayne Pub., 1974.

Daniel, Jerry. "Lewis and Chesterton: the Smell of Dew and Thunder." *CSL: The Bulletin of the New York C. S. Lewis Society,* Sept. 1981.

Lewis, C. S. *An Experiment in Criticism.* London: Cambridge UP, 1961.

—— "Period Criticism." *On Stories and Other Essays on Literature.* Walter Hooper, ed. New York: Harcourt, 1982.

—— *Surprised by Joy.* New York: Harcourt, 1955.

Walsh, Chad. *The Literary Legacy of C. S. Lewis.* New York: Harcourt, 1979.

Wills, Garry. *Chesterton: Man and Mask.* New York: Sheed and Ward, 1961.

# Voices of Fire:
# Eliot, Lewis, Sayers and Chesterton

*John Martin*

And what the dead had no speech for, when living,
They can tell you, being dead: the communication
Of the dead is tongued with fire beyond the language
of the living.

—T. S. Eliot, *Little Gidding*

The four writers this essay will discuss had much to tell us when they were living, but it may be that, as Eliot's lines suggest, they have more to tell us being dead—even if they speak only through their printed words. For indeed, their words seem to shine all the brighter against the sound and fury of the late 1980s. In a world of technical superabundance and cultural vacuity, it's refreshing to know that we can accept Eliot's famous invitation, "Let us go then, you and I," exert ourselves only to the extent of stretching out an arm, and hear again those great old voices. And no Moog synthesizer will we need to fully appreciate them, for we can hear them at any level of our choosing through that greatest of all technological inventions, the non-cassette, non-stereophonic, manually operated book.

T. S., C. S., Dorothy L., G.K.—a fondness for initials would be only the smallest of the shared idiosyncrasies of this distinguished foursome. A far more important common idiosyncrasy would be their attempts, after their separate fashion, to serve as apologists for the truths of the New Testament, to explain the world to the world and the living God to mortal men. The be sure, there have been numerous other great Christian voices in this century—George Macdonald, Charles Williams, and Flannery O'Connor, to name only three—but somehow for me, the four have a special affinity. At least two of my four—Lewis and Eliot—would instantly deny any *literary* affinity, as they did in their lifetime, but we are here to pound the gavel and overrule as we see fit. For no matter in what they differed, they shared very great things: deep learning, high standards, extraordinary talent, a thought-out faith, and a truly childlike enthusiasm for the wonders of Creation.

Even though all four spent their entire professional lives either in or near London, differences of sensibility saw to it that they never formed even the shadow of an idea of a Christian version of the Bloomsbury Group. As to their work, Lewis admired Sayers and Sayers, Lewis; and both admired Chesterton and Sayers admired Eliot; but Lewis did not admire Eliot, nor Eliot Lewis; nor did Eliot admire Chesterton, except for the Father Brown stories. And if Chesterton ever so much as expressed an opinion about any of the other three, I so far haven't discovered it. In any case, they would have made an odd quartet: Lewis, an amiable but most studious professor; Chesterton, a scholarly but winebibbing journalist; Sayers, a curious combination of advertising copywriter and Dante scholar; and Eliot, a stranger combination yet of banker, publisher, critic, poet, arbiter of elegance and practical joker. Whatever their harmonies and dissonances, I think it will be helpful to look at their lives before we look at their works, choosing the amount of biography in direct ratio to their familiarity to what I conceive of as a typical readership.

Lewis of course is familiar enough to readers of this volume as to need virtually no introduction. Yet for those who haven't read *Surprised by Joy* or otherwise become familiar with the large facts of his life, we should note that he was born in Belfast in 1898, grew up there, suffered clumsily and unathletically through the kind of English public schools that suggest Saki's famous line: "You can't expect a boy to be really vicious until he's been to a good school," learned clear thinking from a strong-minded private tutor named Kirkpatrick, read English at Oxford, was wounded in World War I, returned to Oxford to study, teach, and think, and to ultimately find God during a famous busride to the Whipsnade Zoo. He wrote many books ranging from high scholarship to homely apologetics; married very late in life to an American Jewish divorcee; and died a week short of his sixty-fifth birthday, November 22, 1963.

Chesterton, being a considerably less familiar figure, we can treat at somewhat greater length, or to put it more appropriately, at somewhat greater girth. Here, surely, is the most colorful member of our Big Four—a 350-pound giant with a taste for swordsticks, capes, Fleet Street pubs, the conversation of cockneys, and Falstaffian quantities of wine. He had a voice he described as the "mouse that came forth from the mountain" and the mustachioed aspect and bearing of some great caped figure out of a Rubens painting—had Rubens, that is, painted in a mock-heroic vein. He was born in London in 1874 and grew up with a younger brother with whom he debated constantly all through his youth, thus sharpening the skills that would later serve him so well in his famous debates with George Bernard Shaw and Clarence Darrow.

He studied at the Slade Art School and was, if not a first-rate painter, certainly a talented caricaturist. But he was an even better writer and thinker. In fact, he was so good so young that when he was still in his middle twenties, writers of the caliber of Shaw, Swinburne, and Max Beerbohm, delighted by his early articles and art criticism, insisted on meeting him. At 27, he married Frances Blogg, who was five years his senior and, as a devout Anglican, much his elder religiously as well. Her example was persuasive, and G.K.C. embraced her Christian faith with characteristic enthusiasm, eventually, at 48, becoming a Roman Catholic. He wrote as naturally and almost as regularly as he breathed and when he died—at 62 in 1936—left behind him some hundred books and thousands of essays and articles. Most of them were either in defense of the faith or in defense of the working man and social justice—for to Chesterton, they were all one. He wrote at least two superb novels, *The Man Who was Thursday* and *The Napoleon of Notting Hill*, at least two great works of apologetics, *The Everlasting Man* and *Orthodoxy*, a vast quantity of Father Brown detective fiction, and, buried in his numberless short pieces, an Eldorado of epigrams, paradoxes, and other verbal delights.

Dorothy L. Sayers is a somewhat more obscure figure. And that was as she preferred, for she insisted that no biography be written for at least 50 years after her death. As to how much the world respects the posthumous requests of authors we can judge by the fact that she has been dead 25 years and there has so far been not one biography—but three. I will therefore try to keep this *fourth* Sayers biography decently brief. As it happens, that's still fairly long, but some of the events of her life are so disturbing that they should not only be looked at, but looked at in a fairly detailed and balanced context.

Her birthplace was almost a prophecy of scholarship, for when she broke daylight in June of 1893, she found herself under the famous spires of Oxford. Her father was the Reverend Henry Sayers, a kind and wise man who, to her great delight, would get her started on Latin when she was only six. She flourished under this Virginia Woolf sort of home tutelage, and by the time she was 15, was not only rooted and grounded in Latin, but fluent in French and competent in German. But she was no ivory-tower child. There's the story of how as a young girl she rebuked and reported some country-neighbor children who'd been playing a cruel boys' game with sparrows. When their father sent them around to apologize to Dorothy's father, the boys defended themselves: "They were just sparrers, and what are sparrers good for?" Dorothy's answer was simple and immortal: "God made them, so they must be good for something!" (Hitchman 27).

At sixteen she went to a private school. She was very tall, round-faced, long-necked and sensitive about her appearance, and so when an attack of measles cost her most of her hair (not permanently, as it turned out), it's not surprising that she had a brief nervous breakdown and left school. But she recovered promptly, bought a wig, finished her studies, and was at Somerville College, Oxford, in 1912.

As an undergraduate, the clergyman's daughter was almost stereotypically rebellious. Not only was she seen smoking a cigar, but she claimed to be an agnostic, cut lectures, and committed the Oxford version of the sin against the Holy Ghost by talking aloud in the Bodleian Library. But her strong and straightforward personality served her well as Bicycle Secretary. Previous Bicycle Secretaries at Somerville had been powerless, despite much yelling, to get the bicycles' owners to park them in and along the walks. Dorothy L. came down on them like Byron's wolf upon the fold, impounding all vagrant bicycles and releasing them only on payment of a fine to the Red Cross.

After graduation, she taught in a girls' school or two and also worked for a year as an administrative assistant at a snobbish boys' school in the south of France. In 1921, just as she was starting to write what might be called her pistol fiction, she joined Benson's advertising agency as a copywriter at the then good wage of L-4 a week. She also rented a flat in Bloomsbury from where she could walk to work. I'm indebted to one of her biographers for this further detail: "For longer journeys, she invested in a Ner-a-Car motorcycle, which she rode with dignity, sitting bolt upright as if driving a chariot." (Hitchman 55).

She was to remain in advertising for ten years, do very well by it, but then criticize it brilliantly, and also it seems to me, ungratefully, in her detective novel, *Murder Must Advertise:* "Of course there is *some* truth in advertising. There's yeast in bread, but you can't make bread with yeast alone. Truth in advertising," announced Lord Peter sententiously, "is like leaven, which a woman hid in three measures of meal. It provides a suitable quantity of gas with which to blow out a mass of crude misrepresentation into a form that the public can swallow." (74).

Even as Miss Sayers was presumably hiding her own leaven in measures of misrepresentation and writing her early detective fiction, she was throwing herself headlong into the spirit of the Jazz Age. Apart from playing the saxophone at office parties, she acquired a love interest and just about when she was turning thirty, found herself in a family way. She kept the fact secret, removed herself to her parents' home in the country, and had the baby privately. It was a boy, born in January of 1924. She said nothing of his existence even to her closest friends, but nevertheless registered the child in her own name. She was to support him financially, but she left his care and nurture to an eccentric and reclusive cousin, a Miss Ivy Ann Shrimpton, who lived in a remote Cotswold village.

Another bombshell followed in short order. In 1926, two months before her thirty-third birthday, in a Register Office wedding, Dorothy married 44-year-old Oswald Arthur Fleming, who'd been divorced by his first wife a year earlier on the grounds of adultery. He claimed a spectacular military background, including the French Foreign legion, an assertion somewhat perplexing to the French, who've never been able to trace him. But whatever, he moved cheerfully into Dorothy's flat on Great James Street and thereafter passed himself off as a journalist.

And a third bombshell. After the death of her father, in 1928, and of her mother, in 1929, Dorothy behaved in a way that passeth most understanding. She refused to allow solemn hymns at either funeral, and put up neither headstone nor memorial, with the result that even today their graves are unmarked.

And there, I'm glad to say, the bombshells end. At the age of 35, like her beloved Dante, she seems to have found herself in a dark wood and thenceforth proceeded ever more towards the light. Her detective fiction, particularly the Lord Peter Wimsey stories, prospered and she was able to leave the world of advertising after only ten years before the mast. Then, with her characteristic abruptness and decisiveness, she turned to more exalted writing. In 1936, the friends of Canterbury Cathedral asked her to write a play for their festival of 1937—and she wrote a brilliant one, *The Zeal of Thy House.*

The play is seen, as it were, through the eyes of the three great archangels—Raphael, Gabriel, and Michael—looking down from Canterbury's ceiling at the works and sins of William of Sens, the great French architect who was chosen to rebuild the cathedral after fire had severely damaged it in the late 12th Century. The device is extraordinarily powerful, but just as powerful are the words she puts into the mouth of the pride-ridden architect, before he suffers both a literal and figurative fall:

We are the master-craftsmen, God and I—
We understand one another. None, as I can,
Can creep under the ribs of God, and feel
His heart beat through those Six Days of Creation;
. . .
Me hath He made vice-regent of Himself
And were I lost, something unique were lost
Irreparably; my heart, my blood, my brain
Are in the stone; God's crown of matchless works
Is not complete without my stone, my jewel. . . (70-71)

The title, a perfect one, is from the psalms: "The zeal of thine house hath eaten me up; and rebukes are fallen upon me" (Psalm 69:9). As a religious play, I think it ranks with Eliot's *Murder in the Cathedral,* and indeed simply as a play, it can take its place with the best of the century. Miss Sayers wrote some other religious plays, good but not *as* good, including a well-received radio series on the life of Christ, *The Man Born to be King.* But the great work of her late years—it would occupy her from 1944 to her death 13 years later—was her translation of *The Divine Comedy.*

In 1949, Dorothy became president of the Detection Club, which can never be accused of prejudice against the portly. She was delighted to find that the robes made earlier for the 350-pound Chesterton fitted her perfectly.

Her husband died in 1950, a year before their silver anniversary, and life was a little harder after that. Part of the slack was taken up by reading, reading that pointedly excluded modern novels. As Dorothy expressed it:

As I grow older and older
And totter towards the tomb
I find that I care less and less
Who goes to bed with whom (Hitchman 193).

One of her final consolations was receiving an honorary Doctorate of Literature from Durham University. Whatever her difficulties in getting people to call her Dorothy L. Sayers instead of simply Dorothy Sayers—and her correspondence bristles with references to people who have been so heedless or high-handed as to drop the "L" and can therefore go to Dante's Inferno—whatever those difficulties, it was a delight to be called simply "Dr. Sayers."

Dr. Sayers died one day in the Macmillan-Eisenhower years, returning from a weekend in the country. As some of the rest of us sometimes are, she was in a hurry to get home and feed the cats. She got inside the door but not as far as the kitchen. It was a coronary thrombosis—due at least in part, to too much food and too many cigarettes. Her memorial service was at St. Margaret's and among the readings was a panegyric written by Lewis.

And finally Eliot, one of whose favorite lines was always that of Mary Queen of Scots: "In my end is my beginning." That beginning was on September 26, 1888, in what always seems a highly un-Eliotian part of the world—St. Louis, Missouri. Even so, Eliot had so much Harvard in his ancestry and so much Harvard in his future that we can't help but think his first message to the world, there in his nursery in the heart of Mark Twain country, must have been uttered with a broad "a".

The decisive figure in Eliot's life was probably not so much his father as his grandfather, a stupendously successful achiever at whatever he set out to do—a characteristic that was to be mirrored in his grandson. William Greenleaf Eliot was a Unitarian, but no armchair dreamer talking of world peace and universal brotherhood. At the age of 20, he left the Harvard Divinity School and went where he thought the action was—first to Washington, D.C., and then to what was at the time the western frontier, St. Louis. There, he and his young wife founded a Unitarian mission, had 14 children of their own, and adopted 26 others—mostly victims of a cholera epidemic. In 1857, he founded Washington University of St. Louis, and soon after became its president. The patriarch's second son was Henry Ware Eliot, who would become not only the chairman of a prosperous brickmaking firm, but the father of a large family, mostly girls, but including one Thomas Stearns Eliot, later to be known chiefly as T.S., also to bear such improbable nicknames as "Old Possum," as in "Old Possum's Book of Practical Cats," and such more likely monikers as "the Archbishop."

For Mark Twain, Eliot's fellow Missourian, life on the Mississippi was an intensely practical matter: "It seems safe to say it is...the crookedest river in the world, since in one part of its journey it uses up 1,300 miles to cover the same ground that the crow would fly over in 675." For Eliot, as it would seem from *Four Quartets*, the Mississippi had its mystical side:

...I think that the river
Is a strong brown god—sullen, untamed and intractable,
...
Keeping his seasons and rages, destroyer, reminder
Of what men choose to forget. Unhonoured, unpropitiated
By worshippers of the machine, but waiting, watching and waiting.
...
The river is within us, the sea is all about us.... (*Complete Poems* 130)

The sea was for the summers, when Eliot's father took the family on vacation to the large and comfortable house he'd built in 1897 on the Massachusetts shore. It looked out on a cluster of dangerous rocks that are known as the Dry Salvages. They'd caused many shipwrecks, and they would inspire and give their name to the third of Eliot's Four Quartets:

Also pray for those who were in ships, and
Ended their voyage on the sand, in the sea's lips
Or in the dark throat which will not reject them
Or wherever cannot reach them the sound of the sea bell's
Perpetual angelus. (135)

Eliot, who always seems the most cerebral and least athletic of writers, was in fact a highly skilled sailor, expert at threading his boat through the numerous rocky passages off Cape Ann. He got started on it early while he was still at Milton, his Massachusetts prep school.

At Harvard, where he was, needless to say, a brilliant student, Eliot found much of what he passionately believed in—Dante and Eastern wisdom—but also much of what he already despised. Harvard's president at that time—these were the years around 1910—was a distant relative, Charles William Eliot, a believer in the religion of the future, a kind of prophetic Unitarianism. As the comedian Mort Sahl has said of the Unitarians: "Don't get them angry or they'll burn a question mark on your lawn." But just then it wasn't question marks, it was human perfectibility, and the young Eliot wasn't buying it. After all, he'd grown up in an unperfected Unitarian family, and consequently cared little for any religion other than the religion of poetry.

That religion got its greatest impetus when Eliot read Arthur Symons and was introduced to the strikingly original French poets of the 19th Century—Rimbaud, Verlaine, Mallarme, Baudelaire, and above all, Jules Laforgue. Laforgue's influence on Eliot would make a paper by itself, but perhaps we can sum it up by saying it was less an influence than a kind of possession. Laforgue, a Uruguayan of French descent transplanted to Paris, had died at 27, a year before Eliot was born. After that brief limbo, Laforgue's spirit seemed to find a home in that young Harvard poet who, in the words of the old song, had come a long way from St. Louis.

We've all seen those pictures of Eliot, the young banker dandy, with the derby, the high collar, and the rolled umbrella. But all that, it seems, was not banker garb at all—but a costume worn largely in imitation of Laforgue, who dressed just that way. But the more important imitation was literary. If we read Laforgue's poem, "Winter Sunset," we are virtually reading a prophecy of the work of the young Eliot. As the briefest example, it was a short step from Laforgue's "In the waning yellow gaslight of the misty boulevards" to Eliot in *Prufrock*: "the yellow fog that rubs its back upon the window panes."

Ezra Pound once said of Eliot that he was the only man who had ever trained himself to write modern poetry (Norman 169). In Pound's view that meant that Eliot had acquired fluency in other languages than English, had a thorough grounding in the classics, Dante, Provencal poetry and the poetry of the East, and had learned the value of the right sort of slang cleverly juxtaposed. Or put another way, Pound felt Eliot had the classical depth on which to build a modern idiom and could therefore get rid of all cant and make every word count.

The classical roots went deep. After taking his undergraduate degree at Harvard, Eliot spent an additional three years there reading for a Ph.D. in philosophy, studying Sanskrit and Pali, and translating copiously from the French and German. And if that isn't enough to stir up in all of us a dark and malicious envy, he then went on to Oxford's Merton College and followed up with the "Greats"—the chief works of Greek and Latin literature. Yet he was far from being any sort of hair-on-the collar bookworm. In Boston, he took boxing lessons from an Irish tough who would later, incidentally, appear in several Eliot poems as Apeneck Sweeney; and at Oxford, he stroked the Merton four-oar and led it to victory in one of the intercollegiate boatraces.

It was also at Oxford that he met Vivienne Haigh, the daughter of a distinguished painter. They were both 26 when they were married at a registry office near her home in Hampstead in the late summer of 1915—Eliot taking part without so much as notifying his parents. As a result, Eliot did not quite lose the love of his family, but he did lose his allowance—and that meant some very hard times. He and Vivienne were for a time guests of Bertrand Russell, whom Eliot had met—and impressed—at Harvard. Then the Eliots moved into a flat off the Edgware Road—a far from genteel part of London.

Like Miss Sayers, Eliot was highly musical and as a piano player was quite capable of tackling Beethoven sonatas. But he was haunted for years by the thought that his greatest resemblance to Beethoven would be in the matter of poverty, and there was a period when it was. For a while, he made ends meet by teaching at private schools—in one of which, incidentally he had the once and future poet John Betjeman as a pupil. But in 1917, choosing more money and less tension, he joined Lloyds Bank. America was entering the war just about then, and though Eliot volunteered his services to the American navy, he was declared the 1917 equivalent of 4-F on the grounds of a chronic hernia.

Not surprisingly, Eliot made a first-rate banker. In his Jules Laforgue outfit, he looked the part, of course; but more than that, he'd inherited his father's business sense and his grandfather's talent for completing all undertakings efficiently. That included poetry, and when, during these same years, Eliot met Pound, good things began to happen. Pound was instrumental in getting Eliot's poetry published, first in little magazines and then as a collection: *Prufrock and Other Observations,* in July of 1917. And Pound did something else less welcome: he tried to start a fund to get Eliot out of the bank and writing poetry full time.

But Eliot somehow got his writing done anyway, settling into a routine of rising at five and writing for several hours before his banking day began. In the evenings he had to contend with Vivienne, alternately bouncy and melancholy, and becoming ever more mentally troubled, so the mornings were his only real opportunity to turn out his work.

And he was writing not only his poetry, but criticism so acute it would win him a reputation as one of the great English critics ever. It included *The Sacred Wood,* which would be hailed as the most important work of its kind since Wordsworth's *Preface to Lyrical Ballads.*

His schedule and domestic pressures inevitably took their toll on his nerves and in 1921, Eliot had to take prolonged leave from the bank. He and Vivienne rested up at a sanatorium in Lausanne, Switzerland, which turned into a kind of busman's holiday—for it was there Eliot wrote many of the lines of *The Wasteland,* which would appear in 1922 and become *the* poem of its century:

What are the roots that clutch, what branches grow
Out of this stony rubbish? Son of man,
You cannot say, or guess, for you know only
A heap of broken images... (*Complete Poems* 38)

Improbably enough, the heap of images would bring Eliot a heap of money, for *The Wasteland* found an American publisher as well, the Dial Magazine, and won a prize of $2,000. The mind reels at the thought of what that would be in 1987 dollars—and for poetry, mind you, without so much as a musical arrangement by the Boston Pops. The Wasteland also brought Eliot a wealthy patroness, Lady Rothermere, who would put up the money for The Criterion, with Eliot as editor. Thus would be launched perhaps the only fine-arts magazine ever that could claim among its contributors so glittering a combination of immortals as Eliot, Paul Valery, and Marcel Proust.

In November of 1925, at the age of 37, Eliot, with Ezra Pound rejoicing as the angels of heaven over one sinner who has repented, left Lloyds Bank and became a director of the publishing house that would be known, after 1919, as Faber & Faber. He would remain with it, being paid well but never getting rich, until his death in 1965. As an editor, he would undoubtedly make many good decisions, but he would also make at least one bad one. On the grounds of not wanting to offend England's World War II ally, Russia, he would turn down a brilliant allegory satirizing the power struggles and inventive propaganda that followed on the heels of the Russian revolution. The allegory was George Orwell's *Animal Farm.*

To return to the 1920s: If Faber & Faber was a big step, a bigger step was coming. The way had begun to be prepared as early as 1926, when Eliot had gotten interested in a literary personality far more impressive even than Jules Laforgue and far closer to Eliot's almost instinctively liturgical soul. The new discovery was a 17th century divine, the brilliant and devout Lancelot Andrewes, who had been not only a bishop of the Church of England but also one of that glorious company of 54 scholars from Oxford, Cambridge, and Westminster who were to produce, in the brief span of four years, that "noblest monument of English prose," the King James Version of the Bible. The influence was direct and immediate. Eliot's "Journey of the Magi" was based directly on an Epiphany sermon by Andrewes, and such lines as "a cold coming we had of it" were direct quotations (*For Lancelot* 27). The sheepfold was clearly beckoning.

Yet Eliot had other religious influences besides Andrewes, including such living ones as the exemplary Lord Halifax, whose High Church, tolerant-concerning-Rome, and intensely devout views would be those of Eliot as well. On June 29, 1927, St. Peter's Day, Eliot was baptized—to the delight of the Church and bafflement of the world. But to that chorus of righteous rationalist voices from the congregation of Mr. Worldly Wiseman, Eliot had an answer worthy of Bunyan himself: "In a world of fugitives, the person taking the opposite direction will appear to run away."

Eliot I had died, aged 38 years, 9 months; Eliot II had been born and would live almost exactly as long—37 years, 5 months. The poet of Prufrock and the Wasteland would henceforth write lines just as memorable as the old ones—but now the titles would be such as Ash Wednesday, Choruses from the Rock, Murder in the Cathedral.

Yet of course not all the grit of living would be instantly washed away in the waters of regeneration. Above all, there remained the problem of Vivienne, ever more disturbed and ever more disturbing, and always there, just there, like the arrows sticking fast in St. Sebastian. In February of 1933, after 18 years of nerve-fraying marriage, Eliot instructed his solicitor to prepare a Deed of Separation. Whatever her faults, Vivienne was a one-man woman and there are heart-rending, if unconfirmed accounts, of her later coming to his lectures wearing a placard stating, "I am the wife he abandoned."

Eliot lived on his own thereafter until 1945, when he found a housemate in one John Hayward, a young wit, bibliophile, and housebound muscular dystrophy victim, who had a large flat and was happy to share it with a man who knew a little about books himself. Eliot would remain for 12 years, working industriously, and faithfully attending church. As the French housekeeper said of him: "Mr. Eliot was very religious; he never read the Sunday papers" (Sencourt 92).

In the late 1940s, *The Cocktail Party* proved a great box-office success. It brought Eliot L29,000, of which, to his understandable disgust, the tax collector took L25,000. Far worse was the death of Vivienne in a London nursing home. When Hayward informed him, Eliot reportedly buried his face in his hands, crying "Oh God! Oh God!"

That was 1947. In 1948, he received the Nobel Prize for Literature. And his last years were to be brightened even more by Valerie Fletcher, a well-educated young woman from Yorkshire whose interesting ambition in life was to be secretary to a celebrated writer. Fortunately, she had the good sense not to stop there. Secretary and boss were married when she was 30 and he 68. Passionately fond of his privacy, Eliot foiled both reporters and rabble by scheduling the ceremony for the 6:30 a.m. predawn darkness of a January day in 1957. The church was St. Barnabas's in London. Eliot would later discover that this was the same church, incredible as it seems, in which Jules Laforgue had been married 70 years before.

Now, let's move from lives to works—or, as Eliot has again so quotably put it, to "all the works and days of hands that lift and drop a question on your plate" (*Complete Poems* 4). My plate has been resounding with dropped questions ever since I began this essay, and the hardest to answer has been precisely the one of works: How much of the best of four authors can legitimately be set forth in a brief paper, especially when much of that paper is taken up with literary biography? Well, obviously, the number of samples and comparisons must be severely restricted, yet even so I think we can at least get an idea of what each is best at. We will not empty these four oceans with our thimble, but we may get, here and there, a breathtaking view—and therefore be moved to return, at our leisure, for a longer view and a deeper one.

And let's begin with Lewis, the pillar and ground of this society. It seems to me that at his most valuable, Lewis speaks in the accents of that great and simple passage in Isaiah: "Come now, and let us reason together." The tone is never one of "Oh, what a smart boy am I!" but rather, "Let's look at things as clearly as we can and see what conclusions we reach." And indeed, sometimes Lewis is at his spiritual best when he's at his literary worst—when he's sounding just a little too artless, or folksy, or avuncular, as in this passage from *Mere Christianity*:

> So that when we talk of a man doing anything for God or giving anything to God, I will tell you what it is really like. It is like a small child going to its father and saying, "Daddy, give me sixpence to buy you a birthday present." (125)

Yet it was just such a homely passage, also in *Mere Christianity*, the one about Jesus being either devil, lunatic, or the Son of God, that Charles Colson of Watergate notoriety called decisive in his own radical conversion. Since the pre-Lewis Colson was fond of saying, "I'd run over my own grandmother to get Nixon reelected," and the post-Lewis Colson has been, by all accounts, an exemplary believer, one can only be grateful for Lewis's ability to speak directly to the heart. For what is true in the inch is almost always true in the mile, and Mr. Colson is only one of a multitude of doubters, atheists, and quasi-believers to have found instruction for their souls in the pages of a man who wore the robes of an Oxford don even as he was helping carry out the Great Commission as a preacher in print.

And how preacherly he was, how painstaking, how remarkably—in the best sense of the word—Teutonic. If we read Chesterton, we're struck by his exhilarating leaps and fancies; and if we read Sayers, by the sharpness of her focus; if we read Eliot, by his exquisite, Henry Jamesian refinements and distinctions. But with Lewis, to take the military image that immediately suggests itself, it's fix bayonets, we're going forward, foxhole by foxhole, to root out every fallacy and defeat every objection. *Mere Christianity* does this superbly, but so does *Miracles*, and so does, at a metaphorical level, *The Pilgrim's Regress*—and there are elements of that same straightforward and methodical approach in almost everything he writes. This is not to say Lewis doesn't perform the all-important task of *entertaining* as he goes along, for he certainly does, but he's more concerned with the accuracy of his bayonet thrusts than with the beauty of his motion.

Again, however, Lewis is frequently ingenious even as he's being methodical. In *The Four Loves*, for example, to those who think they see evidence of homosexuality in those in whom it shows least of all, he responds with this Mad Hatter-March Hare analysis:

> (They) are arguing like a man who should say, "If there were an invisible cat in that chair, the chair would look empty; but the chair does look empty; therefore there *is* an invisible cat in it (58).

But the more typical Lewis can be seen in this extended passage from *Mere Christianity*, in which he takes on the Life-Force philosophy, or Creative Evolution, the pet of Bernard Shaw and Henri Bergson:

> One reason why many people find Creative Evolution so attractive is that it gives one much of the emotional comfort of believing in God and none of the less pleasant consequences. When you are feeling fit and the sun is shining and you do not want to believe that the whole universe is a mere mechanical dance of atoms, it is nice to be able to think of this great mysterious Force rolling on through the centuries and carrying you on its crest. If, on the other hand, you want to do something rather shabby, the Life-Force...will never interfere with you like that troublesome God we learned about when we were children.... All the thrills of religion and none of the cost. Is the Life-Force the greatest achievement of wishful thinking the world has yet seen? (33-34).

Moving on to Dorothy L. Sayers, merely to look at the titles of some of her books and essays is to see the emphasis she placed on getting things straight intellectually: *The Mind of the Maker*, *"The Image of God," "The Dogma Is the Drama," Creed or Chaos?, What Do We Believe?*, and, at the detective-story level, "The Dates in the Red-Headed League."

Not that she is in any way humorless. On the contrary, she can joke, quip, taunt, and parody with the greatest wits in the language, and the unlucky man who has read her "Are Women Human?" will need an iron will to retain any illusions he may have about male supremacy. Again, in the *The Cosmic Synthesis,* she is very funny both about doubtful religion and doubt-free nonreligion. She includes such holy wonders as St. Lukewarm of Laodicea, the patron saint of railway caterers, and St. Supercilia, the patron of pedants, whose feast is Eyebrow Sunday. She even develops a thoroughly modern creed, The Creed of St. Euthanasia: "I believe in man, maker of himself and inventor of all science...and in a vague, evolving deity, the future-begotten child of man...and I believe in the spirit of progress, who spake of Shaw and the Fabians; and in a modern, administrative, and social organization." *The Whimsical Christian* 1-10)

And what she can do with levity, she can do just as well with gravity. Consider these excerpts from one of her great essays, "Creed or Chaos":

> ...It is fatal to let people suppose that Christianity is only a mode of feeling; it is vitally necessary to insist that it is first and foremost a rational explanation of the universe. It is hopeless to offer Christianity as a vaguely idealistic aspiration of a simple and consoling kind; it is, on the contrary, a hard, tough, exacting, and complex doctrine.... And it is fatal to imagine that everybody knows quite well what Christianity is and needs only a little encouragement to practice it. The brutal fact is that in this Christian country not one person in a hundred has the faintest notion what the Church teaches about God or man or society or the person of Jesus Christ.
> ...We must teach Christianity, and...it is absolutely impossible to teach Christianity without teaching Christian dogma.... If the average man is going to be interested in Christ at all, it is the dogma that will provide the interest. (34)
>
> Teachers and preachers never, I think, make it sufficiently clear that dogmas are not a set of arbitrary regulations invented...by a committee of theologians.... Most of them were hammered out under pressure of urgent practical necessity to provide an answer to heresy. And heresy is, as I have tried to show, largely the expression of opinion of the untutored average man, trying to grapple with the problems of the universe at the point where they begin to interfere with daily life and thought. (52)

I submit these passages only for their flavor, not because I think they are in any way conclusive in themselves. Yet I would venture the opinion that if the Israelites could walk seven times around the walls of Jericho and bring them down at the seventh time with a great shout, that seven readings aloud of "Creed or Chaos" to a modern heretical congregation, the seventh reading accompanied by the alto voice of a vigorous middle-aged woman shouting "Creed!", would not only flatten the walls but bring more sinners to repentance than at any time since the day of Pentecost. If this is beyond the power of my audience to arrange, I urge you at the very least to read it seven times in a quiet corner, taking full precautions against falling plaster.

Once you have that one committed to memory, go and do likewise with another of her great essays, "The Other Six Deadly Sins." Lust she assumes we know all about already, and she mentions it merely to object to its too frequently being used as a synonym for *immorality*. There are, after all, those other, more insidious forms of immorality—pride and envy, gluttony and sloth, covetousness and wrath. Einstein was no more penetrating on the subject of $E=MC^2$ than is Dorothy L. Sayers on the subject of these six great perils to the soul—although we will surely struggle to refute her when she dares apply the concept of gluttony to our consumption of manufactured goods.

And a final example of Miss Sayers at her best. How many times have we had to listen to criticisms of John's Gospel—from Ernest Renan and all the rest—on the grounds that it was written in a style all its own and contains events and quotations not found in the other three gospels? Suffer no more. Dorothly L. Sayers took thought, and if she didn't add a cubit to her physical stature, she certainly grew a foot and a half intellectually when she came up with an almost perfect rebuttal—an airtight analogy. It made use of, no doubt against his will and tastes, of Bernard Shaw—then very old, as John had been very old when he wrote his gospel:

> Suppose, for example, Mr. Bernard Shaw were...to (write) a volume of reminiscences about Mr. William Archer; would anybody object that the account must be received with suspicion because most of Archer's other contemporaries were dead, or because the style of G.B.S. was very unlike that of a Times obituary notice, or because the book contained a great many intimate conversations not recorded in previous memoirs...? (55-56)

That's just part of it, but I think it makes the case. And now for another great maker of cases, G. K. Chesterton. Not everyone agrees that Chesterton is as stupendously gifted as I keep insisting he is, so before I present samples that I think show his extraordinary power, let me put things in perspective by quoting a dissent by a celebrated critic in a review, in 1927, of Chesterton's book on Robert Louis Stevenson:

> I admit that I have always found Mr. Chesterton's style exasperating to the last point of endurance, though I am aware that there must be many people who like it.... In this diffuse, dissipated, but not at all stupid book Mr. Chesterton wastes a good deal of time. He is concerned in part with attacking misconceptions, which we had not heard of and in which we are not interested.... If Mr. Chesterton does not seem to make the most of Stevenson's "cheerfulness," it is, I suspect, in my own case, due largely to the fact that I find Mr. Chesterton's own cheerfulness so depressing. He appears less like a saint radiating spiritual vision than like a busman slapping himself on a frosty day. There is one authoritative sense, to be respected, in which

we are admonished to be like little children. Mr Chesterton seems to think that we must execute these instructions by a romp. Hence his regular outbursts of heavyweight Peter-Pantheism....
...in any case, Stevenson is an author well enough established to survive Mr. Chesterton's approval. (*The Nation and the Atheneum* Dec. 31, 1927)

The author of this undiffuse, undissipated, but not at all unstupid review is, of all people, T.S. Eliot, and I weep copiously as I add that he wrote it not as a petulant youth but as a mature critic in his fortieth year. There may be a worse pun in the language than "Peter-Pantheism" but I haven't heard it, and in any case, "pantheism" fits Chesterton about as accurately as "beatnik" would fit Eliot. I think a fairer assessment can be found in a 1957 Chesterton collection edited by a critic whose stature approaches that of Eliot himself, W.H. Auden:

Chesterton's literary criticism abounds in...observations which, once they have been made, seem so obviously true that one cannot understand why one had not seen them for oneself. It now seems obvious to us all that Shaw, the socialist, was in no sense a democrat but was a great republican; that there are two kinds of democrat, the man who, like Scott, sees the dignity of all men, and the man who, like Dickens, sees that all men are equally interesting and varied;...that the Elizabethan Age, however brilliant, was not "spacious," but in literature an age of conceits, in politics an age of conspiracies. But Chesterton was the first critic to see these things. As a literary critic, therefore, I rank him very high. (*G. K. Chesterton: A Selection* 15)

I rank him higher yet—and not simply as a literary critic, but as a thinker; and I begin by offering in evidence the single most thermonuclear literary devastation I've ever come across, a devastation of that prophet of the Superman, Friedrich Nietzsche:

Turn up the last act of Shakespeare's Richard III and you will find not only all that Nietzsche had to say put into two lines, but you will find it put in the very words of Nietzsche. Richard Crookback says it to his nobles:

> Conscience is but a word that cowards use,
> Devised at first to keep the strong in awe.

...Shakespeare had thought of Nietzsche and the Master Morality; but he weighed it at its proper value and put it in its proper place. Its proper place is the mouth of a half-insane hunchback on the eve of defeat. This rage against the weak is only possible in a man morbidly brave but fundamentally sick; a man like Richard, a man like Nietzsche. (*The Common Man* 23-24)

Now Chesterton is sometimes accused of being windy, and sometimes he is, but like the supremely talented boxer who has coasted through a few rounds doing nothing more than exhibiting his footwork and throwing an occasional jab, Chesterton will suddenly put together a combination that will leave his opponent flatter than a placemat. With the boxer, combinations are usually a matter of hooks, crosses, and uppercuts; with the thinker, and particularly the controversialist thinker, combinations involve a somewhat greater variety of weapons. To name a few: irony, ingenuity, sense of proportion, ability to make surprising connections, memory for specifics, and a talent for generalizing convincingly. There's also the thinker's supreme weapon—analogy—but since that's a knockout punch in its own right, let's leave that for later and look at the breakdown of Chesterton's combination of the example cited:

First, the *surprising connection*: bringing in Shakespeare and Richard III. Second *irony*: "all that Nietzsche had to say put in two lines, and. . .in the very words of Nietzsche." Third, *memory for specifics*: imagine writing about Nietzsche and then recalling the appropriate lines from Shakespeare. Fourth, *sense of proportion*: the lines about proper value and proper place being the mouth of a half-insane hunchback on the eve of defeat. Fifth, *talent for generalizing convincingly:* "a man morbidly brave but fundamentally sick—Richard, Nietzsche."

As to what a talent for specifics can do, consider what happened to Bernard Shaw when he suggested that the story of Calvary was too sublime, too artistic to have really happened. Chesterton responded with an incredible artillery barrage of example that began with the premise: "These things *do* happen. . .at every one of its most important moments the most certain and solid history reads like a historical novel." And then he cut loose:

> A peasant girl, called half-witted [Joan of Arc], did promise to defeat the victors of Agincourt; and did it; it ought to be a legend, but it happens to be a fact. A poet and a poetess [the Brownings] did fall in love and eloped secretly to a sunny clime; it is obviously a three-volume novel; but it happened. Nelson did die in the act of winning the one battle that could change the world. It is a grossly improbable coincidence; but it is too late to alter it now. . . . When the general who had surrendered a republican town returned saying easily, "I have done everything," Robespierre did ask, with an air of enquiry, "Are you dead?" When Robespierre coughed in his cold harangue, Garnier did say, "The blood of Danton chokes you." Strafford did say of his own desertion of Parliament, "If I do it, may my life and death be set on a hill for all men to wonder at." Disraeli did say, "The time will come when you shall hear me." (*Lunacy and Letters* 145-46).

A full Chestertonian analysis must await the graduate school of eternity, but before we pass on to Eliot, I'd like to offer a single example of Chesterton employing his great weapon, analogy. It's from "Christmas and the Aesthetes," an essay so good I would read it and love it were it written in black marker pen inside the heretofore last graffiti-free subway train in all the five boroughs. Here's the immortal fragment:

There has been no rationalist festival, no rationalist ecstasy.... Mr. Swinburne does not hang up his stocking on the eve of the birthday of Victor Hugo. Mr. William Archer does not sing carols descriptive of the infancy of Ibsen outside people's doors in the snow.... Christmas remains to remind us of those ages...when the many acted poetry instead of the few writing it. (*Heretics* 92-93)

And finally we come to Eliot. What Eliot does best is obvious—he writes poetry best. Indeed no one in this century has written it better—not even Yeats, whom Eliot considered the greatest poet in the language since Shakespeare. Nor has anyone since Kipling enriched so much ordinary conversation or dressed up so many solemn editorials as has Eliot with his talent for the unforgettable declarative: "I have measured out my life with coffee spoons.... April is the cruelest month.... In the room the women come and go, talking of Michelangelo.... We are the hollow men.... I have heard the mermaids singing, each to each.... This is the way the world ends, not with a bang but a whimper.... Human kind cannot bear very much reality.... Here were decent godless people: Their only monument the asphalt road and a thousand lost golf balls.... The last temptation is the greatest treason: to do the right deed for the wrong reason."

Nor has anyone since Donne written such great—and unembarrassing—religious poetry as has Eliot in his magnificent, and mysteriously under-read meditation, *Choruses from "The Rock"*:

If humility and purity be not in the heart, they are not in the home: and if they are not in the home, they are not in the City.... Life you may evade, but Death you shall not. You shall not deny the Stranger.... Why should men love the Church? Why should they love her laws? She tells them of Life and Death, and of all that they would forget. She is tender where they would be hard, and hard where they like to be soft. She tells them of Evil and Sin, and other unpleasant facts. They constantly try to escape from the darkness outside and within by dreaming of systems so perfect that no one will need to be good. (*Complete Poems* 104-06).

Nor has anyone, at a somewhat lesser and lighter, but nevertheless very important, level, done as much for any tribe of animals as Eliot has done for those familiar household creatures of fang and fur:

Macavity's a mystery cat: he's called the Hidden Paw—
For he's the master criminal who can defy the Law. (*Old Possum's* 37)

And as to what constitutes Eliot's *best* poetry, we have Eliot's own verdict—Four Quartets. We even have his verdict as to the best of the four. But before I go on to that, I'll enter a brief dissent, simply so I can quote a few lines from my own favorite, "Burnt Norton." Some late autumn when you're standing in a Renaissance garden wondering where all the years went, recall these lines, for in them is all that sad wonder of King Solomon in Ecclesiastes or Rembrandt in his last self-portrait:

What might have been and what has been
Point to one end, which is always present.
Footfalls echo in the memory
Down the passage which we did not take
Towards the door we never opened
Into the rose-garden. (*Complete Poems* 117)

But if, in so remembering, you find that your sense of melancholy becomes too acute, remember also that Eliot had a decidedly nonaristocratic sense of humor, idolized Groucho Marx, and could laugh at and even praise "Chard Whitlow," Henry Reed's hilarious parody of "Burnt Norton":

As we get older, we do not get any younger.
Seasons return, and today I am fifty-five,
And this time last year I was fifty-four,
And this time next year I shall be sixty-two (Reed 218).

In any case, Eliot's favorite quartet was the fourth, "Little Gidding," which includes not only our opening theme-setter about the communication of the dead being tongued with fire, but such sadder-and-wiser lines as the following. The words are Eliot's but in the poem he gives them to Yeats, or rather to the ghost of Yeats, as the two tread "the pavement in a dawn patrol":

Since our concern was speech, and speech impelled us
To purify the dialect of the tribe
And urge the mind to aftersight and foresight
Let me disclose the gifts reserved for age
To set a crown upon your lifetime's effort.
First, the cold friction of expiring sense
Without enchantment, offering no promise
But bitter tastelessness of shadow fruit
As body and soul begin to fall asunder.
Second, the conscious impotence of rage
At human folly, and the laceration
Of laughter at what ceases to amuse.
And last, the rending pain of re-enactment
Of all that you have done, and been; the shame
Of motives late revealed, and the awareness
Of things ill done and done to other's harm
Which once you took for exercise of virtue. (Complete Poems 141-47)

Of special note are those first lines, about speech impelling us "to purify the dialect of the tribe," although, as is so often the case with Eliot's lines, they are not Eliot's lines at all. In fact, they're from a poem by Stephane Mallarme, "The Tomb of Edgar Poe." But the sentiments are so strongly Eliot's that the lines might as well be his. Indeed, with the possible exception of Dr. Johnson, no one has ever worked harder than Eliot at purifying the dialect of the English-speaking tribe—a task that might be compared to purifying the Ganges with a single bottle of chlorine. For what worries me is that computer engineers, interfacing with Madison Avenue ad men, and then all of them traveling and gentling their smoke through the deep space of psychobabble, can seem to corrupt language faster than the Eliots of our world can correct it.

We open Eliot's pages, and we hear a crystal voice talking about an "auditory imagination—the feeling for syllable and rhythm that (should) invigorate every word. . . that fuses the old, the obliterated, and the trite with the current, the new, and the surprising." (*Selected Prose* 94). But if we open the pages of most of what is being written today, we find authors fusing the obliterated and the trite with the dull and the bad. And if we turn on television, God help us, we get verbless sentences and prepositions followed by nominative-case pronouns, to name only two. Worse yet, we will hear respectable academics who are yet to serve time for it, saying they are "into" philosophy or "doing" music.

It would be one thing if we could keep the barbarians outside the gates inside which the books are written. The trouble is that the barbarians too often hammer their way in, lock up the watchmen, and then set about deciding, for example, such virtually sacramental questions as the choice of words in the Holy Bible. Samson may have slain a thousand Philistines with the jawbone of an ass, but their relatives live on. Disguised in Roman collars and Geneva robes, they find their way onto high-ranking committees and exact their revenge by mangling such sacred works as the Bible, the Book of Common Prayer, and the Roman Catholic Mass.

When one of their atrocities—the New English Bible—came out in 1961, Eliot grabbed the nearest jawbone and went after its authors in the best style of a literary Samson. He laid about him left and right, expressing his belief that it was not only symptomatic of the decay of English but that if it were used for religious services, it would become an active agent of decadence. After all, he contended, the life of sacred writing is in the music of the sacred word, which was not to be found in the tone-deaf passages of the new translation. He came down hardest on the change from "neither cast ye your pearls before swine" to "do not feed your pearls to pigs." Obviously, the idea of pearls for the inspection of pigs is quite reasonable, but rare is the farmer who'd use pearls as swill for his porkers. Understandably, Eliot made some enemies. In any case, I shudder to report that three million people immediately bought the new version.

And it is with words from the Bible—happier words—that I would close. For one thing our four authors had in common, deeply in common, was the King James. Its images, its rhythms, its exact words and phrases were everywhere in their work. So, for that matter, was its wisdom, for implicit in all but a little of their important work was the advice of Proverbs: 4:7: "Wisdom is the principal thing; therefore get wisdom: and with all thy getting get understanding."

If *our* generation has a motto, it seems to me it's Tennyson with a tag-line: " 'Tis not too late to seek a newer world—so let's run it through the computer and see what permutates."

That's why I say, " 'Tis not too late to seek an *older* world." Through the valley of desolation—the noise, the radios, the televisions, the billboards, the high technology and the low language—let us walk, in the manner of the prophet Ezekiel, to our boneyard of good books. The King James will surely be glittering there, and perhaps we shall also see in that ancient greatness, the works of Lewis, Sayers, Chesterton, Eliot. Perhaps we shall hear a voice: "Son of man, can these bones live?" And we shall answer with Ezekiel: "O Lord God, thou knowest." And let us think what it truly means when next we hear the voice: "Prophesy unto the wind, prophesy son of man, and say to the wind, Thus saith the Lord God, Come from the four winds, O breath, and breathe upon these slain, that they may live." (Ezekiel 37:9)

## Works Cited

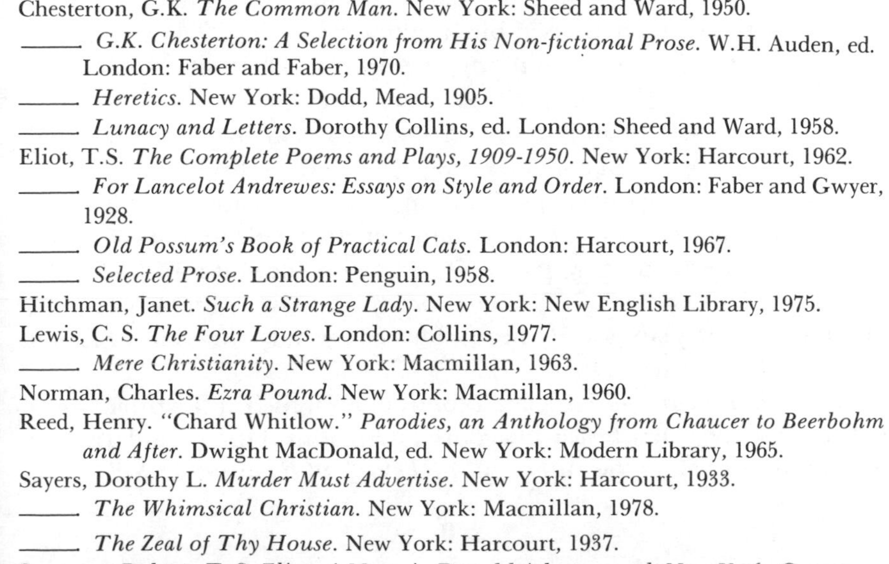

Chesterton, G.K. *The Common Man.* New York: Sheed and Ward, 1950.

_____ *G.K. Chesterton: A Selection from His Non-fictional Prose.* W.H. Auden, ed. London: Faber and Faber, 1970.

_____ *Heretics.* New York: Dodd, Mead, 1905.

_____ *Lunacy and Letters.* Dorothy Collins, ed. London: Sheed and Ward, 1958.

Eliot, T.S. *The Complete Poems and Plays, 1909-1950.* New York: Harcourt, 1962.

_____ *For Lancelot Andrewes: Essays on Style and Order.* London: Faber and Gwyer, 1928.

_____ *Old Possum's Book of Practical Cats.* London: Harcourt, 1967.

_____ *Selected Prose.* London: Penguin, 1958.

Hitchman, Janet. *Such a Strange Lady.* New York: New English Library, 1975.

Lewis, C. S. *The Four Loves.* London: Collins, 1977.

_____ *Mere Christianity.* New York: Macmillan, 1963.

Norman, Charles. *Ezra Pound.* New York: Macmillan, 1960.

Reed, Henry. "Chard Whitlow." *Parodies, an Anthology from Chaucer to Beerbohm and After.* Dwight MacDonald, ed. New York: Modern Library, 1965.

Sayers, Dorothy L. *Murder Must Advertise.* New York: Harcourt, 1933.

_____ *The Whimsical Christian.* New York: Macmillan, 1978.

_____ *The Zeal of Thy House.* New York: Harcourt, 1937.

Sencourt, Robert. *T. S. Eliot: A Memoir.* Donald Adamson, ed. New York: Garnstone Press, 1971.

# Notes on Contributors

*Owen Barfield,* a longtime friend, colleague, and confidant of C. S. Lewis, has served as executor of the Lewis literary estate. Barfield, a lawyer by training and profession, has nevertheless made his most formidable impact on twentieth century thought in the fields of religion, linguistics, and rhetoric. As an anthroposophist, Barfield is widely known as an interpreter and popularizer of the works of Rudolph Steiner. His works include *Poetic Diction* (Wesleyan University Press, 1973), *Saving the Appearances* (Harcourt, 1957); and *History in English Words* (Eerdmans, 1967).

*Robert Boenig* has his Ph.D. from Rutgers University in Medieval English literature and is an Assistant Professor or English at Texas A&M University. He is presently visiting professor of English at Purdue University. He is associate editor of *Studia Mystica,* and has published in such journals as *JEGP, ELN, Mythlore, Neuphilologische Mitteilungen,* and *Speculum,*

*Margaret L. Carter* received her Ph.D. from the University of California, Irvine and is the author of two books, *Spectre or Delusion: Narrative Doubt and the Supernatural in Gothic Fiction* (UMI Research Press, 1987) and *Shadow of a Shade: A Survey of Vampirism in Literature* (Gordon press, 1975); and the editor of *Demon Lovers and Strange Seductions* (Fawcett, 1972) and *Curse of the Undead* (Fawcett, 1970).

*Alzina Stone Dale* is an independent scholar and lecturer who has authored several widely praised biographies, including, *The Outline of Sanity: A Life of G. K. Chesterton* (Eerdmans, 1982) and *Maker and Craftsman: The Story of Dorothy L. Sayers* (Eerdmans, 1978). She also is the editor of several important editions of works by Chesterton and Sayers, and is at work on a literary biography of T. S. Eliot.

*Jerry L. Daniel* received his Ph. D. in Classical History from Rutgers University and serves currently as minister of the Echo Lake Church of Christ in Westfield, New Jersey. Dr. Daniel is the editor of *CSL: The Bulletin of the New York C. S. Lewis Society,* the oldest scholarly journal focusing on Lewis studies. He has published several articles in *CSL* and the *Journal of Biblical Literature.*

*Bruce L. Edwards* is Associate Professor of English at Bowling Green State University, where he teaches courses in rhetorical theory and theories of composition. He is the author of *A Rhetoric of Reading: C. S. Lewis's*

*Defense of Western Literacy* (Center for the Study of Christian Values in Literature, 1986) and two writing textbooks, *Processing Words: Writing and Revising on a Microcomputer* (Prentice-Hall, 1987) and *Roughdrafts: The Process of Writing* (Houghton-Mifflin, 1986) with Alice Calderonello. He has published essays on Lewis, Flannery O'Connor, Walker Percy, and Frederick Buechner, and is currently at work on a book about Kenneth L. Pike and his contribution to rhetorical theory.

*Gracia Fay Ellwood* teaches in the Religious Studies department at California State University, Long Beach. A member of the Society of Friends, she is involved in Sanctuary and related efforts on behalf of victims of violence in Central America. Among her writings are *Good News from Tolkien's Middle Earth, Psychic Visits to the Past,* and (with Doris Robin and Lee Vibber), *In a Faraway Galaxy.* At present she is collaborating with Robert Ellwood on *The Seven Faces of Faith,* to be published by Prentice-Hall in 1988.

*Kath Filmer* received her Ph.D. from the University of Queensland, where she currently teaches courses in Language and Media and the Rhetoric of Science Fiction and Fantasy. She is co-founder of The Inner Ring: The Mythopoeic Literature Society of Australia, and managing editor of its journal, *The Ring Bearer.* She has published articles on polemic literature and on C. S. Lewis in particular in *Extrapolation, Seven,* and *Mythlore.*

*Margaret P. Hannay* is Associate Professor of English at Siena College, Loudonville, New York, and serves as President of the Conference on Christianity and Literature. She is the author of numerous important works on C. S. Lewis, including *C. S. Lewis* (Frederick Ungar, 1981), and is the editor of and contributor to *Silent but for the Word: Tudor Women as Patrons, Translators, and Writers of Religious Works* (Kent State University Press, 1985) and *As Her Whimsey Took Her: Critical Essays on Dorothy L. Sayers* (Kent State University Press, 1979). She is currently at work on a biography of Mary Sidney, Countess of Pembroke.

*Paul Leopold* was born and grew up in New York City. He has attended the University of Rochester, New York University, and is completing his Ph.D. at Yale University in renaissance literature, writing on the English renaissance depictions of Alexander the Great. He has taught abroad extensively, including teaching posts in Sweden and Italy. His "Writings of Joy Davidman (1915-1960)" appeared in *CSL: The Bulletin of the New York C. S. Lewis Society.* He and his wife and four children currently live in Rome.

*Kathryn Lindskoog* is an independent scholar and writer who had the privilege of meeting C. S. Lewis in the late 1950s, receiving his approbation for her M.A. thesis about the Narnian Chronicles, later published as *The Lion of Judah in Never-Never Land* (Eerdmans, 1973). She has authored two other books about Lewis, *C. S. Lewis: Mere*

*Christian* (Harold Shaw, 1987); and *Around the Year with C. S. Lewis and His Friends* (C. R. Gibson, 1986). She is contributing editor to *The Wittenberg Door* and *The Reformed Journal,* and has published more than 250 articles and reviews in various other journals.

*John Martin* is a writer living in New York City. His essays have appeared in such magazines as *Chronicles of Culture, Worldview,* and *The Chesterton Review,* and one of his novels was published by Doubleday. He is also co-author of *The Troll Palace,* a murder mystery produced well off-broadway in 1985, and *Troubadour,* a musical based on the life of Francis of Assisi.

*Joe McClatchey* has his Ph.D. from Arizona State University and is Professor of English at Wheaton College, Wheaton, Illinois, where he has taught since 1970. Professor McClatchey founded and regularly directs the Wheaton-in-England Study Program. He has published articles in *Seven, Studies in Browning, Mythlore, Chesterton Review* and *New Oxford Review.* His "Teaching Individual Characters and Motif" will appear in *Teaching the Arthurian Tradition in Literature,* published by the Modern Language Association.

*Robert B. Meyers* has his Ph.D. from the University of Pittsburgh and is presently Associate Professor of English at Bowling Green State University, where he teaches undergraduate and graduate courses in literary criticism and world literature. Professor Meyers has published essays on speech-act theory and literary theory in such journals as *Boundary 2, Centrum,* and *Research in Education.*

*Paul Piehler* is Associate Professor of English at McGill University, Montreal, Quebec. Born in England, Professor Piehler was a student of C. S. Lewis at Magdalen College, Oxford, 1949-52. He is the author of *The Visionary Landscape: A Study in Medieval Allegory* (McGill University Press, 1971) and *Guide to Medieval and Renaissance Studies in Montreal* (Studia Medievalia, Montreal, 1972). He is currently director of a wide-ranging research project, "Structure and Imagery in Medieval Allegory," an interdisciplinary study of the attempt in medieval visual and literary art to express the shaping principles of the phenomenal universe within a single unified work.

*David H. Stewart* is Professor and former head in the department of English at Texas A&M University, where he teaches courses on Shakespeare and literary criticism. He has published extensively on a variety of topics, and his oeuvre includes a volume on Mikhail Sholokov (*Mikhail Sholokov: A Critical Introduction,* University of Michigan Press, 1967), a rhetoric anthology (*The Wiley Reader* [New York: Wiley and Sons, 1976; 1979), and numerous articles on such topics as the teaching of writing, Northrup Frye, Kipling, Dickens, Faulkner, and, of course, C. S. Lewis.

# Index